Photo: No 44993 Copy Pit. Overleaf: No 44690 Salwick. Both ALAN CASTLE

The author wishes to express his sincere gratitude to all of those who have assisted in the preparation of this book, but in particular to the following: Bill Ashcroft, Joseph Booth, Tony Bowles, Norman Callaghan, Dave Bradbury, John Burnett, Maurice Burns, Bob Clarke, Richard Dixon, Bob Downham, Charles Findlay, Peter Fitton, John Fletcher, Tony Gillett, Robert Gregson, Andy Hall, David Hardman, Tom Heavyside, Ernie Heyes, Derek Huntriss, Mick Kelly, Ian Krause, Steve Leyland, Dick Manton, Eddie May, Terry Millar, Tommy Miller, Peter Norris, Mike Pope, Ken Richardson, Dave Rodgers, Brian Sharpe, Mike Taylor, Ian Thistlethwaite, Malcolm Thistlethwaite, David Tomlinson, Paul Tuson, Jim Walker, Bill Watson and Frank Watson.

Written, photographed, compiled and edited: Alan Castle
Editorial Assistant: Brian Sharpe
Design: Anita Tams-Waters
Production Manager: Craig Lamb
Publisher: Dan Savage
Managing Director: Brian Hill

Published by: Mortons Media Group Ltd, Media Centre, Mortons Way,Horncastle, Lincolnshire LN9 6JR. Tel: 01507 523456
Printed by: William Gibbons and Son, Wolverhampton
Published July 2008
ISBN 978-1-906167-10-3

STEAM
The Grand Finale

A 40th anniversary tribute to the final men & machines

A chronology of 1968

Alan Castle

The year of 1968 was a pivotal year in a period of great change and, with the march of so-called 'progress' that included man being a matter of months away from walking on the moon, the time was up for steam. The first week of August was to see the closure of the final three depots - effectively drawing to a conclusion the century and a half of loyal service provided by a form of transport to which the wealth of our nation owed so much. The steam era ended so poignantly on 4 August, a day on which innumerable steam railwaymen, most of whom had dedicated their entire lives to the railways, were declared redundant. These words, therefore, are a tribute to those *final men and machines*.

On 11 August, did any of those thousands sat in the massive traffic gridlocks up in the high Pennines really believe that this would not be for *ever*? The, then seemingly unshakeable, view from the exalted heights of BR management was that it was *not* to return *under any circumstances*. Indeed, certain individuals then resident on the British Railways Board were so adamantly opposed to steam as to be desirous to see it despatched as soon as was possible… and no matter what the cost!

Indecent haste

Even die-hards accepted that steam had to go one day - but not so hurriedly and with such a disgraceful lack of gratitude, and the indecent haste with which most of the fleet soon came to be disposed of, was a sad reflection upon the state of our emerging society. Even the few privately preserved locomotives in working order did not represent the image that top management wished to create. The view was that steam was the creation of a more primitive age and, quite simply, deserved no place in an era of new technology. For those who did take the time to cogitate upon such matters, there was a sadness felt that reflected an acceptance that the life as we knew it was soon to change, perhaps for the better, perhaps not, but certainly a realisation that changes were inevitable and counted as 'progress'.

There had been a period in the immediate post-war years, during which attempts were made to construct modern and more reliable steam locomotives as the way forward for the then newly nationalised railway, rather than to leap headlong into untried and untested dieselisation. In the pages to follow, we shall discover *why* this was and how things then suddenly changed, both as a consequence of the 1955 Modernisation Plan, and also because of the effects of the later decimation of the national network, as initiated by the infamous Dr Beeching. Despite the ambitious aspirations of the British Transport Commission design teams, many new locomotives ultimately came to be sent for scrap well before their 10th birthdays. Some were hardly 'run-in' – clearly, a shocking and disgraceful waste!

Until as late as 1967, the steam-age railway in the North West of England, in many respects, really did still remain relatively untouched. North of Preston, steam working still continued - and in some quantity – particularly on the remoter moorland main line stretches over Shap and along the Settle & Carlisle line, where, in both places, even large Pacifics were still very much in evidence. However, when Carlisle Kingmoor, Tebay and Workington depots finally closed to steam working on 31 December, this proved to be a dramatic and major downturn in steam's sphere of operation. Maurice Burns made a sentimental journey to witness first-hand the very last steam workings over Shap Summit. After 122 years, it really was the end of an era and Maurice provides some fitting words in appreciation. His own personal epitaph encompasses, in particular, the passing of one essential, but otherwise little-addressed, aspect of railway operation – the men and locomotives of the Shap Bankers.

Come the dawn of the 1968 New Year, the 360-odd steam locomotives nominally still in service at the *'lucky thirteen'* surviving depots found themselves basically restricted to essentially short sojourns in and around Lancashire, north Cheshire, a corner of the Peak District and an occasional foray a few miles into West Yorkshire. With no alternative motive power to call upon, staff at depots invariably had to 'make-do-and-mend', often against almost impossible odds with little or no spare parts back-up, just to keep a bare minimum of engines available for traffic. Everywhere that one looked standards of cleanliness had deteriorated noticeably. This, of course, had gradually been taking place for many years and, for some enthusiasts, it became a sad fact of life that having to go to the extreme extent of having to clean one's own engines, if only in order to stand any chance of securing a reasonable photograph, was to become very much a part of the accepted routine. Maurice Burns recounts one or two of the numerous cleaning sessions in which he personally became involved and Paul Riley continues on a similar theme with a few further words on the last days of the *'Great Steam Chase'*… or the trials and tribulations of steam photography in the 1960s.

The noose tightens

For that handful of surviving depots still in business, the noose was ever-tightening. The first three to go, all on 4 March, were Trafford Park, Buxton and Northwich, the latter two being at the extremities of the route traversed by intensive limestone minerals traffic. These closing weeks fortunately coincided with some very wintry conditions in the Peak District which, when trains actually were able to run, did provide some spectacular photo opportunities. Within another couple of months, four further depots succumbed, with Stockport Edgeley, Heaton Mersey, Edge Hill and Speke Junction closing on 6 May 1968. It was a near miracle that steam survived to such an advanced stage as May regularly hauling a prestigious titled train. Nevertheless, despite more than one previous attempt at dieselisation, Stanier 'Black Fives' remained firmly on the roster of the *'Belfast Boat Express'.* We examine the reasons behind this and hear about some of the more outstanding runs.

Elsewhere, life went on much as it always had done and nowhere more so than in the Yorkshire Dales. The limestone traffic from quarries on the former Skipton-Grassington Branch took ballast trains to destinations from which steam had otherwise long-vanished and we follow one such train on an outing to Appleby. The remaining three depots in the Manchester Division; Newton Heath, Patricroft and Bolton closed at the very end of June and Steve Leyland provides an account of the demise of his own local shed of Bolton.

The final three

With but a single month to go, this chronology is brought to a conclusion with an in-depth focus upon 'The Final Three'. During those final hectic weeks, the otherwise totally unassuming and quite 'matter of fact' steam depots at Carnforth, Lostock Hall and Rose Grove had fame literally thrust upon them and the area around soon became inundated with visitors of totally unprecedented proportions. Right up until the very last weekend of all, it was still possible to travel on one or other of two 'portions' of main-line expresses that, from Preston, completed their final few miles onwards to their destinations behind steam power. Tom Heavyside provides a personal insight to the final passenger workings of 3 August.

Most of the special train activity in the closing weeks concentrated upon the last day, when each of the major railtour operators of the time vied for custom with their individual *'Farewell to Steam'* sorties. With severely limited itineraries being available and with the, perhaps inevitable, Sunday late-running scenarios, on 4 August it soon became almost impossible for those witnessing events to predict from which direction the next special would appear! Published here, for the first time ever, is a comprehensive list of all the footplate crews involved in that historic day.

One week later, three 5MTs and a Britannia were engaged in operating various stages of a BR-organised final steam excursion upon which history has since imparted the infamous sobriquet, *'The Fifteen Guinea Special'.* Some reflections upon that historic day are provided from three very differing viewpoints - a passenger, a 'linesider' and a footplate inspector involved in the behind-the-scenes planning and preparations.

After it really was all over and the masses had departed, what happened then? As we now know, a handful of engines - from all three depots - survived the cutting torch, but there was no escape for the remainder. A few lingered on for some months, rusting away in forlorn lines awaiting their inevitable destiny, but the *'Barry phenomenon'* was really some years to the future and with neither the funding being available, nor the preservation mania yet really having taken off, all would eventually be towed away for scrap. With the end of steam, so also disappeared most of the steam age infrastructure and, as a postscript to those unforgettable final months, Robert Gregson visited the derelict and decaying remains of Lostock Hall shed which, remarkably, survived for 22 years after its last steam locomotive had departed.

The age of the steam railway. The decision to develop existing steam power had been made as long ago as 1948, being greatly influenced at that time by the parlous state of Britain's economy and the low capital-cost necessary in preference to massive expenditure required to get large-scale and totally untested dieselisation off the ground. One of the 999 'Standards' that came to be constructed by British Railways between 1951 and 1960, Class 4MT 4-6-0 No 75019 passes through Rose Grove station in April 1968, en-route to Skipton to take up its duties on 'No 94 Target' – which will involve working a train of new ballast from the quarries at Spencers Sidings on the Grassington branch. BILL WATSON

British Railways 1948-1968...
The first 20 years
Alan Castle

I t must have occurred sometime around the springtime of 1956 when, from a primary school playground on the outskirts of Preston, I glimpsed my very first main line diesel locomotive. Although very few youngsters growing up in such halcyon days of steam could really pretend to appreciate much of what was happening, that vision witnessed from the little schoolyard in Middleforth really was a portent of the future railway as this was to evolve.

At that period in time, of course, British Railways possessed just seven examples and the pioneer LMS Co-Co, No 10000, had actually been constructed some time previously, in 1948. Having sojourned for much of their earlier years on the Southern Region, No 10000 and its twin No 10001 had now returned to their earlier stamping grounds. Not long afterwards, they came to be joined by another three former SR stable-mates, in the form of the Bulleid-designed Co-Cos Nos 10201/2/3, all of which soon came to truly exemplify the astonishingly swift metamorphosis from steam to diesel that was so very imminent.

British Railways' standardisation of steam power
On 1 January 1948, Britain's railways had been nationalised and the newly created 'British Railways' had come to inherit more than 20,000

steam locomotives from the 'Big Four' companies (as well as some other smaller railways that went into public ownership at the same time). Over the course of the next 12 years, production of steam continued apace with, initially, many pre-nationalisation classes being perpetuated, until designs for new BR Standard classes were unveiled in 1951. These were largely based on LMS practice, but incorporating ideas and modifications from other constituent companies and, in some respects, also from North America - characteristic features being taper boilers, high running plates, two cylinders, rocker grates and streamlined cabs.

A total of 999 'Standards' came to be constructed between 1951 and 1960. In addition, more than 750 ex-WD locomotives were also taken into stock; many having seen service abroad during World War II. Remarkably, within just 20 short years, even all of these much newer engines had gone and steam was dead.

This part of the story really begins on 25 January 1955 with the announcement of a £1240-million Modernisation Plan, spelling-out the British Transport Commission's scheme for large-scale modernisation of the rail network, the principle feature of which was to be the ultimate total replacement of steam by diesel and electric traction. Naturally, diesels were still something of a novelty, but, nevertheless, following soon after

the Plan was published, the proposed 1956 Building Programme for steam came to be drastically slashed. From a total of 263 proposed engines deleted from the previous schedule, these included 36 additional Britannia Pacifics - for three Regions, 20 Clan Pacifics for the North Eastern Region and the first of a new Class 8F 2-8-0 design. Notwithstanding the transparently clear 'writing-on-the-wall' for steam, a further few did actually come to be constructed - these comprising 84 9F 2-10-0s and 61 mixed traffic engines of various types – all authorised as an 'additional build'.

In the event, it was to be the former GWR Swindon Works that assumed the honour of turning out the very last of that final order. Taking longer than expected to complete its batch of 9F 2-10-0s, No 92220 *Evening Star* only came to be released to traffic in as late as March 1960. With its copper-capped double chimney and other Swindon embellishments (such as being the only named 9F), it naturally found itself allocated to the Western Region. With careful maintenance, the majority of these brand-new and modern machines could probably have worked for up to 50 years. Nevertheless, the first withdrawals were not far away and, ultimately, it was all proven to have been a quite shocking waste.

The question did beg asking as to why such large numbers had actually been constructed, particularly when it was already known that their usefulness would be limited to such a few short years. But, the BTC's decision to develop existing steam power had been made as long ago as 1948, being greatly influenced at the time by the parlous state of Britain's economy and the low capital-cost necessary to build a series of new steam, in preference to the massive expenditure required to get large-scale and, of course, totally untested, dieselisation off the ground. Within eight years and following the radical changes ensuing, no sooner had the first batch of 32 Class 9Fs been completed at Crewe in December 1954, than the bottom-line of the Modernisation Plan dictated the total obliteration of steam. Although the BTC had previously pushed ahead in good faith, the argument for coal and steam, based on cheap fuel and efficiency, was very soon to be lost. Coal was becoming more and more expensive and the otherwise ageing fleet of steam power was becoming increasingly difficult to maintain.

Figures produced claimed to show that the cost of crewing and fuelling a steam locomotive was some 2½ times that of diesel power, and the daily mileage achievable was far lower, as well. As labour costs rose, particularly after World War II, non-steam technologies had become much more cost-efficient. This was a trend by no means restricted to the UK for, by the end of the 1970s, most Western countries had completely replaced steam in passenger service and very soon afterwards likewise those remaining in freight usage.

Progress and the decline of steam

Before any final decision was taken regarding bulk delivery of the anticipated 2500 diesel locomotives required, British Railways had stated that they wished to spend time evaluating the results of the diesel experiment. A 'pilot scheme' of about 170 examples was to be constructed for design assessment. Orders were placed with many different locomotive builders (the majority of whom possessed absolutely no experience of main-line locomotive construction) and prototypes came to be hastily 'cobbled together' essentially for this evaluation. However, the

The age of the steam railway. At one time there were three magnificent gantries like this one in the Preston station area, but following shortly on the heels of the end of steam, the 1970s saw the commissioning of Preston power 'box, which swept away all semaphore signalling and the numerous manual signalboxes controlling this. Not long afterwards, the West Coast Main Line electrification inevitably brought with it unsightly overhead catenaries, which further marred the outlook from the station towards the magnificent spire of St Walburge's church. Here, the road is set for the main line north, up which Stanier 'Black Five' 4-6-0 No 45390 is heading with 'No 78 Target'. A trip working, consisting of a couple of coal wagons bound for Garstang and Catterall, this was the sort of traffic that was also soon to disappear for ever, for road competition had dictated that there was no longer a place for it in the modernised and cost-conscious railway network. ALAN CASTLE

project then came to be abandoned under pressure from the Conservative government, resulting in BR having no real option but to place large orders for unproven machines and with designs straight off the drawing board. Sadly, many steam engines which were less than ten years old came to be sacrificed in the ensuing totally unnecessary haste, but some of the diesel classes that replaced steam soon proved to be so unreliable that they saw even less service than their immediate forebears. Some transformation that proved to be!

Furthermore, the infamous Dr Beeching had also chopped the national rail network down in size by a third. The scale of changes occurring can be gauged from the fact that, the 20,000 or more steam engines in service up until the late 1950s, came to be replaced by a mere 5000 diesels and electrics.

That ceaseless march towards total dieselisation/electrification gradually ensued and the soon-to-be-termed 'British Rail' coined such titles as 'Inter-City' and gradually painted all of its carriages blue and grey, this presumably in an early attempt to present a 'corporate image' that was thought vital to accompany its new trains. Naturally, steam engines had no place in such visions, for they were too obviously mechanical, labour-intensive and possessed embarrassing and allegedly unhealthy emissions.

The demise of steam came at different times around the country. East Anglia had become largely dieselised by the end of the 1950s, with all bar one remaining steam depot having closed by 1962. With some notable exceptions, much of Scotland north of Glasgow and Edinburgh also saw steam give way to diesel traction by 1962, while Western Region steam faded into the history books at the end of 1965 with the Southern and North Eastern Regions following suit in 1967.

The release back to traffic from Crewe Works, on 2 February 1967, of Britannia Pacific No 70013 *Oliver Cromwell* proved to be the very last steam locomotive to receive an overhaul at any BR workshop. From that date forward, the by now vastly reduced number of surviving railway workshops were to concentrate merely on the maintenance of diesel/electric traction. Any overhauls necessary to keep steam engines in traffic had to be undertaken at those few depots still with equipment and machinery capable of doing such work. Clearly, boiler-lifts and heavy overhauls were out of the question, even by those prepared to retain their alliance with steam.

No more spare components were to be manufactured, or even refurbished, and if a part could not be cannibalised from elsewhere, depots were faced with no other option but to withdraw locomotives for scrapping.

The first day of January 1968 was to dawn with but about 360 steam locomotives remaining in service at a mere 13 depots – all situated in the North West of England and this is where we take up the story.

The age of the steam railway. All that epitomised the archetypal country station goods yard, that had existed almost unaltered since the 19th Century, can be seen somewhere in this superb picture. Rose Grove shed's Stanier 8F 2-8-0 No 48423 has paused between shunting duties at Kirkham, while in the course of working 'No 25 Target' which trips between Blackpool North and Preston NU Yard. Seen storming away from the station is Lostock Hall's 'Black Five' No 45444 at the head of the 12:44 Preston to Blackpool South – a through portion of the 09:05 from London Euston. The road coach is one of the Ribble Motor Company's 'Burlingham Seagull' bodied Leyland Tiger Cubs built in 1956 and is, presumably, providing transport for a permanent way gang employed in the neighbourhood. Some Sunday work in the area is clearly anticipated, as the sidings contain wagons of fresh ballast that have undoubtedly originated from quarries on the Grassington Branch. PETER FITTON

After a night-time snowfall, a weak wintry sun is barely over the towering mass of Langdale Fell as 'Black Five' No 44884 with safety valves blowing-off slowly moves forward onto the hill with a Christmas extra parcels working. Providing some much-needed muscle at the rear is Fairburn 2-6-4T No 42210. In the distance, another 2-6-4T prepares to leave the shed to bank a following train. MAURICE BURNS

Last of the Shap bankers

Steam over Shap ended on 31 December 1967

Maurice Burns

The railways across the northern fells have always held a special fascination for me and none more so than that over Shap Fell with steam. In the early 1960s, railway periodicals were liberally sprinkled with photographic masterpieces recorded by those such as the late Eric Treacy and Derek Cross. A superb landscape and memorable visions of steam engines working hard were, after all, the perfect combination, especially if the weather was kind! Indeed, the sight and sound of a heavy northbound train, with locomotives both on the front and also at the rear, toiling up the Shap incline, was one of the finest displays of raw steam power one could see – a truly unforgettable experience. It was against this background that I, and countless other enthusiasts, headed for these parts at the end of BR steam to capture on film those images of steam that would soon be no more.

My own Shap memories spanned just three years, starting on a hot summer's day in August 1964, but did leave a lasting impression. I had reached the summit cutting the hard way from my home on Teesside, on my 'Jack Taylor' cycle, arriving just after lunch. For the next four hours, there followed a procession of steam; these including a 4F light-engine, a Duchess No 46245 *City of London*, a filthy Britannia No 70013 *Oliver Cromwell*, a 9F on a Ford car train, a Jubilee and a large handful of Class 5s on freights. I had hoped to see some trains banked up the incline but, remarkably, on this, my first visit here, none of these required a banker. Just my luck!

However, all that was to change on my next visit to Tebay (another cycle ride), this time on a Friday evening after work, on 27 November 1964. For the crossing of Stainmore, the weather had been perfect and I arrived at Tebay just before midnight. My first visit to the shed would not be forgotten in a hurry, it created such a huge impact, with the noise of exhausts and whistling in the darkness throughout the night. There was just so much traffic at that time, either speeding south downhill or heavy freights stopping for a banker and then restarting.

There were two banking-engines on duty, Fairburn 2-6-4 tanks Nos 42210 and 42110, which were both sat outside the 'bothy' ready for action. Inside the bothy, the enginemen made me most welcome; they were such a friendly bunch and, as I sat round the coal fire drinking tea, I heard a freight slowly plod through the station, then on to the foot of the bank to whistle up for a banker. The driver and fireman went outside and, climbing aboard No 42210, moved off the shed

A Fairburn 4MT 2-6-4 tank comes off Tebay shed, to buffer-up against the rear of a Stanier 'Black Five'-hauled freight patiently waiting under the shadow of Loups Fell ready to do battle with the four miles of 1-in-75 to the summit. MAURICE BURNS

and eased up to the guards van at the rear of the freight. Following the customary exchange of whistles, the train disappeared noisily up the bank and into the darkness. Just how the people in Tebay ever slept, I will never know!

Moments later, another freight, hauled by one of the last of the Patriots, No 45531 *Sir Frederick Harrison*, whistled for assistance and it was now that the driver of banker No 42110 offered me a trip to the summit. After the buffers of the tank engine touched the guards van and following the exchanging of whistles, it was soon full-regulator for the banker.

Looking forward into the darkness, there was so much exhaust noise and almost constant shovelling of coal into the firebox by the poor fireman, that the Patriot at the front could not be heard at all.

Indeed, we joked that the crew were taking it easy and leaving all the work for the banker! After the Scout Green 'box, we were soon passing the distant lights of Shap Wells Hotel and into the steep-sided summit cutting. Approaching the then Summit signalbox, the driver of No 42110 slammed shut the regulator and, slowly, the guards van tail-light moved away and, as if by magic, we could now hear in the distance the exhaust of the *Patriot* at the front end of the freight. A quick descent of the bank followed, to discover another freight with a Class 5 waiting for assistance. I did two more trips up to the summit, but as 03:00 approached, tiredness set in and, in the warmth of the locomen's bothy, I crashed-out in my sleeping bag!

The next morning, I could not believe my eyes - it was snowing! However, by mid-morning, the sky had totally cleared and I cycled up to Shap Wells, where I caught several Class 5s on freights or parcel trains, all banked by the Fairburn tanks.

The lighting conditions were perfect, with a combination of snow, sun and steam! For black and white pictures, I used a 35mm Practica camera, some being taken with my new 135mm telephoto lens, while, for Kodachrome slides, I was also fortunate to have brought my father's British-made Ilford Advocate camera.

Throughout 1965, I made many more return visits; often it has to be said, in dreadful weather! However, I made a conscious decision several times to travel on the banking engines in daylight to take photographs from the footplate. Getting a footplate ride was easy - one just had to ask! Tebay shed staff were a friendly bunch and nothing was too much trouble. So, once more, I travelled on the footplate of No 42110.

The heavy freight traffic always required a banker, but one train stands in particular. It was immense. I do not know its exact weight, but it could have been about 1000 tons, consisting of a riding van, a crane and a long train of concrete track panels intended for re-laying the West Coast Main Line. Hauled by two 8F 2-8-0s at the front, both with a full head of steam, and with a Fairburn tank at the rear, this train passed me at Greenholme cutting at just walking pace, about 5mph, but the crews and engines were in full command of the job, reaching the summit without stopping.

By 1967, the type of banking engines had changed. The 1960s had started out with a stud of Fowler 2-6-4 tanks, but these came to be displaced by the Fairburns in 1964. As the latter, in turn, became worn out, they were ultimately replaced by BR Standard Class 4 4-6-0 tender engines.

During the bitterly cold night of 27 November 1964, the two engines on Shap banking duties, Fairburn 4MT 2-6-4 tanks Nos 42110 and 42210, take a short break in the yard in between turns up the hill. MAURICE BURNS

Well into the climb, Stanier 'Black Five' No 45312, banked at the rear by a Standard Class 4MT, battles against the gradient and a stiff easterly wind as it passes Greenholme with a northbound fully fitted freight. MAURICE BURNS

For those who enjoy the great outdoors, there is no wilder place than the southern slopes of Shap Fell. This bleak and forlorn stretch of moorland is one of howling winds and horizontal rainfalls, where only ragged sheep and railway photographers might roam. With one of Tebay's Standard Class 4MT 4-6-0s working hard at the rear, for Springs Branch's Stanier 'Black Five' No 45321 the hard work is nearly over as it approaches Shap Wells with a summer Saturday Euston-Glasgow relief. MAURICE BURNS

These were to become the last steam banking engines at Tebay; this prior to the end of steam at Carlisle and the closure of Kingmoor and Tebay sheds from 1 January 1968. While man enough for the job, compared to the Fowler and Fairburn tanks, they proved not to be so popular with the Tebay crews, due to the draughty cabs when tender-first descending from Shap! First to arrive, in April 1967, were Nos 75019, 75026 (fitted with double chimney), 75027 and 75039.

A month later, Nos 75024, 75030, 75032 and 75035 were added to the allocation. Nos 75035 and 75039 did not last long and were soon withdrawn, but the remainder lasted to the very end of steam at the shed.

After closure of Tebay, Nos 75019 and 75027 saw further service at Carnforth, indeed right until the very end of steam on BR in August 1968. Happily, one Tebay banking engine is still with us today, in the form of No 75027 - now preserved on the Bluebell Railway.

Towards the end of 1967, in the last months of steam over Shap, the chances of getting any more decent photographs of the bankers were rare. Carlisle Kingmoor shed (12A) had a declining number of working locomotives and, with closure occurring during the Christmas holiday period, it was hard to pin down the very last workings. However, all of a sudden, along the grapevine travelled news of a football excursion from Carlisle to Blackpool and back… planned to run on Boxing Day.

Looking back upon how this actually happened, it being before the days of the internet, emails and mobile phones, is quite amazing! We even knew the booked motive power. It was scheduled to be the last working Britannia, No 70013 *Oliver Cromwell* – the special leaving Carlisle about 10:00 and returning after dark at about 21:00.

During the evening of Christmas Day and that night, ten or so photographers descended on Kingmoor shed to seek out No 70013 and to give it a thorough cleaning with oil and paraffin. It would be one of the engine's last Kingmoor working, prior to movement to Carnforth to work

A pair of Standard Class 4MT 4-6-0s, including the green-liveried No 75026, await their next turns of duty in the shed yard at Tebay during the final week of steam. MAURICE BURNS

out its last days before the end of steam on BR on 11 August 1968.

Boxing Day morning was a photographer's dream. Full sun, a clear blue sky… and a frost! Now with a super-shine finish, *Oliver Cromwell* looked superb – could this really be the last BR steam working ever over Shap from Carlisle?

Most opted for the curves at Strickland Woods, south of Penrith. The accompanying pictures explain it all. With the pictures 'in the bag' and with no other steam trains to photograph, everyone went home happy. We had seen what was likely to be the last steam over Shap… and in perfect conditions.

That should have been the end of this story but, for me, it was not quite. While sat back at home on Teesside having my tea, I thought, *Oliver Cromwell* will be on the return working in just four hours' time and, really, I should be there, if only to make a tape-recording of the train climbing towards the summit for the very last time. Should I go all the way back to Shap - that was the question? It would be far easier to take the easy option and to remain at home? Well, I did make the effort and I have never regretted it – coming to witness what turned out to be a memorable spectacle.

In darkness, I arrived at lonely Scout Green

signalbox. There was little traffic on the evening of Boxing Day and the friendly signalman appreciated the company, offering to let me know when the return football excursion was due. Eventually, I got the word that No 70013 was passing Grayrigg 'box, so, with my Phillips reel-to-reel tape-recorder and torch, I then walked up the line beyond the 'box.

It was a magical evening… especially for such an occasion as this. While it was dark, there was no wind, a clear sky, stars above and a heavy frost. Indeed, it was so quiet, you could hear a pin drop! I listened for the sound of a train in the distance, expecting to hear the distant roar of *Oliver Cromwell* in the Lune Gorge below, as it gathered speed to charge the bank of Shap. What I heard, though, was just a faint rumble and then… total silence. This could only mean one thing… *Oliver Cromwell* had stopped for a banker!

There would appear to be just one snag. On Tebay shed, all the fires appeared to have been dropped, so there was no banker available. No 70013 would now have to tackle Shap with its heavy train, from a standing start.

I heard the chime whistle faintly in the distance, then the first beat of the exhaust but, soon, the engine was accelerating up to 30mph by Greenholme - the noise being so loud in the still night air, the regulator was obviously 'in the roof'.

After Greenholme cutting, the train came into view, with the glow of the firebox reflecting in the exhaust and the illuminated carriage lights in the distance.

It was certainly going well, as it approached Scout Green 'box, with occasional sparks going skyward from the chimney. Just as it had passed me, it went into a slight wheelspin, which was quickly brought under control by the driver, before eventually regaining its feet and plodding over the summit at over 20mph.

I had, therefore, witnessed every beat of *Oliver Cromwell* from a standing start in Tebay Station to Shap Summit - a memory I will never forget! As the train passed over the summit and accelerated on towards Penrith, it eventually went totally silent again... steam over Shap and the banking engines were now no more.

31 December 1967 marked not only the end of steam over the Northern Fells, but also, sadly, the real end of main line steam in Britain.

The last remaining steam engines on BR were now to be concentrated in a small area in the North West, with no real place to go, but, for many enthusiasts such as myself, the great memories of BR steam over Shap - with its banking engines - live on.

Boxing Day 1967 and the last southbound steam passenger working over Shap rounds the curve through Strickland woods headed by No 70013 *Oliver Cromwell*. In the darkness of a frosty winter's evening, Maurice would be a lone spectator later this day at the lonely Scout Green signalbox to witness the return working of this Carlisle-Blackpool football special climbing the bank unassisted. MAURICE BURNS

'To a dignified end'
The last engine cleaners on British Railways

Maurice Burns

In the final years of BR steam, thousands of enthusiasts travelled from one part of the UK to another, as each region saw its last engines disappear for scrap. Most would carry a camera and take the odd shed or station photograph. However, with engines in quite appalling condition mechanically, many had been patched up using parts from other withdrawn locomotives and, although each shed had 'cleaners', these had stopped cleaning engines long before the end of steam. For freight engines in particular, the only time that these were seen to be clean was when they had been repainted following works' overhauls, but that was now a long time ago…

There were one or two exceptions, where shedmasters took a pride in keeping their locomotives clean and where cleaners did do the job for which they had been employed. The differing management styles were never more obvious and starkly apparent than during the well-documented 'Indian Summer' of the A4 Pacifics, running between Glasgow and Aberdeen. Here, one could see freshly cleaned Aberdeen Ferryhill A4s passing filthy ones from Glasgow St Rollox which had not seen cleaning rags for many a year.

Aberdeen did clean its A4s right to the very end and, when its last LNER pacific, No 60532 *Blue Peter*, was retained on standby duties until December 1966, this, too, remained clean until withdrawal.

It was against this background that, in July 1965, while on a holiday near Perth, I bumped into the late Paul Riley - a great guy who shared my passion of going to that little bit extra in order to capture on film the last of BR steam. We were both fans of the late WJV (Bill) Anderson and his style of photography and how we envied the chance to photograph immaculate Pacifics at exotic locations, such as Glenfarg Bank in Fife, much as Bill had so often done.

Just then, a truly filthy A4 – No 60027 *Merlin* passed by. Once the immaculate pride of

The cleaning of one's first steam engine is something one would never forget - especially when this was an A4! Being caught in the process by the Perth MPD running foreman in August 1965, equally memorable was the fact that he did not throw us off the shed, but did want his picture taken! Here he proudly poses in front of A4 No 60027 *Merlin* while Dave Hartas (left) and Paul Riley continue with their task unabated! MAURICE BURNS

Haymarket and frequently working 'The Elizabethan', it had now been relegated to work out its final days at St Margaret's, on freight or occasional passenger work. At Perth this day, it had been booked to work the 14:55 to Edinburgh, over Glenfarg, so Paul suggested we clean it up ourselves!

In the chapter 'Never Again', later in this book, Paul describes in detail what actually happened, but, suffice to say, in itself, for me it was a momento

us event to clean an A4. This would however lead, in future years, to meeting up with numerous other enthusiasts, all of whom possessed the same drive and guts to get their hands dirty if necessary, in order to transform filthy engines back to their former glory – and all in the interests of photography!

In the final years of steam, we, the enthusiasts, had to become the real - if unofficial - last engine cleaners on BR!

However, with no training, Paul and I leant a few lessons as a consequence of this initial experience. Firstly, we needed to add more bearing oil to the paraffin that we used in order to produce a better shine. Secondly, to avoid friction with crews, we should always dry-off the handrails and tidy-up when finished. We did see our shining A4 climbing the 1-in-75 of Glenfarg, but noticed to our horror that we had left some cleaning rags jammed between the boiler and handrail, right next to the *Merlin* nameplates. We did not do that again, either!

Paul and I soon came to be joined by an expanding group of like-minded keen photographers, mainly from the Midlands, who came to nickname themselves the MNA.

The next engine earmarked for cleaning was Dundee's single-chimney A2, No 60530 *Sayajirao*, which worked a passenger to Glasgow. Following this, we then travelled to Ayr to clean Hughes Fowler 'Crab' 2-6-0 No 42789. With the greater numbers now involved, cleaning became quicker and, at Ayr, we found we could clean more than just the one locomotive.

The first cleaning adventure of 1967 for me

The transformation of the filthiest A4 ever seen is now complete and the crew prepare their engine for an early afternoon Perth to Edinburgh passenger departure over Glenfarg Bank. MAURICE BURNS

5 November 1966 saw the end of one of the most popular locomotive classes built by the LNER - the Gresley V2 2-6-2s. The very last working example, No 60836, was scheduled by the Scottish Region to make one final run from Edinburgh Waverley to Perth and Aberdeen, before being sent for scrap. To ensure that it went out in a blaze of glory, the engine was cleaned overnight at Edinburgh St Margaret's shed. MAURICE BURNS

In the summer of 1966, the last handful of V2s at Dundee had a regular summer passenger working to Edinburgh Waverley. Having received an overnight facelift on Dundee shed, No 60919 makes a fine sight as it accelerates off the Tay Bridge at Wormit on an August Saturday. MAURICE BURNS

turned out to be the last run of the 'Cambrian Coast Express' from Aberystwyth, with steam over Talerddig Summit to Shrewsbury. On 4 March 1967, Paul had organised the event to perfection, this including the borrowing, from a retired former manager of the Cambrian Railways, of the original 'CCE' headboard. Rostered motive power, by this time, no longer being the immaculate Machynlleth Manors, quite filthy Standard 4MT 4-6-0s were provided by Shrewsbury, a shed by now part of the re-vamped London Midland Region. These usually no longer possessed either front number plates or shedplates and, being LMR engines, also had the wrong type of top lamp-bracket for the Western Region headboard!

No problem! A suitable bracket was 'borrowed' from a withdrawn ex-WR 78xxx 2-6-0 at Shrewsbury shed (photographer Alan Castle spent the major part of an uncomfortable night in the empty tender, removing the rusty bolts securing this!). Meanwhile, Chris Weston had organised in York carriage works the manufacture of an 89C shedplate and Dave Williams had made an assortment of different numerals to glue onto a blank number plate – we did not know in advance which engine would be rostered! Half-a-dozen other photographers descended upon Aberystwyth station to clean the engine - at the platform end - with officialdom totally turning a blind eye!

There, in just over an hour, a 75033 number plate was manufactured, shedplate and new top lamp-bracket fitted, bufferbeam repainted and, using cleaning material brought from Shrewsbury shed on the inward working of No 75033, the loco was transformed. Finally the 'Cambrian Coast Express' headboard was proudly placed in position and, with the assistance of car-borne colleagues, the last run of this famous train was photographed climbing to Talerddig Summit.

Such an event would be a hard act to follow, but I did then discover, right on my own North Eastern doorstep, an idyllic three-mile long steam-hauled passenger branch line running between Alnmouth and Alnwick. At Alnmouth, there was even a small loco shed - a sub-depot of 52D Tweedmouth. Motive power was provided by Peppercorn LNER-design K1 2-6-0s, which had a layover at the attractive Alnwick station between duties. It was here, on the platform end, that I asked the crew if I could clean their engine – this being the one-time Fort William No 62011.

A few weeks later, I cleaned another one, No 62021, and on that occasion the crew joined in! Even later, in May 1966, upon returning from a weekend in Scotland, I popped into Alnmouth shed, only to discover to my astonishment that one of the very last V2s, No 60836, had been 'acquired' as a result of a motive power shortage, and that it had been rostered to work the two-coach branch passenger. In one hour, the V2 was cleaned up!

Eventually, this superb steam branch line operation went diesel as from 18 June 1966, but not before I had cleaned No 62011 overnight ready for the last day and then posed the entire Alnmouth shed staff in front of it. In the mid-afternoon of that final day, one of Tyne Dock's 9F 2-10-0s, No 92099, turned up - to see steam go out in a blaze of glory. It was filthy, of course, and I hastily suggested to the mass of enthusiasts present, that a rapid cleaning session was desired. This commenced on Alnmouth shed, but, such was the shortage of time, that the

Remarkably, Montrose depot became one of the final outposts of BR steam in Scotland, lasting until March 1967. A sub-shed of Dundee, elderly ex-North British Class J37 0-6-0s were retained here for working the daily freight to Brechin. In September 1966, No 64620, polished overnight to perfection, stands in the old wooden shed, prior to setting out on its daily trip to Brechin. MAURICE BURNS

The North British line from Morpeth to Riccarton Junction on the Waverley Route, had been cut back to Woodburn by the 1950s, but, somehow, a Thursdays-only freight survived until closure of the line. Having cleaned ex-NER J27 0-6-0 No 65842 on South Blyth shed, at the conclusion of a memorable day's photography, in perfect weather, a group of unofficial engine cleaners, Maurice Burns (left), Paul Riley, Tim Stephens and Dave Gouldthorp, pose on the bufferbeam at Woodburn on 22 September 1966. MAURICE BURNS

The Northumberland hills and autumnal colours are captured in this picture of ex-NER J27 0-6-0 No 65842 departing Woodburn with the Thursdays-only freight of 22 September 1966. It was pictures such as this that made the cleaning effort so worthwhile - even more so for the fact that this was the very last occasion a J27 worked the train from Woodburn and, within days, the line then closed for ever. MAURICE BURNS

cleaning had to be finished in Alnwick station! As news of such unofficial activities spread along the grapevine, the cleaning of engines by enthusiasts was gaining momentum. At the time, York shed had on loan Leeds Holbeck's 'Jubilee' No 45675 *Hardy* for passing-out firemen, this occurring on a York to Newcastle parcels turn. In the event, No 45675 was not only cleaned (in what is now the NRM), but the smokebox and bufferbeams were also totally repainted.

Over in the North West at Carnforth, another group of photographers had discovered that the unique Stephenson-Link 'Black Five' No 44767 was booked for a mid-day Morecambe to Leeds summer Saturday extra passenger. This particular engine cleaned up really well. The photograph, however, of the train climbing to Clapham, was only achieved after the gang had waded through Clapham Beck, the infant River Lune in bare feet, to reach their chosen location!

By the summer of 1966, every enthusiast was in Scotland, or so it appeared. Steam did not have long to go, yet it still consisted of a remarkably wide variety of engine types, from B1s and V2s, to A2s and A4s, besides some other attractive North

British products. Dundee was my favourite shed and, during that summer, its V2s were regularly rostered for a Dundee to Blackpool passenger. V2 No 60813, the one with the mini smoke deflectors, was the booked engine one day and came to receive the full overnight treatment. Seeing their immaculate engine as they turned up for duty, the crew were quite in disbelief. They did, however, kindly arrange some smoke for us as the train came off the Tay Bridge. No 60919 was cleaned for the same duty on yet another occasion. Clearly, this clandestine practice was now becoming commonplace and not only in Scotland, but anywhere from Blackpool to Aberdeen and maybe even farther afield.

One of my own favourites were Dundee's North British J37s, which were rostered on freight turns to Montrose. At the sub-shed at Montrose, another J37 was usually out-stationed. Being of wooden construction, this was a little dream of a depot, with its own coaling dock and turntable nearby. The normal duty for the loco was a daily freight turn on the Brechin branch and the shed was the scene of countless cleaning operations and the subject of numerous stories. On one

occasion, the steam-raiser came to work without a box of matches, only to ask us if we had any! On another day, a photographer, Chris Weston, freely admitted that he had cleaned the J37 overnight and, while waiting in his chosen spot on the branch on a hot summer's day, had fallen asleep - only to be awoken by the noise as the loco passed by... and far too late to photograph it!

Other adventures in 1966, included great times cleaning ex-NER J27s Nos 65842 and 65874 at South Blyth, for the operation of the Woodburn branch in rural Northumberland. Sometimes things would not turn out right, for example, when as usual we only cleaned one side of the engine for the photograph and the driver then forgot to turn the engine! Similarly, we once cleaned Q6 No 63387 at Sunderland, only for it to work just 'engine and van' up Seaton Bank – this was not what we had in mind! Worse though, was an ex-Crosti-boilered 9F cleaned at Leeds Holbeck, whose turn was cancelled altogether and, we being 20 miles away waiting at the lineside, we never knew! This is what it was like in the final year of steam, trying to capture engines we had made respectable – but there was

The rugged ex-NER J27 0-6-0s had outlasted many more modern machines, even when steam was in rapid decline. By 1967, their last stronghold had become at Sunderland South Dock, where four of the very last survivors, Nos 65855/11/94/79, all suitably cleaned, stand in the roundhouse prior to their very last day in traffic in the September. Very fortunately, one of these engines, No 65894, survived the scrapyards, thanks to donations made to the NELPG by enthusiasts from all over the UK. MAURICE BURNS

never any absolute guarantee of success. The autumn of 1966 saw a flurry of Scottish Region 'last runs'. First was the last A4, No 60019 *Bittern*, working between Glasgow and Aberdeen on 3 September, whose buffers I had painted white – the paint still being wet as it left Glasgow! The following month, on 8 October, was the final trip of the Peppercorn A2s. On that occasion, I spent the night on Edinburgh St Margaret's shed cleaning No 60532 *Blue Peter* and the steam-raiser was so sympathetic to the cause that he allowed me to drive the engine, at 02:00, from the running shed to the coaling plant, prior to departure – I just could not believe it! Later, I

photographed it at Shankend on the Waverley Route, but, in true *Blue Peter*-efficient style, the double chimney was clear - a total contrast to the single-chimney *Tudor Minstrel*, seen some time earlier over the same route.

On 5 November, I was back in Edinburgh, cleaning the last V2, No 60836, for its final run to Aberdeen and travelled on the train on its unforgettable southbound run. It was so off-beat, but sounded magnificent when climbing out of Montrose and, despite the dubious mechanical condition, it fully completed what was its final official task - before withdrawal. Finally, the last Scottish B1, No 61278, worked over the

Waverley Route on 3 December and, super-cleaned, was photographed as it laid a smokescreen over Whitrope Summit in the day's failing light.

1967 was to be the last year of truly main-line steam, but, remarkably, the J37s still held on to the Brechin branch until as late as March. That year did bring to an end these memorable trips to Scotland, but there were still other places to go. The real highlights by now were in the North East, where the last pre-grouping engines - the old Q6 and J27s - were still working 'bonus turns' from Sunderland South Dock and Hartlepool. Many J27s were cleaned, my hands being dirtied on Nos 65817, 65882, 65879 and 65894. The Q6s were not forgotten, with Sunderland's No 63395 and Hartlepool's No 63387 ending their working lives immaculate.

I never thought I would ever clean a WD 2-8-0, until, just three days before the end of steam in the North East, the Sunderland roster board said, '90009 coal from Easington to Consett'. Consett? I could not believe it! This would obviously be the last steam to Consett, so, on my own, I cleaned No 90009, to duly photograph her on the stiff 1-in-35 climb at Beamish - with arranged black smoke.

Leeds Holbeck, at this time, still had three 'Jubilees', No 45593 *Kolhapur*, No 45562 *Alberta* and No 45697 *Achilles* on its allocation. One of these became rostered for the relief 'Thames Clyde Express' on Saturdays throughout the summer and, on every occasion, they were cleaned by enthusiasts on the Friday night before. Upon starting to clean No 45697, when the layers of dirt were removed, the green boiler was found to be unlined, but its tender was lined out, but painted black! This had obviously come from a 'Black Five'.

The end of September saw the cleaning of the last B1, No 61306, at Low Moor, prior to the last

Aberystwyth station, Saturday 4 March 1967, the day of the final steam-worked 09:45 Aberystwyth-Paddington – the 'Cambrian Coast Express'. As it was not known in advance which engine would be rostered on the day, Dave Williams had enterprisingly provided an assortment of different numerals to glue onto a blank number plate. The plate itself was actually crafted literally from a piece of Aberystwyth shed obtained by Mr Riley, the unwanted remains of which still lie on the platform! Members of the cleaning gang include (left to right) Chris Weston, Dave Gouldthorp, Maurice Burns, Dave Lacey, Paul Claxton and Paul Riley. ALAN CASTLE

A rather grubby Standard 4MT 4-6-0 No 75033 stands at the platform at the head of the stock which will form the final steam-worked 'Cambrian Coast Express', and in this view, the transformation has commenced. A hand-painted 6C Croes Newydd shed-code has already been replaced with a more appropriate 89C Aberystwyth plate and a front number plate will also be constructed in due course. Notice also, the Western Region top lamp-bracket and the latter-day location of the previous LMR-style bracket (which has been temporarily removed). MAURICE BURNS

At the request of enthusiasts who had cleaned one of the last Q6 0-8-0s, the friendly crew from Sunderland South Dock shed, lay on a smoke-screen, as No 63395 engine climbs Seaton Bank with empties to Hetton on its very last day in traffic on 9 September 1967. It was photographic images such as this that created a big impact in the later NELPG fundraising campaign to save this particular engine from the scrapyard. MAURICE BURNS

Metamorphosis complete! Although neither a Machynlleth Manor nor chocolate and cream rolling stock were available, the original 'Cambrian Coast Express' headboard *was* and, given the changes that have clearly taken place in the intervening years, it, in no way, seems out of place! MAURICE BURNS

With the A470 road alongside remarkably free of traffic (for very few people knew about it), the final steam-hauled 'Cambrian Coast Express' climbs Talerddig Bank in fine style! ALAN CASTLE

Bradford to Leeds working with steam at the head of the 'Yorkshire Pullman'.

Carlisle Kingmoor still had the Britannia Pacifics, which were a fine attraction over Shap - when they could be tracked down. On December Saturday mornings, one of their final workings included the Carlisle to Manchester (Red Bank) empty parcel vans. On three consecutive weekends, the rostered Britannia was cleaned and, on two occasions, photographed climbing to Shap - with steam leaking from everywhere… and in driving rain. Hopeless! The final one we cleaned – No 70045 *Lord Rowallan* - was however caught on camera at Low Gill in the Lune Gorge and, at last, the sun shone! Kingmoor's last passenger working of all was, of course, the Carlisle to Blackpool football excursion, when No 70013 *Oliver Cromwell* was cleaned to perfection on Christmas Day. This occasion did bring to a close the real end of cleaning of express passenger engines in Britain.

In early 1968, with steam now banished from the Northern Fells and, with that, also from the main line, life would no longer be quite the same. I would now be venturing to new parts of the country – in the North West. The year got off to a bright start with several weekends at Buxton cleaning 8Fs in the old LNWR loco shed; Nos 48775, 48744, 48532 and 48191 being among those to receive the treatment. Unexpectedly, this produced some better than expected results. However, those glorious images of snow and steam hard at work, captured in frosty weather, would provide the very last opportunities to do this with BR steam - it only having months to go before the end.

Railtours kept the pulse racing and every engine on every railtour was now polished to perfection, usually almost entirely by the enthusiasts. After transfer to Carnforth, the last Britannia No 70013 *Oliver Cromwell* had become a celebrity engine and, now being cleaned just about every weekend, its paintwork was always immaculate.

I did take a week's holiday, concentrating on the final freight workings from Carnforth. There were a few highlights, such as on the Barrow line, with Arnside viaduct, Grange- over-Sands and Kents Bank, where coal, freight and parcels

On a perfect sunny morning at Carnforth shed in May 1967, Carlisle Kingmoor's unique Stephenson link motion LMS 'Black Five' No 44767 is cleaned by (L to R) Christopher Weston, Paul Claxton, Dave Gouldthorp and Ian 'Bert' Robb, as well as the photographer, prior to working a Morecambe to Leeds passenger train. MAURICE BURNS

The cleaning gang having waded in bare feet through the River Lune... reaching their chosen photo location the hard way, the end result was well worth it, as the, now immaculate, 'Black Five' 4-6-0 No 44767 climbs Bentham bank towards Clapham with a Morecambe to Leeds passenger train in May 1967. Thankfully this engine was preserved. MAURICE BURNS

Having been cleaned every Friday evening by enthusiasts at Leeds Holbeck shed, the last three active Jubilees – Nos 45593 *Kolhapur*, 45697 *Achilles* and *45562 Alberta* - pose in the roundhouse in August 1967. Every Saturday throughout the summer of 1967, one of these magnificent engines worked over the Settle and Carlisle line on the relief 'Thames Clyde Express'. MAURICE BURNS

trains still operated. My favourite, however, was the Windermere branch – a line that went to the hills and a goods yard that still had a daily delivery of wagons for the coal merchant. We cleaned Nos 45017 and 45025 at Carnforth.

The Grassington line from Skipton was another branch that saw steam to the very end and No 75034 was once cleaned up at Carnforth for that duty. The loco eventually being loaned to Rose Grove specifically for the purpose, Nos 75019, 75027 and 75048 also came to regularly attain their own super-shine finishes at the latter establishment.

On one occasion near the very end, 'Black Five' No 45134 had a layover at Kendal goods yard where the front end was quickly cleaned up prior to working back to Carnforth, producing one of my last decent shots of BR steam on freight – the footplate crew even co-operating with the smoke! Cleaning occurred at Kendal and Windermere on other occasions as well.

On 28 July 1968, there was a major session at Rose Grove, cleaning engines for the weekend's railtours. My own contributions were to 8F

No 48773 and 'Black Five' No 45156 *Ayrshire Yeomanry,* on both of which the paintwork did come up really well.

It was while on top of the boiler of No 45156 that day, that I noticed a light-blue Morris Minor police car driving right up to where we were working. We feared the worst. Had the shedmaster called in the law to remove the trespassing engine cleaners? Were we all to be 'booked' and fined... on the penultimate weekend of BR steam? I then could not believe my eyes, as the two policemen got out of the car to just stand and watch, but taking no action whatsoever! Realising this was a major photographic opportunity in the history of steam (!), I carefully walked behind the policemen (not that I had done this before, you understand) to take a picture of them watching us - the last engine cleaners on BR – cleaning engines. They never did realise!

So, upon reflection, what we did all those years ago in trying to photograph the last engines of BR was, for those involved, great fun, working with good company. From my first engine-cleaning experience with A4 No 60027 *Merlin* at Perth, to the last time with No 70013 *Oliver Cromwell* at Lostock Hall on 4 August 1968, there are a thousand happy memories in between.

Although what we accomplished was frequently without permission, on shed most of us were never challenged for trespassing. We possessed neither overalls nor safety boots, and no-one ever showed us the correct methods for climbing onto boilers, or onto the tops of tenders, but, despite this, no-one ever got hurt. More importantly, perhaps, we had no idea of what was supposed to be the proper method to clean engines, but, somehow, we did manage it, and managed it very well.

So what was left behind for us all today? Certainly, countless memorable photographs exist of our immaculate engines, of which only a few can be shown here, but there is something far more fundamental that has survived. For those involved in working so close to steam, many of us dearly wished that we could have saved all of those locomotives that we took such great pains to work upon.

My final photograph in this chapter, taken at the conclusion of the very last cleaning session at Lostock Hall, depicts some of our youthful group, posing on Lostock Hall's 8F No 48476 – the very last engine cleaners on BR. Among that gathering are faces that many readers may recognise today as later going on to assume major roles in the steam preservation movement. Some helped the NYMR or the Severn Valley. Others assisted in the fund-raising for and purchase of engines from BR by NELPG. Yet others later went on to rescue locomotives from Barry scrapyard. Some became volunteer firemen, or engine drivers, while others became engineers, involved in the restoration of steam engines to working order. One or two others even ended up in BR management roles.

Many of those depicted in that photograph have been in the steam preservation movement for a lifetime and I sincerely believe that, for them, it may very well all have started with cleaning the last engines on BR. A great deal more than just old photographs remains from those activities of 40 years ago and more. Those engine-cleaning pursuits sowed some of the seeds for the enthusiasm that has help shape, in no small way, the preservation movement that we know so well today.

The last active LNER B1 4-6-0, No 61306, having been cleaned overnight in Bradford Low Moor shed, departs Bradford Exchange on 30 September 1967 with the Bradford to Leeds portion of a King's Cross express. Luckily this engine was originally saved from the breakers yard by the B1 Locomotive Society. MAURICE BURNS

On 27 July 1968, enthusiasts get to work at Rose Grove shed on two locomotives rostered for railtour duty, 'Black Five' 4-6-0s Nos 45156 and 45073. A premature curtailment in activities was anticipated, when the long arm of the law was seen to enter the premises. Fearing the worst... and this on the penultimate weekend of BR steam, somebody's prayers must have been answered, for the two policemen were observed to get out of their car merely to stand and watch. In their taking no action whatsoever, this was a major photographic opportunity not to be missed! Certainly, there were, perhaps, more supporters of steam than anyone realised! MAURICE BURNS

At the conclusion of the final engine cleaning session of 3-4 August 1968, some of those involved pose on 8F 2-8-0 No 48476 at Lostock Hall shed. They are left to right on the running plate – Bob Clarke, Geoff Simpson, John Barnes, Dave Lacey, Dave Wilkinson, the late Ken Groundwater and Ian Krause... and below left to right – Jim Bodfish, Pete Proud, Kev Gould, Dave Gouldthorp, Tony Bending, Barry Buckfield, Neville Stead, Dave Williams and Mick York. It should be noted that many of those named, even in 1968, were already involved in the steam preservation movement and were later instrumental in shaping the railway preservation movement we all know so well today. MAURICE BURNS

Raw steam power at its finest! Greenholme, December 1967. In the failing light of a winter's afternoon, during the final week of steam over Shap Fell, a northbound fitted-freight hauled by a Stanier 'Black Five' is assisted to the summit by one of Tebay shed's Standard 4MT 4-6-0s. PAUL RILEY

Never Again!

The trials and tribulations of steam photography in the 1960s

Paul Riley

The 'MNA', an acronym for the 'Master Neverers Association', was an organisation founded upon a common desire to travel by train, while avoiding paying for the privilege. Its members also cleaned steam engines in their spare time and countless enthusiasts in the mid-1960s came to be in the debt of this group of young men, in recognition for those sterling efforts so selflessly extended to permit steam to die with at least some dignity. In the period in which the group flourished, between the mid-1960s and that final dramatic finalé at Lostock Hall on 4 August 1968 (when 13 engines were cleaned in one final, marathon, overnight session), there was a feeling of almost Masonic brotherhood about the organisation. The unspoken and unopposed leader was Paul Riley, who went on to create what is arguably one of the most exciting steam photographic collections of the period. Attempts to obtain the ultimate 'master-shot' were never going to be easy and usually required considerable effort, often resulting in little reward.

Railway photography, to me, was more of a way of life than a hobby. It began early in 1961, at a time when I chased trains on a push-bike. Photographically speaking, the first 12 months weren't up to much - a sort of trial and error period. However, cycle trips became longer and faster particularly when, in 1963, I chased LNWR 'Super D' 0-8-0 No 49361 around Birmingham on an SLS special, photographing it in no fewer than eight different locations.

On 3 March 1963, when the country was still in the depths of the 'Big Freeze', I left Coventry on that bicycle at 02:00 for Aylesbury. It was the last day of steam-hauled local passenger services on the Great Central and I obtained photographs at every station from Aylesbury (at first light) to Charwelton (at dusk) in the one day. Every few miles, I had to get off and sprint some distance, in an effort to keep my circulation going. Even so, my hands and feet stayed completely numb, but I am sure it was worth the effort!

My first Pentax SLR camera came on the scene in April 1963; its first outing being to Hatton Bank to photograph all 12 FA Cup semi-final specials on the occasion of Southampton's visit to Villa Park. The sight of Bulleid Pacifics, in addition to the regular diet of Castles and Halls, made quite a spectacle. Before the arrival of the Pentax, all my work was done on colour film. Initially using Perutz, I switched to Agfa CT18, before deciding upon Kodachrome II for the last 18 months of steam. For my black and white photography, I

mainly used Kodak Plus-X, but when conditions demanded I used Tri-X and Pan-X.

Saturday 26 September 1964, was the date of my first of many pilgrimages to the Waverley Route. The trip was basically to photograph Gresley A4 class Pacific No 60007 Sir Nigel Gresley on an RCTS special to Edinburgh, but, as it turned out, the picture was to be one of the worst I ever took on the line. The position I chose was just north of Riccarton Junction and, being some ten miles up the l-in-70 from Newcastleton, I anticipated that it would be struggling with 12 bogies (450 tons) behind the tender. There was even a V2 on standby at Riccarton, but in the event, No 60007 broke all records, clearing Whitrope summit at 38mph, with a clear chimney.

Paul Riley (left) with fellow engine cleaners Dave Gouldthorp and Tim Stephens on 65842 at Woodburn, September 1966. MAURICE BURNS

Scout Green, December 1967. The very last of the low winter sunlight highlights the exhaust from BR Standard class 5MT 4-6-0 No 73067 climbing Shap bank near Scout Green with a down freight banked in the rear by a Standard Class 4MT 4-6-0. PAUL RILEY

During subsequent visits to the Waverley Route, to photograph the only four steam workings per day, I became acquainted with a crowd of 'gentlemen' from the Midlands and, one weekend in the winter of 1965, six of us met up at Crewe. Taking the overnight Birmingham-Glasgow train as far as Carlisle, we transferred to the 04:45 to Edinburgh, as far as Hawick. Arriving in 20 degrees of frost, we then walked the 18-odd miles back to Steele Road and returned in the early hours of Sunday morning replete with only one shot. This was of a V2 at Shankend with the 08:06 Millerhill-Carlisle freight. Surprisingly, everyone was happy, perhaps due to the unsurpassed peace and beauty of the Border Country in winter which almost made the photography a secondary exercise.

During the summer of 1964, I travelled to Beattock, on the last day of the Glasgow Fairs Holiday, to photograph the returning specials from Blackpool and Morecambe, always an interesting affair, as Carlisle Kingmoor was invariably short of locomotives. I left Carlisle on one of those specials, after first checking with the crew that they would be taking assistance up the bank. At Beattock, I transferred from train to banker, for a lift to the summit and then started to walk back down the bank. Before first light (a fortnight at f2 exposure!), A2 Pacific No 60535 *Hornet's Beauty* went up the bank, to be followed by Stanier Pacific No 46255 *City of Hereford*.

After a good day, photographing a varied assortment of motive power, I waited at Beattock station for a southbound train and was not disappointed when No 46235 *City of Birmingham* drew into the platform. To my amazement, the Duchess was not taken off at Carlisle and continued south to Crewe. Having travelled back behind steam from Beattock, I was determined to continue behind steam to either Rugby or Birmingham - no matter how long it took! Six hours later, my prayers were answered in the form of another Duchess, this time No 46240 *City of Coventry*. The engine took over the relief 'Irish Mail', which departed some 40 minutes late with 14 bogies behind the tender and Riley on the footplate trying his hand at firing. Having uprated a roll of Tri-X to 3200ASA and still only managing to get an exposure of a thirtieth of a second at f2, I managed a shot of the speedometer reading 90-plus mph, quite an achievement on a locomotive footplate!

The year of 1965 was a very eventful one in Scotland. I had three separate weeks' holiday to

Unquestionably one of the finest steam action photographs taken in the Lune Gorge. On 25 February 1967, Stanier Jubilee 4-6-0 No 45562 *Alberta* creates an almost mystic effect in taking on slightly more than a full load of water as it thunders over Dillicar Troughs with the 'Border Countryman' railtour from Leeds to Beattock. Some slight adjustments (allegedly) having been made by the photographer to the water level in the troughs (a somewhat lower level by that time having been established for diesels with steam-heating boilers), the fireman had clearly not anticipated such an unexpected bonus! It, perhaps, goes without saying that Mr Riley's public-spirited efforts would not have been appreciated by any 'window-hangers' in the leading coach! PAUL RILEY

Express power at rest! A nocturnal interlude at Leeds Holbeck depot in Summer 1967. Having been polished to perfection by the MNA, two of the three remaining members of the Jubilee class 4-6-0, Nos 45562 *Alberta* and 45593 *Kolhapur*, await their day's duties, which will include working a couple of summer Saturday reliefs over the Settle & Carlisle line. PAUL RILEY

concentrate on the Glasgow-Aberdeen route. Daytime was spent taking photographs, usually finishing at Perth in time to catch the southbound 'West Coast Postal', which continued to Stirling, before the passenger Glasgow portion was split. The first night that I travelled on this train, I got chatting to the Carstairs crew, who adopted me as fireman as far as Stirling, following which I continued to Glasgow, where I picked up the 23:00 to Aberdeen. This was a regular A4 turn

and, by 'kipping on the cushions', I arrived at 03:00 in time to go down to the fish market for breakfast. These arrangements continued for most of that week and, occasionally, I would fire the A4 back to Aberdeen. One night, while noshing an Angus steak butty in Perth refreshment rooms, the fireman of the 20:25 'Postal' entered in a fuming temper and threw his gloves at me, uttering obscenities about a Britannia (although that wasn't what he called it!) that wouldn't steam. I

took the hint and, as it was 20:00, I had 25 minutes to sort it out. I first tried the pricker, but the clinker was absolutely solid. So, all I could do was to build up the fire very carefully, but at 20:25, only 160psi showed on the gauge. The driver opened the regulator fully, allowing No 70041 *Sir John Moore* to slip violently (a last resort to break up the fire), but, after firing steadily to Gleneagles, there was still only 160psi on the gauge. This remained constant to Stirling, where the idle fireman talked me into carrying on to Carstairs. Here, he was relieved by the Carstairs crew, who were equally happy to let me continue to Carlisle and where we arrived at midnight with Riley completely knackered. However, after a wash and breakfast in the railwaymen's bothy, I boarded the 02:25 to Perth behind another Britannia, No 70048 *The Territorial Army 1908-1958*. By Beattock, I was back on the footplate back to Perth, where I took a well-earned couple of hours 'kip' in the three-star 'ECS Hotel'.

It was during this same week, while busy working Hilton Junction box, that I met Maurice Burns, just as A4 No 60027 *Merlin* came past with the 10:15 ex-Edinburgh. Both Maurice and I decided to go round to Perth MPD to ascertain the return working. When questioned, the foreman replied that it would be returning to Edinburgh at 14:55. Just as we were about to go off shed and back up the line, we looked at No 60027, then at each other, realising that it was quite the filthiest A4 that we had ever seen. We decided it could do with cleaning. Tongue-in-cheek, we returned to the foreman and asked if we could clean it. His reply was that he hadn't any cleaners on shed. To this, we said again that WE would clean it. Very mildly and half-

It's April 1967, but winter still has a firm grip on the slopes of Wild Boar Fell. Slogging up the final few yards to Ais Gill Summit is Holbeck Stanier 'Black Five' No 44912 heading for home with the morning Carlisle-Leeds (Hunslet) freight. Once the last of the wagons has passed under the bridge, the work will be over for the crew and they can settle back for the mainly downhill run from here to Settle Junction. PAUL RILEY

heartedly, he said that we couldn't do that. Not getting the inevitable marching orders, we decided to hunt round for some cotton waste and paraffin. Working very fast, we had the engine clean in no time, but hit problems with the tender. A ladder was needed, so I slipped back into the gloom of the shed and laid my hands on one. Heading hack to the yard and No 60027, I was spotted by the foreman. After all, I was a bit conspicuous with a damned great ladder over my shoulder. Carrying on, I sensed I was being followed, all the time fearing the big crunch and having to photograph a clean locomotive and dirty tender. By the time that he had caught up with me, I had the ladder up on the tender and was going like mad with the cotton waste. To our amazement, he stood watching with his hands behind his back and mouth wide open.

Eventually, the silence broke: "Ach, a've noo ever seen anything like it in 40 years of service!" He then insisted on being photographed with us and No 60027! (See previous chapter) Even so, the final photograph at Glenfarg was a dead loss - but the cleaning session was very significant in being the first of a very long line of similar tasks. This procedure spread so rapidly and with such keen interest that crowds of us would leave our homes on Friday evenings to clean up anything from the Lymington branch engine to A4s at Aberdeen (Ferryhill).

In 1965, BR approached me for the use of some of my photographs taken on the West Highland line for a Highland Railway exhibition in Inverness - and asked me to name my own price. I asked for 30/- (£1.50)… and a bit of co-operation regarding LNER A2 No 60530 *Sayajirao* of Dundee (62B). These single-chimney A2s had haunted me and I couldn't get one working on an ordinary passenger train. This was annoying, particularly after seeing all the WJV Anderson masterpieces - yes, I was jealous! My request was that No 60530 should be rostered to work the 10:15 Dundee-Glasgow and the 18:15 return for one week, commencing 30 August. To this, BR agreed in part, namely to roster it for the Monday only. As Sundays were fairly quiet in Scotland, Dave Gouldthorp and I decided to spend the afternoon cleaning No 60530 on

Such is the sedate progress of this heavy train, that No 48448 is seen again a mile or so further on from the picture at the foot of the page, this time leaving Holme Tunnel and within yards of Copy Pit Summit, where brakes will be pinned down for the switchback descent to Hall Royd Junction, Todmorden. PAUL RILEY

Dundee MPD. Unfortunately, we hadn't allowed for the temperament of the shed foreman, who just wouldn't hear of us cleaning one of HIS engines. Not to be outdone, we crept back at 02:00 and spent three hours cleaning the loco, until you could have eaten your dinner off the top of the boiler! Next, it was off to Auchterarder for the outward journey and to Dunblane for the return. As BR had informed me that it was for one day only, we took off for Ayrshire and the Fowler 'Crabs' on the Tuesday, only to find on our return to Glasgow that No 60530 had worked the same turn again. Back to Dundee we went, to check the roster board for the Wednesday which read '10.15am Glasgow - 44718'. During the wee hours this mysteriously became '10.15 am Glasgow - 60530' !

As luck would have it, we just happened to be at Hilton Junction to photograph the outward journey and St Rollox for the return. Although Monday evening's shot was useless, the other three were quite acceptable - all this in just three days… after three years of trying.

In April 1967, I procured a provisional driving licence and, after three or four hours' tuition, I purchased a beat-up Vauxhall Wyvern for £40. The first jaunt, to Birkenhead, was obviously a trial and error affair, although the normally steel nerves of my passengers began to soften well before we got back to Birmingham.

After only a couple of months, the old Vauxhall began to break up - literally. The Buxton-Glossop road claimed the front bumper and the back one disappeared while chasing a special on the

A cold frosty morning at Cliviger in February 1968. There is absolutely no wind about to disturb the stillness and the exhaust of Rose Grove's Stanier 8F 2-8-0 No 48448 hangs along the valley as the loco climbs to Copy Pit Summit with 7N82, the 06:53 Farington Junction to Cudworth coal empties. PAUL RILEY

With steam leaking from blowing piston glands on both side of the loco, 8F 2-8-0 No 48448 appears still to be very much in command of its task, when seen near Cornholme with a westbound coal train climbing to Copy Pit summit in March 1968. PAUL RILEY

before the day was out) in the boot, and with two passengers on the back seat, we left Coventry at 05:00 for a trip which usually takes an hour and a half. It soon became evident that things were not going to be easy, with the M6 looking more like a battlefield than a motorway. Vehicles were abandoned everywhere - not only on the hard shoulder, but over all six lanes as well. I managed to pick my way through these and got to Macclesfield at 07:00, although the town had, officially, been cut-off since midnight.

The snow was still falling, but after much discussion we decided to attempt to reach Gowhole via Whaley Bridge. We soon started to encounter problems on the climb out of Macclesfield, as the route was up a l-in-10 out of the town. Nevertheless, I managed to pass everything that was stuck, including a milk float with snow-chains. At the top of the hill, with snow drifting to depths of over 4ft in places, two lorries had collided and closed the road, so we had to turn back and try another way out. This time, we tried the direct road to Buxton (the A537) known locally as the 'Cat & Fiddle Road', after the pub high on the moors and much renowned in this type of weather - but I'd never heard of it - then. I soon learned!

The first few miles were relatively easy, but then we hit snow drifts up to 8ft deep. I soon discovered the only way of continuing was to hit the drifts at 30-40mph, first knocking a hole in them and, of course, getting stuck, before reversing about 200 yards and blasting through the gap. Inevitably, the car eventually became embedded, so at that point the shovels came out and we started digging. This process continued for over an hour, with our making only minimal progress, probably about two miles in that time.

We were now heading into the country, with little sign of habitation, and from here the rate of progress was very slow and strenuous. It must have been sheer lunacy, but we pushed on… until it happened. I completely missed a Y-junction and embedded the motor in 4ft of snow. I had become almost completely buried in a particularly deep drift, with the car partly off the road, when out of the blizzard came two large headlights. It was a huge snowplough, which stopped just short of our car. The driver got out of the cab, came over to us and asked where we were heading. "Buxton," was our reply, to which his response was, "Are you crazy? This road's been closed for the last 24 hours!" It was at this point that we decided to dig the car out, turn it round, and head back to Macclesfield, trailing the snowplough.

Back in the café, we recovered from the hypothermia/exhaustion with mugs of hot tea, and then referred to the map to plan our next move. We decided that a safer bet would be to head north on the A523 and then take the A6 south of Stockport. This we managed to do, without too much bother, although a number of trees had been brought down across the A6 south of Chapel-en-le-Frith, but by this time the route had been cleared for traffic.

We finally arrived in Buxton sometime in the early afternoon, and headed straight for the sheds. I remember attempting to drive down an alleyway on the approach to the MPD, but the car became stuck in another snowdrift. "You go and see what's working and I'll dig the car out," I said to Allan Stewart, so he headed away from the car and up a banking, only to discover the sheds standing in an oasis of undisturbed snow. It was pretty obvious that no engines had moved that

Southern near Andover. The last trip with it was certainly the most interesting. With the usual complement of five in the car, we chased a Stanier Class 5 up Shap, from Tebay, and when cornering fairly hard, it started to handle very strangely. Upon investigation (naturally, after the shot) we discovered that a 2ft length of leaf spring had come through the boot. The following day, we continued to Berwick to see preserved A4 No 4498 *Sir Nigel Gresley* and, upon checking the oil and water levels, I noticed that the engine had developed a ten-degree list to one side (due to shattered engine mountings). This really put the wind up me, to the extent of imposing a 30mph speed limit for the rest of the trip, for fear of having a 1500cc engine on our laps. Having taken the shot of No 4498 on Cockburnspath Bank, we commenced the return journey from Grantshouse to Coventry. Thirteen hours of solid

driving later, with stops only for black coffee, it was straight into work - and they called this enjoyment!

The next arrival on the scene was a beautiful blue 12-year-old Mk 1 Ford Zephyr, which was to outlast BR steam - just. Eighteen months and 60,000 miles takes some stamina, especially for a 12-year-old. It was with this motor that I discovered radial tyres, especially after getting only 6000 miles from a set of cross-plies. This change to radials definitely increased consumption - shots per mile that is!

On Monday 5 February 1968, it snowed heavily and the forecast was for more, so I thought conditions would be perfect for the Buxton area with 8Fs off Gowhole and working up to Chinley and Chapel-en-le-Frith. So, with two 1cwt iron castings (borrowed from work) and two large shovels, (these would be well used

Having worked a train of empties earlier in the day over to Healey Mills Yard, No 48448 now returns home with a Healey Mills to Wyre Dock load of coal. On a line that even today continues to produce seemingly endless new photo opportunities on its climb from Todmorden to Copy Pit summit, the 8F is seen winding its way through the rooftops on the reverse curves near Portsmouth. PAUL RILEY

day. Determined to find the answer, Allan stumbled across the hidden tracks and into the building. At the shed foreman's office, he politely asked, "What engines will be working today?" - only to be met with the reply: "You don't think we'd send engines out in this weather, do you?" Allan headed back to the car to give me the bad news and, in fact, we both then had a good laugh at the foreman's rhetoric!

After that, there was only one place to go and that was to the local alehouse, before the return journey to Coventry, which was a little easier and did involve no shovelling. Nine 8Fs and one 'Black Five' were on shed that day and we didn't get a single photo - even of RDU 290 stuck in the drifts!

The following Saturday, we were off up to Buxton again, with another 05:00am start. We made it this time and managed to photograph steam in the last of the clearing snow.

Yes, RDU 290 certainly did herself justice and ended her life in a blaze of glory. On Boxing Day 1967, with new engine just run-in and tuned to perfection, we took off for Shap with five for Britannia No 70013 Oliver Cromwell on a football special to Blackpool.

We arrived at Strickland Woods in frosty, foggy weather, but as No 70013 appeared, the sun broke through, just like magic and, contrary to expectations, stayed out all day. From Strickland to Shap Summit, we caught the train at six different locations and then decided to continue chasing to Preston, this with the help of 105mph from RDU 290.

On the M6 we overtook the train and then, from 90mph to a dead stand on the hard shoulder, we halted under a bridge with the car-bonnet up, scrambling up onto the bridge to shoot 70013. Then it was back to the car to slam the bonnet shut, with 37 shots of Oliver Cromwell

in the bag… all in immaculate condition and ideal weather!

After all these years, there is still a weekend in August when we all get together at The Station Inn at Ribblehead. After drinking to all hours and singing all those educational rugby songs, the following morning sees us collecting all the stragglers - who have the knack of ending up anything up to two miles away from everyone else. This annual reunion is now the high point of the year and will continue, I am convinced, until the last one of us has drawn his last breath!

Paul Riley (1945 to 1976)

● The above text is based upon 'Railway Rantings', a set of notes Paul Riley compiled some time before his untimely death in August 1976, with additional contributions by Allan Stewart, Ian Krause and Alan Castle. Part of Paul's words and some of his work can be viewed today online, courtesy of The Restoration & Archiving Trust, custodians of his slide collection, at http://www.gwrarchive.org/site/sitel2ph/sitel3ph/autobiography.html

Copies of Paul's photographs, as illustrated in this book and on the website, can be obtained by contacting r_and_a.trust@btinternet.com

Snaking round the reverse curves between Cornholme and Portsmouth, 8F 2-8-0 No 48247 climbs to Copy Pit summit with a Healey Mills to Wyre Dock coal train. Banking assistance at the rear is provided by sister engine number No 48257, which, as yet, is still out of sight. 24 February 1968. PAUL RILEY

Closed

3 March 1968

Northwich MPD

Trafford Park MPD

Buxton MPD

On the very last day of steam, 2 March 1968, Stanier 8F 2-8-0 No 48744 has been rostered to work a stone train up the Hindlow branch to Briggs Sidings As this duty produced the last engine to be booked off Buxton shed in revenue-earning service and, having been specially cleaned the previous night, it is now the centre of attention for railway men and enthusiasts alike as it is turned to work chimney-first up the hill out of town. MAURICE BURNS

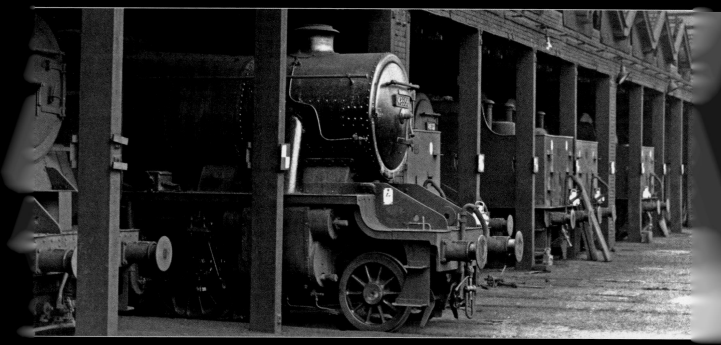

Trafford Park MPD in early 1968. The former 'joint' depot was particularly interesting for the variety of engines, including Great Central and Midland types until the end of the 1950s, augmented briefly by some of Great Northern and even of Great Eastern origin. Here, Stanier 8F No 48356 pokes its nose out from under a roof that has seen much better days. With a continuing lack of maintenance to the structure, most of the remainder of the roof had already been removed altogether. TOM HEAVYSIDE

The propensity of 8-coupled and 10-coupled motive power depicted in this view is the clearest possible indicator that, in its final years, 8E Northwich was very much a freight-traffic orientated depot. Situated on the Cheshire Lines Committee Manchester (Central) to Chester (Northgate line), much of the shed's work originated from large chemical works in the locality. The former ICI Mond Division soda ash works set up in the 1920s, with its need for tons of limestone every day from the Peak District has also been a mainstay of the line and still generates much of the freight traffic in the locality today. In this view the engines nearest the camera, on

Peak steam farewell
The last winter of steam in Derbyshire

During the first two months of 1968, the attention of most photographers had transferred from the now steamless Shap and Ais Gill to an area south-east of Manchester, where steam was still employed on freight duties. Working along part of the Midland Railway's highly scenic Manchester to Derby main line, through the Derbyshire Peak District, steam still handled minerals traffic from the Manchester area to Buxton and to large lime-works complexes around Peak Forest. During the course of several successive weekends, and with snow often heavy on the ground, a series of apparently never-ending freights, hauled by specially cleaned 8Fs 'performed to the gallery' in the area between Gowhole Yard and Dove Holes Tunnel. Here, on 3 February 1968, LMS 8F 2-8-0 No 48442 passes Chinley South Junction with a mixed freight including wagon-loads of coal bound for Buxton Yard. DEREK HUNTRISS

LMS Stanier 8F 2-8-0 No 48442 approaches Chinley Station on 3 February 1968 with a mixed freight bound for Buxton. With rationalisation having taken place in recent years, only the two tracks nearest the camera remain in situ today. Although heavy limestone trains still ply the route between Tunstead and Northwich, freight traffic of the order shown here has now become another aspect of a long-vanished era. DEREK HUNTRISS

Always a location popular with photographers is Chinley North Junction. The home signal is pulled off, permitting 8F 2-8-0 No 48744 to cross over the junction to head a train of 16-ton mineral wagons up the former Midland main line towards Peak Forest. January 1968. PAUL RILEY

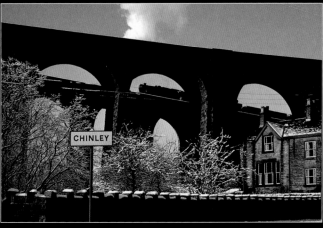

There is no doubt as to the location of this photograph! Heading for Buxton, 8F 2-8-0 No 48442 passes over the lofty viaduct forming Chinley North curve, with a freight working bound for Buxton Yard on 3 February 1968. DEREK HUNTRISS

In early 1968, operational difficulties became compounded, when problems in Dove Holes Tunnel dictated that single-line working had to be initiated for weeks on end, while engineering work continued. This meant that up trains had to reverse onto the down line at Chapel-en-le-Frith, in order to work 'wrong-line' as far as Peak Forest, this, at times, producing inevitable bottle-necks to traffic. At nearly 1000ft above sea level and at the summit of a long climb at 1-in-90, 8F 2-8-0 No 48191 emerges from the 2984 yards-long Dove Holes Tunnel with a Gowhole Yard to Buxton train of mineral empties in February 1968. MAURICE BURNS

Buxton shed's 8F 2-8-0 No 48465 shunts loaded coal wagons in the sidings adjacent to the quarry of the Buxton Lime Company (now RMC Roadstone) at Peak Forest. Although the quarry still despatches stone by rail today, most of the buildings depicted in this January 1968 view have since disappeared. DEREK HUNTRISS

On 17 February 1968, 8F 2-8-0s Nos 48775 and 48424 double-head a heavy rock train past Peak Forest summit, bound for Port Talbot in South Wales. It will be noticed that No 48775 still possesses its WD-type top-feed and that No 48424 has a larger than normal vacuum ejector on the side of the boiler – having been allocated to the Western Region for some years before moving to Buxton. The pilot engine will travel as far as Edale on the Hope Valley line, where it will be removed. MAURICE BURNS

The Torrs at New Mills is a dramatic gorge, above which the town perches and along the bottom of which lie 18th century mills and weirs on the River Goyt. The railway, too, hugs the walls, before disappearing into two separate tunnels at the junction of the Hayfield branch with the Midland main line from Chinley to Manchester. Here, in the early weeks of 1968, Edge Hill's 8F 2-8-0 No 48056 heads a Gowhole Yard to Garston freight towards New Mills Central Station. The Hayfield Branch (closed in 1970) is seen behind the train. ALAN CASTLE

The swan-song for steam at Buxton. On the very last day, 2 March 1968, Stanier 8F 2-8-0 No 48744 has been rostered to work a stone train up the Hindlow branch to Briggs sidings on the steeply-graded remnant of the old Ashbourne line (at 1267ft, reputedly the highest point on BR in England). The working proving to be the final revenue-earning turn at 9L, the major concern of the photographers is that locomotives invariably worked tender-first up the hill. Nevertheless, someone did successfully persuade the crew to take such a significant working engine-first, this permitting numerous pictures to be secured of the train as it slowly made its way through the snow-clad moors. IAN KRAUSE

Ashwood Dale is a spectacularly narrow deep-cut and tree-lined valley just outside Buxton, along which the former Midland route towards Millers Dale fights for space with both the River Wye and the A6 trunk road. Here, Stanier 8F 2-8-0 No 48191 threads one of the most scenic sections, past Lovers Leap, with a Gowhole freight to Buxton in February 1968. ALAN CASTLE

The majority of enthusiasts had more than enough to occupy them during the opening months of the year, what with intense activity in the scenic Buxton area and a mad dash to cover the rapidly vanishing number of remaining passenger workings. It was not surprising, therefore, that the first specials to be hauled by steam did not operate until the middle of March. On 17 March, two tours organised by the Williams Deacons Bank Club ran on the same day between Stockport and Carnforth, via Blackburn and Skipton. The first special being heavily over-subscribed, a relief train was soon arranged to run 30 minutes behind the first one. On the Stockport-Accrington leg, the first special was hauled by No 4472 *Flying Scotsman* and 'Black Five' No 45290. The second train, seen here halted at Waltons Sidings due to single-line working in Sough Tunnel, was worked by No 70013 *Oliver Cromwell* and 'Black Five' No 45110. PETER FITTON

Springtime steam specials

Three weeks later, on 6 April, the LCGB ran its 'Lancastrian' Railtour. Using Edge Hill's 'Black Five' No 45305, this ran from Liverpool Lime Street to Manchester Piccadilly, via Warrington Arpley and Northenden, then on to Wigan Wallgate via Tyldesley, before then heading for Edge Hill via the Southport avoiding line and the Bootle Branch. Here No 45305 is seen passing Gathurst, on the Wigan-Meols Cop leg. PETER FITTON

At Edge Hill, shortly before the LCGB special returned to Lime Street station, the itinerary included a short diversion from the main line to head down through Waterloo Tunnel to the Riverside station of the Mersey Docks & Harbour Board. This steeply graded branch had been specifically constructed for American boat trains arriving directly on the quayside, from London Euston and No 45305 is seen here crossing a dock entrance bridge just outside the Riverside terminus. With the ending of transatlantic sailings from Liverpool, the line saw little further use and the final working occurred in 1971 when a troop train was run in connection with the 'troubles' in Northern Ireland. The station has since been demolished and the site is now occupied by new waterfront office accommodation. DAVE RODGERS

One week later, it was the Easter weekend and on 13 April, BR (Scottish Region) operated its traditional 'Easter Grand Tour'. Running from Edinburgh Waverley, via the now late and lamented Waverley Route and the Settle & Carlisle line, with diesel power, No 70013 Oliver Cromwell was waiting to take over at Hellifield. The route then lay via Blackburn, Bolton and Manchester Victoria to Stockport. Here, Oliver Cromwell is seen climbing away from Wilpshire Tunnel towards Blackburn. ALAN CASTLE

The following weekend, on 20 April, it was the turn of the RCTS to run its 'Lancastrian No 2' railtour from Liverpool. No 70013 Oliver Cromwell is seen here heading through typical Southern Lakeland scenery along the Oxenholme-Windermere branch. MAURICE BURNS

At Morecambe, Carnforth's 'Black Five' No 45342 joined No 45156 to take the RCTS train forward to Preston. A vacuum fault had been discovered on No 45342, which necessitated swapping Nos 45342 and 45156 around, putting the extremely polished No 45156 next to the coaches, much to the disappointment of lineside photographers. Here the duo are seen climbing to the eastern portal of Wilpshire Tunnel. ALAN CASTLE

Also on 20 April 1968, the Manchester Rail Travel Society, in association with the Severn Valley Railway Society, ran 1Z77, the first of their two 'North West Tours' from Birmingham New Street. 'Black Five' Nos 45110 & 44949 took over at Stockport to head the special up the ex-LNW line to Buxton. Here they are seen working hard past Lyme Park on the climb up to Disley. ALAN CASTLE

A few minutes later and the MRTS/SVR tour of 20 April is now in the majestic Peak District National Park. Climbing along the valley side between Whaley Bridge and Chapel-en-le-Frith, 'Black Fives' Nos 45110 & 44949 are seen between Chapel-en-le-Frith South and Dove Holes, soon after crossing over the Midland route to Millers Dale. PETER FITTON

Having traversed both routes to Buxton, a later stage of the 20 April MRTS/SVR tour and an engine change at Stalybridge sees Standard 5MT 4-6-0 Nos 73134 & 73069 working the leg via Standedge to Huddersfield and then down the Calder Valley line through Hebden Bridge onto the Copy Pit route. Here the train approaches Marsden Station. PETER FITTON

On the Blackburn-Bolton line, Standard 5MT 4-6-0 Nos 73134 & 73069 are in charge of the MRTS/SVR tour and are seen climbing past the little-used goods yard at the closed Spring Vale station, shortly before passing through Sough Tunnel. This section of the route has been singled in recent times. DEREK HUNTRISS

A somewhat circuitous stage of the MRTS/SVR tour of 20 April was between Bolton and Stockport, but via Rochdale and Oldham. Stanier 8F 2-8-0 No 48773 worked this section and is seen here climbing Broadfield Bank, being driven by Rose Grove's Roy Burton and fired by Alan Roberts. Apart from a distinct lack of factory chimneys in the skyline of today, the location may nevertheless be familiar to some, for it is now part of the East Lancashire Railway's Heywood extension. PETER FITTON

On the section between Stockport and Liverpool Lime Street, a further engine change on the MRTS/SVR tour of 20 April saw one of the last remaining 9F 2-10-0s, No 92160, take charge. This was indeed the penultimate occasion on which a 9F would haul a passenger train; the final time being with 92218 on a repeat to the tour on 27 April. No 92160 is here seen passing the closed Northenden station on the CLC route to Liverpool. A Speke Junction engine at this time, it will shortly move to Carnforth to become one of the last two working members of the class. DEREK HUNTRISS

On 28 April 1968, GC Enterprises operated their 'NW Circular Tour', hauled throughout by Britannia Pacific No 70013 *Oliver Cromwell*. Just as the train title suggests, the special is seen here on the Southport-Burscough stage of a circular journey round Merseyside prior to venturing up the Calder Valley line to Todmorden and Copy Pit. DEREK HUNTRISS

On 27 April 1968, the MRTS/SVR ran the second of their two 'North West Tours' from Birmingham New Street. In a repeat itinerary, but with some changes in individual locomotives, in this splendid hillside vista, ex-LMS 'Black Five' 4-6-0s Nos 45073 & 45156 are seen climbing round the long curve above Coombs reservoir on the LNW route into Buxton. BOB CLARKE

Carnforth's 'Black Five' No 45025 lays a smokescreen along the cutting past Skew Bridge signal box, one mile south of Preston, with the 06:15 Heysham Harbour to Manchester Victoria – the last-ever steam-hauled up 'Belfast Boat Express', Sunday 5 May 1968. ALAN CASTLE

'Belfast Boat Express'

A significant event in the run-up to the very end was the demise of steam at the beginning of May 1968 on Britain's last steam-hauled titled express

Alan Castle

It is 7am on 4 May 1968. At the start of another glorious spring day, the sun climbs ever higher in the sky, gradually warming the untamed vegetation through which butterflies are lazily fluttering. Apart from occasional birdsong, solitude is absolute at such an hour in the four-track cutting carrying the West Coast Main Line southwards from Preston to Farington Junction.

There is little or no freight or passenger traffic about this early on Saturday mornings, particularly as the commencement of the frenetic seasonal holiday reliefs and excursions to the coast are yet a couple of months hence.

From the open doorway of Skew Bridge signalbox, the strains of Satchmo's recent number one hit, *What a Wonderful World*, waft gently across the permanent way, being emitted from a small transistor radio sat by the track diagram panel. Peter Kellett, booked signalman on 6 to 2 shift, has his feet up, heavily engrossed in the morning paper.

All of a sudden, 'clang!', one of numerous bells on the block telegraph clamours out 'call attention!'. This unwarranted intrusion has emanated from Ribble Sidings 'box, about half a mile to the north.

Pete puts down his *Daily Mirror*, leaping up to respond to the call. The up fast line instrument

now emits four more rings in quick succession, indicating the request: 'Is line clear for express passenger train?' Pete responds in the affirmative and moves along the instrument shelf to contact Farington Curve Junction, the next 'box to the south, in similar fashion.

'Line clear!' is again received and Pete, placing his left foot on the lever frame casting, swings purposefully back on his 'home' and then his 'distant' signal levers. These are long hard pulls, for some of the cables are well over ¼ mile in length. Task completed, he steps back and turns to log the time of the movement in his train register, then moves to open the end window of the 'box in order to observe the spectacle now beginning to emerge from the platform ends of Preston station in the hazy distance one mile to the north.

The telegraph rings twice more, as a billowing white exhaust hanging in the still cool air starts to materialise beyond the massive signal gantries. The low head-on sunlight reflects off a gleaming smokebox door as an indistinct shimmering vision at last begins to take on form. Working hard on the rising gradient, it takes another minute or so to reach the 'box before an immaculate ex-LMS 'Black Five' 4-6-0 No 45342, with Carnforth's legendary Ted Fothergill at the controls, steams majestically by with seven Mk1 coaches in uniform blue and grey livery in tow.

A quick glance at the red-backed headboard on the loco confirms the train to be the 'Belfast Boat Express' en route for Manchester Victoria. It is the very last officially titled train on BR to be steam worked – and, after some 40 years of running from Heysham, this is the penultimate time that steam will work it.

As the last vehicle disappears around the curve under the massive Leyland Road bridge, a smoke screen slowly settles in the still air, bringing with it one of, arguably, the most delicious smells in the world – that aroma of hot oil and steam that permeates every fibre of one's being.

With some almighty crashes, the levers are thrust back in the frame and solitude returns to the valley once more. Pete slides the window shut and returns to his armchair, ever conscious that he has just signalled his very last steam-hauled train transporting passengers from the Irish boat via Heysham. Agreed, the final two runs of all are scheduled to take place the following day, but as this particular 'box will be switched out from 22:00 Saturday until 06:00 Monday, Pete regrets that he will not be there to witness either of these.

In the event, it would be up to No 45025, another 'Black Five' from the Carnforth stable, to assume responsibility for the very last out and home duties. Quite fitting is the fact that these particular two locomotives had been selected to share the final honours, for between them, they had accounted for appearances at the head of the train on no fewer than 90 days during the previous six months – indeed with No 45025 taking the lion's share on an amazing 47 occasions!

The previous four decades

The history of the Irish boat traffic through Lancashire is complex, dating back to 1843, at which time sailings commenced from Fleetwood, but it was, somewhat surprisingly, the Midland Railway that originally developed the deep-water port at Heysham, this opening in 1874.

The precursor of the Manchester service extant into the 1970s was initially known as the 'Manchester Boat Train' and started life in the 1920s as a through train from Leeds via the L&Y routes through Manchester.

Precisely when the change in title came about is somewhat unclear, but, unlike the far more celebrated 'Ulster Express' connecting Heysham Harbour with London Euston, no formal title ever appeared to have been bestowed upon the rolling stock in the form of dedicated carriage roofboards.

Perhaps such an unfortunate omission arose as a consequence of the fact that as it was essentially a nocturnal operation for the majority of the journey, running mainly under the cover of darkness, any public relations element was likely to be minimal. Certainly, the Belfast steamer connecting with the Manchester train (and with the 'Ulster Express' of course) normally left Heysham at around 23:40, so the train's passing would normally have gone virtually unnoticed by all but a mere handful of the travelling public.

In early LMS days, the title 'Ulster Link' at Carnforth 'Western' shed indicated that the depot had been allocated the duties of working the 'Ulster Express' non-stop from Morecambe to Crewe.

This was a most important train and such was the interest created that instead of providing additional LNWR engines, the motive power department decided to transfer eight three-cylinder Midland Compound 4-4-0s to the depot.

Yet further into its journey and now having branched off the West Coast Main Line, No 45025 makes good headway beyond the Chorley stop, near Adlington on the Euxton Jct-Bolton section, with the final steam-hauled up 'Belfast Boat Express', on Sunday 5 May 1968 PETER FITTON

Eight senior drivers were each allocated a Compound and in order to make up a full eight weeks' work, they were also alternately rostered to work the 'Manchester Boat Train' from Heysham Harbour to Manchester Victoria.

Right up until the very last workings in the early 1970s, the latter was always diagrammed to follow the 'Ulster Express' from Morecambe every morning, but scheduled to stop to pick up passengers en route at Lancaster, Preston and Chorley.

In the wartime years, upon arrival in Manchester, the loco uncoupled and made its way to Red Bank sidings to turn and to pick up a set of coaches to return to Morecambe.

After the end of the war, Carnforth-based Jubilees and 'Black Fives' worked the service for many years, until the controversial D57xx

'Metrovick' 1200hp Co-Bo two-stroke-engined diesels took over in about 1963.

Based on Barrow shed, the unique locomotives had been operating for a further number of years within the Workington-Preston-Carlisle triangle before a local decision was made to try them on a more prestigious duty, namely the 'Belfast Boat'.

This move, however, was destined to be short-lived for, seemingly, after having duly returned all 20 locomotives of the particularly unreliable class to Metropolitan-Vickers' works at Manchester to receive modifications; such efforts produced little improvement in terms of reliability. Unfortunately, or fortunately, depending on one's point of view, it then became an undeniable fact that steam was often called upon to substitute and by 1965, the failure rate of the Co-Bos had got so out of hand that it was finally acknowledged that a mistake had been made.

In the summer of 1964, still interspersed with the odd 'Metrovick', Nos 45606 *Falkland Islands* (10A), 45017 (9D), 45284 (8A) and the most appropriate engine of all, No 45526 *Morecambe and Heysham* (12B), asserted themselves on 1P02. On 5 Sept, No 45588 *Kashmir* (12A) was identified and on 19 April 1965, within days of being condemned, No 45666 *Cornwallis* (8B) worked the train.

During this spring, motive power for the evening train was clearly Newton Heath-based but using Agecroft crews and with 'Black Fives' being the norm, albeit with sundry variations both in class and depot. Nevertheless, the train was attracting attention locally and 9D 'Brits' and 'Jubs' such as Nos 45600 *Bermuda* and 45632 *Tonga* managed an occasional look in. When Agecroft shed itself finally closed, Patricroft men once again assumed control.

Shortly after a switch back to 10A Carnforth locomotives in the diagram, following 10J Lancaster Green Ayre's closure on 18 April 1966, 10 'Black Fives' were transferred from 10J to 10A. Engines of this type were still being outshopped at Crewe, or even released from store, and Carnforth was combining the best ex-Green Ayre engines with its own top-condition examples. Ex-works No 45374 (10A), for example, was consistently active on the working in late May and June 1966.

On the grey morning of 1 May 1968, Stanier 'Black Five' No 45435 slows to a crawl on the approach to Euxton Junction with the 06:15 Heysham Harbour-Manchester Victoria – the 'Belfast Boat Express'. On this date there was a complete possession of the slow lines of the West Coast Main Line in the area to facilitate track renewal. The points are set for the Bolton line and No 45435 will soon accelerate again for the hard climb up to Chorley, the next booked stop. ALAN CASTLE

A classic study of rain, wind and steam in the darkness of a gloomy winter's night. With injectors full on for the steep climb out of the station, No 45025 departs from Preston's platform 4 on Wednesday 28 February 1968 with the 20:55 Manchester Victoria-Heysham boat train. ALAN CASTLE

Meanwhile, the last recorded Metrovick sighting came on 18 June 1966. This was, of course, a quite unique scenario – a rare instance of where a regularly diesel-hauled service had to permanently revert to steam operation. Obviously, it was a considerable victory for the steam die-hards, particularly at such a late stage in that age of ever-encroaching dieselisation. The trusty Stanier 'Black Five' 4-6-0s once again had come to the rescue, assuming their places back on the roster – and being warmly welcomed by crews and enthusiasts alike.

One significant outcome of this decision was that the train eventually came to be the very last named express on BR to be regularly steam-worked, being (most unusually for the period) formed of a rake of coaching stock in uniform livery – latterly, a blue and grey set.

In latter days, the outward working for the 'Belfast Boat' engine started with the 0615 Heysham-Manchester (1J05). During the day, a fill-in turn existed in winter in the form of the 09:15 Manchester (Victoria)-Blackpool (North) via Castleton parcels working (3P04) plus the 14:50 Blackpool (North)-Manchester (Victoria) parcels (3J06).

In summer, however, the loco worked the 0927 Manchester (Victoria)-Barrow (1L12) plus the 14:35 Barrow-Manchester (Victoria) and a nine-coach set all day. The final part of the diagram for the locomotive was the inward-bound 'BBE', the 20:55 Victoria-Heysham (1P02). Except on Saturdays, between duties in the early evening, the boat train locomotive was kept at Patricroft MPD and 9H men now worked it to Preston.

In the summer of 1967, 'foreign' engines were tending to creep in only between lengthy runs of 10A machines. Caprotti Standard 5MT No 73137

of Patricroft got involved on 26 May, whereas 1967's first of two Britannia appearances was with No 70023 *Venus* (12A) on the evening 1P02 of 31 July. Only five locomotives otherwise broke up the 10A monopoly during the whole of the remainder of that summer.

Straight after the end of the summer timetable, No 45342 (10A) came into 'Boat Train' prominence, but its late October session was cut

short by sudden and unexpected dieselisation, when D214 settled on the diagram for all of a full week. Nevertheless, after seven days, an equally unexpected reversion to steam occurred, starting with No 45017 (10A) on 7 November. This proved not to be a 'flash in the pan', the diesel interlude, it then being concluded, was merely a driver-training exercise on Type 4s.

The 1968 New Year was to bring with it renewed

Carnforth's Ted Fothergill with No 45342, seen striding away in purposeful fashion from the booked Chorley stop and crossing over the Leeds & Liverpool Canal, with the 06:15 Heysham-Manchester (Victoria) on Saturday 4 May 1968. As referred to in the text, 'unprecedented speeds' were achieved throughout this section of the journey. ALAN CASTLE fears that the 'BBE' would revert irreversibly to diesel haulage – this as a consequence of some new diagrams being introduced specifically to eliminate steam-hauled passenger trains.

Nevertheless, steam working continued unabated until the beginning of May and to within three months of the very end of steam. It was not surprising, therefore, that during the first four months of 1968 enthusiasts turned up in ever-increasing numbers to travel on the two trains. As the workings ran mostly in darkness for much of the year, photography was often difficult and the main interest essentially lay in locomotive performance.

Outstanding 1968 performances

Standards of performance varied, but now and again, with the combination of a good locomotive and an enthusiastic crew, it was still possible to experience some fine runs. For instance, on 30 January 1968, No 45342 working the 20:55 ran well over each section between Manchester and Preston, but the Patricroft driver complained that his engine was priming on the first part of the journey to Bolton so could not be fully extended. Nevertheless, three nights later, the same man was in charge of No 45017 on the 20:55 and his inferences that he could have achieved even better were now proved to have born some substance. Who could have anticipated the spectacular performance that ensued?

Making what can only be described as an electrifying start out of Victoria, No 45017 stormed through Salford station, this despite having seven coaches plus a long wheelbase van behind the tender (see Table 2). Once under way, Driver Sullivan showed some mercy and wound back the reverser to a shorter cut-off. This method of driving proved to be effective, for the engine sailed up the three miles from Clifton Junction to Kearsley (average gradient of 1-in-200) with a barely audible exhaust beat. Indeed, by Kearsley, the speed had risen to 58mph, but the safety valves were still about to lift! Supplemented by a rapid, well-judged approach to Bolton (Trinity Street), the 'Black Five' drew to a halt in a time of 14min 12sec from Manchester, showing a gain of almost three minutes on the fairly tight schedule – a really brilliant effort.

At Preston, Driver Ted Fothergill of Carnforth MPD, already established on the steam scene as a bit of a 'thrash man', took over for the remainder of the run. On this occasion, it was observed that Ted was allowing his fireman to drive, resigning himself to the shovel, and an inauspicious trip was therefore anticipated. That fireman, however, was soon to establish himself as something of a hero, for he was seen to drive the 'Black Five' with considerable competence.

Approaching Greenbank Sidings, not far out of Preston, No 45017 was accelerating fiercely when an amber signal showed ahead. The amber was passed with the engine only being eased very slightly – more as a gesture than a precaution, or so it seemed. Fortunately, the next signal showed a clear road and No 45017 continued to accelerate through a hail of falling cinders up to a maximum speed of 74mph before slowing for the scheduled stop at Lancaster (Castle).

It was No 45017 again that returned south the following morning at the head of the 06:15 ex-Heysham. The 21 miles from Lancaster to Preston took nearly 26 minutes, signal delays having been experienced soon after departure.

The 'Belfast Boat Express'

Rostered locomotives during the final months - August 1967 to May 1968

Date	Aug-67	Sep-67	Oct-67	Nov-67	Dec-67	Jan-68	Feb-68	March	April	May
1	44874	44709	Class 5	D214	44894	45342 (M) D378 (E)	45017	45025	45025	45435 (M) 44899 (E)
2	44874	44709	45342	D214	44894	44894	45017	45025	45025	45342
3	44874	44709	45342	D214	44894	44894	45017	45025	45025	45342
4	44874	44709	45435	D214	44894	44894	45017	45025	45025	45342
5	44874	44709	45342	D214	44894	45134	45017	45025	45025	45025
6	44874	45342	45342	D214	44894 (M) 45342 (E)	45134	45133	45025	45025	D1617
7	44874	45342	45342	45017	45342	45134	45017	45025	45025	(diesel)
8	44874	45342	Class 5	45017	45342	45134	45342	45025	45025	(diesel)
9	44874	45342	Class 5	45435	45342	45134	44683	45025	45025	(diesel)
10	44874	45342	Class 5	45390	45342	45134	45025	Class 5	45025	D1617
11	44874	45342	Class 5	45390	45342 (M) 73010 (E)	45342	45025	45025	45025	(diesel)
12	44874	45342	45017	45390	70004	45342	45025	45025	45025	(diesel)
13	44874	45342	45017	45390	45493 (M) 45342 (E)	45342	45025	45025	44894	Class 25
14	44874	45342	45017	45390	45342	45342	45025	45025	45134	(diesel)
15	44874	45342	45017	45390	45342	45342	45025	45025	Class 5	D5212
16	44709	Class 5	45017	45390	45342	45390	45025	45025	44942 (M) 44874 (E)	(diesel)
17	44709		45017	45017	45342	Class 5	45025	45025	45025	(diesel)
18	44709	44822 (M) 45259 (E)	44697	45017	45342 (M) 45493 (E)	Class 5	45025	45025	45025	(diesel)
19	44709	44874 (M) 45134 (E)	45232	Class 5	44894	45390	45025	45342	45025	(diesel)
20	44709	45342	45232 (M) 44897 (E)	45330 (M) 45134 (E)	44709 (M) 73134 (E)	45390	45025	45025	45025	(diesel)
21	44709	45342	45342	45411	73134 (M) 45287 (E)	45390	45025	45025	45025	(diesel)
22	44709	45342	45342	45206 (M) 45227 (E)	45287 (M) 73134 (E)	44848	45025	45025	45025	(diesel)
23	44709	Class 5	45342	45227	73134 (M) 45345 (E)	44894	45134	45025	45025	(diesel)
24	44709	Class 5	45342	44894	Class 5	45212	45134	Class 5	45025	(diesel)
25	44709	44709	45342	44894	-	45212	45134	45435	45025	(diesel)
26	45390	44709	45342	44894	44709	45342	45134	45212	45025	(diesel)
27	45390	44709	45342	44894	44711	45342	45134	45212	45394	(diesel)
28	45390	44709	45342	44894	45017	45342	45025	45212	45435	D5198
29	45390 (M) 73071 (E)	Class 5	D214	44894	45017	45342	45025	45212	45435	(diesel)
30	73071 (M) 45390 (E)	Class 5	D214	44894	45017	45342		45025	45435	(diesel)
31	44709				45017	45017		Class 5		(diesel)
KEY TO TERMS										
(M)	Morning 06.15 Heysham - Manchester Victoria working (1J05)									
(E)	Evening 20.55 Manchester Victoria - Heysham working (1P02)									

However, after leaving Bolton very serenely, an astounding effort commenced, the Carnforth driver ramming the regulator up towards the cab roof, causing the 'Five' to break into an exhilarating roar. Speed rose rapidly on the downhill stretches towards Manchester with 73mph being recorded before the brakes went on for the 50mph speed restriction round the curves at Clifton Junction. After this slowing, the hot pace resumed, Windsor Bridge No 2 box, 9.1 miles from Bolton, being passed in a breathtaking 10min 4sec from the start, giving a start-to-pass average speed of approximately 54mph. The journey of 10.6 miles to Manchester Victoria took 15min 1sec, but this included a call of 38sec at Salford. The equivalent non-stop journey would have taken about 13 minutes.

Steam's final hours

On Friday, 3 May 1968, about 100 enthusiasts gathered on Manchester Victoria's No 12 platform to await the 20:55 to Heysham. That coming weekend, the reign of steam on the 'BBE' was due to end. The empty stock rolled in from Red Bank carriage sidings at about 20:35 and it was quite a pleasant surprise now to see No 45342 at the head, instead of the ubiquitous No 45025.

Despite clearly faulty valve settings, No 45342 had a propensity towards heavy flogging and some tremendous outputs of power, which gave a syncopated exhaust beat (two blasts and a wheeze, followed by an explosion!); but as it had been an earlier 'regular' on the job, it did seem fitting that it was present for The Finale.

Another surprise came as by a quirk of fate, the driver present on this historic occasion was Patricroft's Jack Sullivan, our friend who made that stupendous Manchester-Bolton dash with No 45017 back in February! Hopes were boosted instantly.

At about this time, too, the Lancashire Life magazine had contained an article featuring the stronghold of steam at Carnforth, which included a photograph of No 45342. Enthusiast Dave

On 1 May 1968, passengers are all on board and No 45435 blows off impatiently as its driver awaits the signal to depart from Preston's platform 7 with the 06:15 Heysham Harbour-Manchester Victoria – the up 'Belfast Boat Express'. ALAN CASTLE

Bradbury showed this item to Driver Sullivan, reminding him of one of the opinions he had expressed on his previous 'BBE' exploits: "45342 is a better engine than 45017."

Sullivan now had been presented with one of his pet locomotives – this accompanied by an audience eager to appreciate his driving capabilities. A glorious swan-song for steam on the train would be fittingly appropriate, so was Sullivan the man to provide this?

No 45342 left Victoria punctually, skidding twice on the inclined start round the curves, before the regulator was thrust further open and the wheels bit into the straight track. Rapid acceleration produced 39mph through Salford and the rate quickly increased with the noisy off-beat exhaust to 52mph by Pendleton. The engine was emitting some exquisite smoke and sound effects with a shower of cinders raining down on the carriage roofs before the permanent-way slack slowing after Agecroft Jct caused Sullivan to ease to 32mph.

Recovery, though good, was not brilliant, to 53mph by Moses Gate. Despite the setback and a badly-impeded approach to Bolton – 8mph past the depot – the express stopped in 17min 41sec.

It was interesting to note that the starts from Manchester Victoria to Deal Street of both No 45017 on 2 February (1min 36sec) and No 45342 on 3 May (1min 48sec), both with Sullivan driving, were quicker than any of the other 58 runs that David Bradbury eventually came to log on this route, with the one exception of No 45025 on 19 April (1min 42sec). The recovery from the Agecroft slack was good, but not outstanding, and the latter stages of the run were hampered by a signal check near Bolton MPD, yet the overall journey time was no more than 17min 42sec.

Eight minutes were regularly allowed for the loading of parcels at Bolton, and when this time had elapsed No 45342 made a magnificent start, being utterly thrashed up the rising gradients to Horwich Fork Junction, where a 60mph speed restriction dictated that it be eased considerably, which resulted in the safety valves lifting. The actual acceleration was excellent, but to maintain the boiler pressure at just below 225lb/psi during this hard effort was a brilliant piece of

enginemanship by the combined efforts of Driver Sullivan and Fireman Barry Smith.

The entertainment continued, in less spectacular fashion, but with a maximum speed of 71mph on the descent to Chorley. The dynamic start had enabled the 11miles 49chains from Bolton to be covered in 13min 31sec, giving an average start-to-stop speed of 51mph and slashing the schedule by 2⅕ minutes. The previous best timing over the Bolton-Chorley section hitherto

With the dull conditions now having turned to rain on 1 May 1968, the route indicator shows that the road is set for the Manchester line, as No 45435 threads the cutting on the final approach to Bolton (Trinity Street) with the 0615 Heysham Harbour-Manchester Victoria – the up 'Belfast Boat Express'. ALAN CASTLE

had been 14min 15sec and that by Caprotti-fitted Standard 5MT No 73134 on 22 December 1967, so the time taken by No 45342 proved to be a long way inside the then existing 'record'!

At Chorley, there was time to reflect on the excellence of the run thus far. Ahead lay 8miles 45chains of falling gradients to Preston, punctuated by a 30mph speed restriction at Euxton Junction when joining the West Coast Main Line, so the prospects of any further sensational performance appeared slim.

Being aware of the imminent slowing for Euxton Junction, Sullivan did not push his engine unduly hard, but, after negotiating this, the offbeat No 45342 erupted into action, accelerating like a whirlwind down the main line towards Preston.

The syncopated roar from the chimney appeared incredibly loud in the cutting between Euxton Junction and Leyland. Speed was shooting up through the 40s and 50s, reaching about 65mph passing Leyland station with the regulator still wide open, the exhaust crackling healthily and steam blowing from the gland packings of the left-hand cylinder.

It was a marvellous sight to behold as the engine swayed gently on the slight curvature through Leyland, lights on the station illuminating the bellowing steam machine for a few memorable seconds. Then it was out into the darkness Speed rose to 74mph at Farington Junction and the fast pace continued until braking began for the difficult approach to Preston, this being aggravated by a crossover from the Down Fast to Down Slow line to access the old Platform 1 that the down 'Belfast Boat Express' often used.

Doors opened and enthusiasts spilled out onto the platform to gather round the engine. The journey time of 11min 35sec had been the swiftest recorded on any steam hauled train ever between Chorley and Preston, and the arrival was five minutes early.

Driver Sullivan made his appearance and there was a spontaneous reaction from the crowd – everyone singing 'For he's a jolly good fellow'; indeed one of the most open and unanimous appreciations ever witnessed and a deserved tribute to a driver who, it was felt, had always tried to produce his best from any engine that he was given.

After that outstanding performance, with a fresh crew at the controls, the Preston-Heysham section ahead could only have been an anti-climax – or so it initially would have seemed. At Barton & Broughton, the train traversed a 20mph pw slack, but once this was passed, any decidedly placid start from Preston was redeemed by a session of absolute thrashing by Driver Eric Jones – all the pent-up power and vitality being again released in a mighty eruption from the chimney! As showers of glowing red cinders streaked past the carriage windows, No 45342 accelerated up to no less than 78mph at Oubeck, this certainly testifying to the excellent steaming capacity of the boiler.

Throughout this tremendous acceleration, the engine was working on a long cut-off, in contrast to the shorter cut-offs that Sullivan had used at higher speeds. The 21 miles to Lancaster took only 26min 14sec even though, of this, 10min 14sec had been taken up by that first 4½ miles.

The fun was not yet over – not by half! On the section near Bare Lane Station where the line runs parallel to South Road, passengers were treated to a final furious volley of cinder-slinging, causing even late-evening pedestrians to turn and

TABLE 1   3 May 1968 20.55 Manchester Victoria - Heysham (1P02)
Loco: Class 5MT 4-6-0 No 45342 (10A)   Load: 7 coaches (239 tons tare)
Driver: Jack Sullivan (9H)   Fireman: Barry Smith (9H)

Mileage	Station / Signalbox	Actual time min.sec	Sched. time min.sec	Actual speed in mph	Other notes
0	**MANCHESTER VIC.**	0	0	0	
0.32	Deal St.	1.48		13½	
0.71	Salford	2.25		39	
2.38	Pendleton	4.38		52	
3.37	Agecroft Junction	6.01		43	
				32	pws
4.7	Clifton Junction	8.22		40	
7.72	Kearsley	12.18		50	
8.38	Farnworth & Halshaw Moor	13.05		52	
9.08	Moses Gate	13.56		53	
	(passing Bolton MPD)			8	sig check
10.62	**BOLTON (TRINITY STREET) arr.**	17.42	17	24½	
0	**BOLTON (TRINITY STREET) dep.**	0	0	0	
3.03	Lostock Junction	4.57		57	
6.06	Horwich Fork Junction	8.02		59	
6.57	Blackrod	8.29		65	74 max
11.6	**CHORLEY arr.**	13.31	17	0	
0	**CHORLEY dep.**	0		0	
3.09	Euxton Junction	4.46		53 max	35 over jct
4.67	Leyland	6.3		50½	
5.94	Farington Junction	7.41		70½	
7	Farington Curve Junction	8.34		76 max	
8.68	**PRESTON arr.**	11.35	16	0	

Crew change - Driver: Eric Jones

0	**PRESTON dep.**	0	0	0	sig. check
0.41	Preston No. 5	2.15		5½	
1.11	Oxheys	4.45		34	
				35	20 pws
4.6	Barton & Broughton	10.14		35	
7.4	Brock	13.42		47½	
9.47	Garstang & Catterall	15.39	13.00	69	
12	M.P. 12	17.52		67½	
17.77	Oubeck	22.47		73	
19.74	Lancaster No. 1	24.33		66½	
21	**LANCASTER (CASTLE) arr.**	26.14	22.00	0	
0	**LANCASTER (CASTLE) arr.**	0	0	0	
2.55	Bare Lane	5.31		-	
4.23	**MORECAMBE (PROMENADE) arr.**	8.47	10.00	-	

TABLE 2   2 February 1968   20.55 Manchester Victoria - Heysham (1P02)
Loco: Class 5MT 4-6-0 No 45017 (10A)   Load: 7 coaches+ 1 LWB van (257 tons tare)
Driver: Jack Sullivan (9H)

Mileage	Station / Signalbox	Actual time min.sec	Scheduled time min.sec	Actual speed in mph	Other notes
0	**MANCHESTER VIC.**	0	0	0	
0.32	Deal St.	1.36		15	
0.71	Salford	2.13	0.67	30½	
2.38	Pendleton	4.23		46½	
3.37	Agecroft Junction	5.31		52½	
4.7	Clifton Junction	6.55		57	
7.72	Kearsley	10.13		55	
8.38	Farnworth & Halshaw Moor	10.57		54	
9.08	Moses Gate	11.46		51½	
10.62	**BOLTON (TRINITY STREET) arr.**	14.12	17	38	

TABLE 3   3 February 1968   06.15 Heysham - Manchester Victoria (1J05)
Loco: Class 5MT 4-6-0 No 45017 (10A)   Load: 7 coaches (239 tons tare)

Mileage	Station / Signalbox	Actual time min.sec	Scheduled time min.sec	Actual speed in mph	Other notes
0	**BOLTON (TRINITY STREET) dep.**	0	0	0	
1.54	Moses Gate	2.59		55	
2.24	Farnworth & Halshaw Moor	3.4		64	
2.9	Kearsley	4.15		71	
5.92	Clifton Junction	7.05	9	72 / 59	
7.25	Agecroft Junction	8.22		70	
8.24	Pendleton	9.18		67	
9.91	**SALFORD arr.**	11.31	14½	45½	
	SALFORD dep.	12.09	15	0	
10.62	**MANCHESTER VIC. arr.**	15.01	18	0	

TABLE 4   2 March 1968   06.15 Heysham - Manchester Victoria (1J05)
Loco: Class 5MT 4-6-0 No 45025 (10A)   Load: 7 coaches (239 tons tare)

Mileage	Station / Signalbox	Actual time min.sec	Scheduled time min.sec	Actual speed in mph	Other notes
0	**BOLTON (TRINITY STREET) dep.**	0	0	0	
1.54	Moses Gate	3.15		53	
2.24	Farnworth & Halshaw Moor	4		58	
2.9	Kearsley	4.38		64	75 max
5.92	Clifton Junction	7.18	9	62	50
7.25	Agecroft Junction	8.3		73	
8.24	Pendleton	9.15		64	
9.91	**SALFORD arr.**	11.38	14½	0	

Carnforth's 'Black Five' 4-6-0 No 45134, having just arrived with the 06:15 ex-Heysham, peers out into the morning sunshine at Manchester Victoria on 19 March 1967. Once all the mails are unloaded and the signal is given it will take its empty stock up to Red Bank carriage sidings. ALAN CASTLE

stare at the fearsome holocaust approaching!

On reaching Morecambe Promenade, No 45342 ran round and hauled the train 4½ miles tender-first to Heysham Harbour – even this including a maximum of 57mph and more volcano-like eruptions from the chimney!

Doubtless more enthusiasts than ever before had travelled through to Heysham on one train and most, if not all, of these with no intention of sailing onwards to Belfast. The trip had certainly been worth the effort! They had been lucky enough to have two successive drivers who were equally eager and willing to hammer their locomotive, so much so in fact that their captive audience now came to remember No 45342 above all others!

During the night, at Carnforth shed, Nos 45025 and 45342 awaited the attentions of that celebrated group of clandestine amateur engine cleaners-cum-photographers, the MNA . Yet others from the BBE's travelling supporters' society (the 20.55 Club) soon arrived to assist. Notwithstanding the high standard of work clearly being performed, such well-intentioned efforts did not receive unanimous approval, resulting in the railway police soon pouncing, apprehending in the process a few of the less nimble. Once the honourable gentlemen of the law had made their departure again, work continued unabated and, come the dawn, two absolutely gleaming locomotives stood awaiting their final moments of glory.

So it was on Saturday 4 May that from Morecambe Promenade onwards, No 45342 came to assume charge of the 06:15 Heysham-Manchester, sister engine No 44963 having brought the seven-coach train in from Heysham, the latter giving a good account of itself on the climb past Torrisholme.

A very authentic looking 'Belfast Boat Express' headboard had now been affixed to the smokebox door handrail to complete the picture. Some thought must have been put into the design of this, for apart from being a fairly accurate facsimile of the standard BR headboard format, care had also been taken to revise the mountings, now that the top lamp-irons of locos, upon which headboards were normally affixed, had been positioned at a lower level and to one side of centre on the smokebox door.

The driver in charge turned out to be none other than the redoubtable Ted Fothergill and the train set off in fine style, but due to the severe speed restriction at Morecambe South Junction, any excitement had to wait until Lancaster had been passed.

On the one-mile climb at 1-in-98 out of Castle station, Driver Fothergill attempted his first rapid acceleration, No 45342 responding immediately to his skilful handling with a swift increase in speed. Unfortunately, however, the effort proved to be a little too much for the engine and it soon lost its grip on the damp rails.

At first, recovery was slow, but Lancaster No 1 'box at the top of the bank was passed at 34mph. Henceforth there was nothing that could hold back the unbeatable combination of Fothergill and No 45342! Within one further mile, speed had leapt from 34mph to 50mph; Bay Horse being passed at 69mph and for some 2½ miles in the vicinity of Garstang, speed was averaging 82mph.

The maximum speed recorded at any point was 82½mph, which, it has to be said, was not unusual for express trains on this stretch of fast main line, but the adverse effect of the off-beat valves on No 45342 was more pronounced at short cut-offs and high speeds than at long cut-offs, so the performance was in no way second-rate.

Some six miles from Preston, the 'Black Five' was still doing 78mph, before the brakes had to be applied for the pw slack at Barton & Broughton, speed dropping to a minimum of 24mph before the regulator was again opened. Milepost 4¼ was passed at 27mph and in a further mile speed had risen again to 43mph. This acceleration was accomplished with no evidence that the engine was being hammered; 60mph was just reached passing Oxheys, before slowing began for the Preston stop. Thanks to recovery time, the train was six minutes early after a journey time of 24min 37sec and the net time from Lancaster had been no more than 22 minutes.

Punctually, at 07:14, the 'BBE'' erupted into action again and in no uncertain terms! It wasn't often that Fothergill was known to have thrashed an engine, but now, as No 45342 surged up the hill out of Preston, the noise from the chimney was drowning even the wheel-beats of the coaches over the track joints! Such a rip-roaring start enabled Farington Junction to be passed at 56mph, Leyland at 58mph and a full 61mph was attained only five miles out, before steam was shut off and the brakes applied at the last minute for the swing to the left over the Euxton Junction restriction.

No sooner had the last of the seven coaches passed over the point blades than No 45342 was opened up again in terrific style, 50mph being sustained on the top part of the 1-in-128 Chorley bank, but Fothergill making one of his fast, accurately calculated approaches to Chorley station, drawing 1J05 to a stand here in no more than 11min 48sec from Preston, 2¼ early.

This was very close to the optimum that could be achieved, so it was all the more astounding then to discover the journey had taken a mere 13 seconds longer than Jack Sullivan's excellent effort in the downhill direction the previous evening – and yet speed had at no point exceeded 60mph! The secret, of course, lay in the stupendous acceleration from Preston, the very last-minute braking for Euxton Junction, a power-packed recovery and a rapid approach to Chorley.

Ted made a timid start from Chorley, but then gave No 45342 plenty of steam on the rising gradients to Horwich Fork Junction. Once again, No 45342 walked away with the job, achieving unprecedented speeds over this section. Adlington to Blackrod was run at an average speed of 58mph and 70mph was attained on the downhill before Lostock Junction, where a crossover to the slow line interrupted the speedy progress. Bolton was not absolutely ready for the train and it was checked by a signal outside Bolton West; nevertheless arrival was still all of two minutes early!

Curiously, like the Chorley start, that from Bolton was again rather leisurely, but then Mr Fothergill made amends and gave his audience what they had been anticipating – more high speed flogging. Commencing just before Moses Gate, No 45342 broke out into a high speed roar and just after Kearsley, speed was up to 72mph before steam was shut off and No 45342 coasted downgrade for some distance. The brakes went on for the Clifton Junction curve and speed was further reduced to 15mph for the pw slack at Agecroft. After clearing this, the engine was again under steam and she ran on to stop at Salford, as booked.

Manchester Victoria was reached at 08:08 and most of those enthusiasts with a bed to go to finally retired for some much needed rest! Since 21:00 the previous evening, No 45342, in its twilight days, had produced one of the biggest concentrations of thrashing ever experienced in the space of 12 hours from one locomotive. It was, indeed, a glorious finale for steam power on the 'Belfast Boat Express'.

Notwithstanding this, it was with some jubilation and considerable delight that for the final appearance of steam on the 'BBE', No 45025 appeared at Morecambe Promenade the next morning, 5 May, to haul the 07:30 to Manchester Victoria. (The train ran one hour later on Sundays). As booked, No 45025 was at the head again that evening on the 20:55. Again, being a Sunday, the train departed from Victoria Platform 11 Middle (almost in Exchange Station along what was then the longest platform in the UK.) and took a diverse route via Pendleton (Broad Street), joining the usual route at Agecroft Junction.

The Preston crew, who had No 45342 the night previously, was again in charge. The driver seemed to have undergone a transformation, or at least a definite change of attitude, for he now proceeded to drive No 45025 hard as far as Chorley, the engine responding splendidly. After passing over the 25mph pw slack at Agecroft Junction, No 45025 accelerated up the climb to Farnworth; the 3.02 miles of rising track from Clifton Junction to Kearsley, begun at a slow speed, being run at an average of 49mph, with Farnworth itself being passed at 57mph. Needless to say, the sound of No 45025 being thrashed was quite stunning too. Steam was not shut off until after Moses Gate, indicating that a rapid approach to Bolton was imminent, but it was painstakingly slow in the latter stages.

Leaving Bolton, No 45025 made a poor start out to Bullfield West, due in part to some wheel-spin on wet rails, but the remainder of the journey to Chorley transformed this into a good run, the total journey taking a shade over 15 minutes. The

Shortly after dawn on an overcast April morning in 1968, Stanier 'Black Five' No 45342 rouses the slumbering residents of Torrisholme, between Heysham Harbour and Morecambe, with the 06:15 Heysham Harbour-Manchester Victoria – the up 'Belfast Boat Express', which it will work as far as Morecambe Promenade. ALAN CASTLE

start out of Chorley, viewed from the platform, was fiery indeed, with glowing red cinders shooting high into the dark sky, raining onto the roofs of the carriages behind, and the exhaust developing into a distinct roar. This amazing spectacle provided a fitting conclusion to the months of pleasure that the two locos, No 45025 and No 45342, had provided to so many enthusiasts and to the end of the reign of steam on its last titled express duty.

Four decades on

Moving 40 years into the future, excursion trains to the Lancashire Coast and boat expresses to Heysham Harbour are no more. The Pacific-hauled 'Ulster Express' has long gone and the 'Belfast Boat Express' also transported its final passengers to the quayside (behind a Class 40 diesel) on 3 May 1975, this occurring almost exactly seven years to the day since the last steam working.

A through commuter service survived between Morecambe and Manchester (Victoria), but latterly this only ran one way (07:45, or thereabouts, from Morecambe) and even that

finally vanished from the timetables in the mid 1980s. All that remains today is a single-line track along which, at lunchtimes, meanders a solitary two-car Sprinter unit from Lancaster, connecting into the arrival and departure sailings of the Isle of Man Steam Packet Co's boat to Douglas … and that is about it!

The near miracle of steam's survival on such an important train until such an advanced stage in the elimination of steam and the experience of following its operation through to the end, with all the attendant memories that that left with its many regular supporters, could not be eradicated by BR. Just as enduring have been the many friendships cemented by the common interest in the steam locomotive at the time of the 'Belfast Boat Express', that have survived 40 years on.

The author wishes to acknowledge the considerable assistance in loco performance details provided by '20.55 Club' members David Bradbury and Steve Leyland, without whom the preparation of this article would certainly not have been possible.

Its passengers and mail safely on board the train, No 45025 waits time at Bolton (Trinity Street) on Thursday 29 February 1968 with the 20:55 Manchester (Victoria) - Heysham Harbour boat train. ALAN CASTLE

Springtime 1968
Everyday steam around the north west

Latchford Viaduct was opened on 8 July 1893 and carried the former LNWR Stockport to Warrington line over the Manchester Ship Canal. It has a span of 250ft and weighs more than 1200 tonnes. Although the structure still survives today, its closure to rail traffic was due in no small part to its poor condition - the line seeing its last passengers in 1962, but continuing to carry some freight until July 1985. Here, in January 1968, Speke Junction's Stanier 8F No 48168 heads a Garston-bound fitted goods. ALAN CASTLE

Badly leaking steam locomotives, grimy rolling stock, BRUTE trolleys, mailbags lying unattended on station platforms... and duffel bags! All integral components of the typical 1960s steam scene and all now vanished with nary a trace. A Manchester engine for the whole of its life, but now relegated to duties which are a far cry from when it arrived brand new at Patricroft shed 20 years previously, the now Newton Heath-allocated No 45420 is Manchester Victoria station pilot on 30 March 1968. The loco is stood in the celebrated Platform 11 which, at 2194ft, was the longest platform in the UK. TOM HEAVYSIDE

Another picture taken on 30 March 1968. In between other duties, station pilot No 45420 takes on water from a column at the south end of Platform 17. Notice the high-level shut-off valve, enabling the fireman to monitor the water supply more accurately from the tender-top. The driver stands on the platform ready to pull the arm away from the tender, but notice also that he stands well clear from any possibility of a soaking! TOM HEAVYSIDE

Conveying coal for Micklehurst Power Station, Stockport Edgeley's Stanier 8F 2-8-0 No 48549 departs from Stalybridge, along the truncated spur of the former Micklehurst Loop to Diggle, with 'Target 27', the 06:10 from Guide Bridge to Staley & Millbrook. Both the loop line and the power station are now long demolished. DAVE RODGERS

High above the rooftops of Bolton, 'Black Five' No 45312 crosses the viaduct carrying the Blackburn line out of town, in the process of working between Horwich and Halliwell on Bolton shed's Turn No 11, which supplies the motive power for 'No 212 Target'. Upon arrival at Halliwell, No 45312 will then return tender-first with a load of wagons destined for Moston Sidings. ALAN CASTLE

Routed via the Calder Valley line, Newton Heath's No 44809 approaches Elland on 16 June 1968, with a Manchester-bound coal train of 16-ton wagons believed to be the 18:10 from Healey Mills to Brewery Sidings. With the closure of the last Manchester steam depots in a fortnight's time, the remaining steam traffic in this locality will then only travel over the Copy Pit line. DAVE RODGERS

With a heavy coal train, banked in the rear by No 48519, Stanier 8F No 48410 slogs past Portsmouth and up the last half-mile to Copy Pit Summit, on 18 May 1968. This particular engine was a former Western Region locomotive, having spent several years allocated to Old Oak Common and is easily distinguished by its different design of vacuum ejector. MIKE TAYLOR

A Copy Pit Banker. Stanier 8F 2-8-0 No 48257 assists a coal train to Copy Pit Summit on 24 February 1968. In between trips, the locomotives stood at Todmorden on a siding that used to form part of the former north curve to the station. That siding still exists today and has never been taken up since the last steam bankers used it. Now there is a buffer stop hidden in the bushes, but banking engines have not been seen here for many a year. DEREK HUNTRISS

Stanier 8F No 48393 passes the site of Holme-in-Cliviger station with a Yorkshire-bound load of coal-empties on 30 April 1968. Although the climb to Copy Pit was steeply graded from both sides, most workings in this direction were coal empties and thus few trains normally required the assistance of a banking engine. MIKE TAYLOR

The fireman checks that his injector is working as Stanier 8F No 48730 passes over the summit at Copy Pit with another load of coal empties from the Lancashire power stations on 27 April 1968. PETER FITTON

Lostock Hall 'Black Five' No 44971 passes Rose Grove shed, with coal empties on 15 February 1968. In this view the LMS Standard No 2 coaling plant and the pre-1937 coaling stage (still supporting its original water tank) are clearly visible. MIKE TAYLOR

A very clean No 45350 passes through Rose Grove station with an eastbound load of coal empties on 23 April 1968. Apart from the platforms themselves, nothing else in this view survives today. Where the houses on the right stood, there is now the M65 Motorway. MIKE TAYLOR

Stanier 8F 2-8-0 No 48062 assists Standard 4MT 4-6-0 No 75019 away from Rose Grove past Gypsy Bridge with a heavy ballast working that had originated on the Grassington branch. The 8F had only come onto the train at Rose Grove Up Sidings. The double-headed combination of a Standard and an LMS 'Black Five' was about to pass at the head of a railtour and hence the number of enthusiasts present. MIKE TAYLOR

Until the closure of Newton Heath depot at the end of June, one of the few daytime steam workings over the Bolton – Blackburn line in 1968 was 5J13, the 17:05 (SX) Burnley Central to Moston fitted freight. This picture, taken shortly before steam finished on the working, depicts an unidentified 'Black Five' heading downhill over Entwistle Viaduct. With gradually encroaching forestation, views of the viaduct like this one are no longer possible. DICK MANTON

Approaching Todd Lane Junction on 17 February 1968, on the now-closed direct East Lancs route into Preston station, is Stanier 8F 2-8-0 No 48533 at the head of 4P21, the 13:35 (SO) Darwen-Heysham oil tanks. The line to Lostock Hall and Liverpool Exchange diverges in the foreground. PETER FITTON

Still a regular steam diagram for Lostock Hall shed throughout the early months of 1968 was 1P08, the 09:00 (MSO), 09:50 (SuO) Liverpool Exchange to Preston (through coaches to Glasgow and Edinburgh). Seen here passing Croston on 14 April is 'Black Five' No 45212. PETER FITTON

Unusually with steam still on over the junction, later confirmed to be because the driver was looking out for the photographer, the 09:50 (SuO) Liverpool Exchange to Preston joins the West Coast Main Line at Farington Curve Junction on 5 May 1968 with 'Black Five' No 44713 at the head, driven by Lostock Hall's John Burnett. ALAN CASTLE

Another regular steam diagram for Lostock Hall shed during early 1968 was the 16:53 (SuO) Preston to Liverpool Exchange (through coaches from Glasgow and Edinburgh). On 7 April 1968, No 44713 had been specially cleaned for this job and is seen here taking the Liverpool line at Farington Curve Junction. Forty years on, No 44713's fireman John Fletcher still fires steam on the main line! ALAN CASTLE

Again specially cleaned at Lostock Hall shed for the duty, 'Black Five' No 44806 climbs towards Moss Lane Junction with the 16:53 (SuO) Preston to Liverpool Exchange in early 1968. The steeply graded Farington Curve from the WCML to Lostock Hall Engine Shed Junction can be seen in the background. Today, with the line having been singled and Liverpool Exchange having completely closed in 1977, there are no longer any through trains from Preston and a change of train is necessary at Ormskirk. ALAN CASTLE

A very rare scene, taken on the former Preston to Longridge branch (closed to passengers in 1931). Lostock Hall's No 48679 passes through the remains of Deepdale Station with 'No 63 Target'; a working which took coal to the Red Scar Works of Courtaulds and to a coal yard at Deepdale. No 48679 was notable for ending its career attached to a lined-green tender (which, clearly, had originated from a Jubilee 4-6-0). The part-time engine-cleaning gang at 10D resisted the temptation to clean this particular engine! ALAN CASTLE

Its transfer from Speke Junction shed to Lostock Hall having been effected shortly before the former closed to steam, 'Black Five' No 44806 eases up to uncouple from the 09:50 Liverpool Exchange to Glasgow and Edinburgh on 28 April 1968. The stock will combine here with a portion from Manchester Victoria which has just arrived in the adjacent platform, the diesel on which will work the train forward. TIM STEPHENS

The last duties for the remaining Ivatt 4MT 2-6-0s – all based at Lostock Hall in 1968 – mainly consisted of station pilot duties at Preston Station. On 12 April 1968, No 43027 is seen awaiting its next task in the sidings between the old Platforms 2 and 3. DAVE RODGERS

Heading for Fleetwood with a mixed freight consisting almost entirely of coal is Rose Grove's No 48423, seen here approaching Bradkirk, near Weeton on 18 April 1968.
PETER FITTON

8P19, the 12:00 Burnley Central to Burn Naze, was a regular coal train working into the Fylde. On 24 April 1968, 8F No 48400 speeds past Weeton with a load of 22- ton twin-doored wagons, specifically used on this turn. PETER FITTON

A historic photograph depicting the very last wrecking train to work off the Marton line (the former direct route from Kirkham to Blackpool South). The date was 3 May 1968 and No 48033 passes Lytham with the final trainload of recovered materials. PETER FITTON

Patricroft's 8F 2-8-0 No 48491 is the sole occupant of Blackpool North shed on 5 April 1968. A 9H or 10F locomotive was regularly scheduled to work' Target 25', which serviced yards at Blackpool North and South, Kirkham, Salwick, Preston NU (North Union) and Farington; the locomotive ending its day at Blackpool North, having finally worked 6P25, the 18:30 Preston EL (East Lancs) to Blackpool North via Ribble Sidings. PETER FITTON

A regular diesel plus steam combination by 1968, but nevertheless providing one of the final regular duties for the remaining Standard 9F 2-10-0s at Carnforth, No 92167 is piloted by Holbeck depot's D5181 on 4N28, the 12:12 Heysham Moss to Neville Hill oil tankers, seen passing Wennington on 29 May 1968. PETER FITTON

On 11 June 1968, one of the three last working Standard 9F 2-10-0s at this time, No 92160, comes off the Midland line at Carnforth with a special oil-tanker working from Neville Hill to Heysham. This engine and No 92167, both Carnforth engines, were withdrawn some 18 days later, thus rendering the class extinct.
MIKE TAYLOR

Saturday 4 May 1968 was the last day of steam working from the former Cheshire Lines Committee shed at Heaton Mersey. The allocation had fallen gradually to 20 by the end of 1967 and after rising to 27 in March 1968 again fell to 10, all 8Fs, during the last week of operation. All 10 saw further service with some lasting until the very end of steam in August. At closure, there were 15 listed weekday diagrams for 8F 2-8-0s and a further two for 5MT 4-6-0s; these duties taking engines to such diverse destinations as Dewsnap, Earles Sidings, Gowhole, Tunstead, Godley Junction, Northwich, Garston, Glazebrook, Chester and Healey Mills. The last booked working off the shed befell to No 48115, which took over from No 48493 (8C) outside the shed on 7E81, the 12:25 Runcorn-Godley Jct and it is seen here preparing to depart. TOM HEAVYSIDE

Closed 5 May 1968

Edge Hill MPD

Speke Junction MPD

Stockport Edgeley MPD

Heaton Mersey MPD

Left: The scrap line at Speke Junction on 6 April 1968 includes 8F No 48371 and 'Black Five' No 44772. TONY BUTCHER

Right: Heaton Mersey's LMS 8F 2-8-0 No 48191 stands at Speke Junction shed on 6 April 1968. Visible are two of the shed's 9F 2-10-0s including No 92218. TONY BUTCHER

Stockport Edgeley shed on 30 March 1968 with two of the shed's allocation, LMS 'Black Five' 4-6-0 No 44855 and 8F 2-8-0 No 48549, in residence. At this time, most longer distance work had been lost or was being handled by diesels, but the depot still provided motive power for numerous trip workings serving most of the yards in the East Manchester area, along with occasional forays further afield, to diverse locations such as Birkenhead, Widnes, Garston, Partington, Oldham, Mifield and Healey Mills. At closure, there were nine 'Black Five' 4-6-0s and four 8F 2-8-0s on the active allocation. TOM HEAVYSIDE

The end at Edge Hill. Where once the Stanier Pacifics had reigned supreme, LMS 'Black Five' 4-6-0 No 45284 withdrawn from service the previous day stands inside 8A shed on the first day of steamless operations, 5 May 1968. TERRY FLINDERS

On Sunday 5 May, Stanier 8F No 48170 arrived on Edgeley shed having travelled home from Heaton Mersey (which was also closing), but then departed soon afterwards light engine at 11:00 for its new home at Patricroft. Although there were some instances of steam locomotives being left on the shed area for a short time after official closure, No 48170 was the last Edgeley-allocated locomotive to leave under its own steam. Its departure was marked in grand style by a bagpipe recital from 9B fireman, Tommy Baker - a skilled player of the instrument – as he escorted the engine from the premises. The event was accompanied by the sound of detonators as well as the bagpipes. TR SMITH

A hive of industry amid the rolling fields of the Yorkshire Dales. On 1 June 1968, a very nicely polished Standard 4MT No 75019 (notice the burnished brass cab spectacles) pulls away from Spencers Sidings with a full load of ballast wagons destined for any one of a dozen destinations around the North West. DAVE RODGERS

Steaming into the Dales
The last steam branch line Alan Castle

I suppose that it must have been the prospect of a journey for the first time in my life, actually being hauled by a London & North Western Railway locomotive, that was, very indirectly, the innocent cause of my first introduction to the Grassington Branch.

Along with the 'Lanky' Class As, the LNW 'Super D's occupy a major proportion of the surviving train-spotting memories of my earlier youth. In the late 1950s, these two types were synonymous with the contemporary goods yard scene in the Preston area, they were everywhere! I recall being absolutely fascinated watching one after another 0-8-0 emerging from underneath the supporting gantry of Preston's No 2A signalbox, at the head of heavy freight trains, appearing literally to have surfaced from the bowels of the earth, as they roared up the last few yards of that fearsome 1-in-29 gradient from Preston Docks, and invariably being banked at the rear by other members of the class.

With the burning-down and subsequent closure of Preston MPD in June 1960, although much of the allocation was transferred to Lostock Hall, it became only too apparent, even to the casual observer, that the latter establishment was a bastion of all things L&Y and such 'intruders' were apparently unwelcome, any such being fairly rapidly banished to the nearest surviving 'Wessy' establishments to the north and south and where crews were more accustomed to their sometimes temperamental handling traits.

Many of the 0-8-0s damaged in the fire, in fact, did not see service again, being destined to storage for many years in the roofless shell of the shed building and the last few working examples from that time onwards coming to be seen on only exceptionally rare occasions. So scarce in fact, were they, that by mid-1962, I actually thought they had all finished in the North West. Nevertheless, it was at that time that a quite

unexpected opportunity presented itself, which appeared to be far too good to miss out upon. Through the grapevine, I came to learn of a forthcoming railtour being planned to run in my locality and, not only was a 'Super D' booked to work one of the stages of this but, for lucky passengers, there were numerous other equally enticing delights in store. The adventurous itinerary promised the chance to venture upon many lines that, even then, had not seen a passenger train for many a year.

The 'icing on the cake' for me, however, was the chance to be able to depart from a local branch terminus that, although within easy walking distance of my home, was one at which I had not observed more than one or two trains in my whole lifetime, let alone a full-blown real passenger train! Indeed, Preston (Fishergate Hill) had despatched its last regular passenger workings to Southport over 60 years previously.

Absolutely the last fare-paying passengers had crossed its threshold way back in 1951, descending from one or two of the intentionally diverted specials associated with that frenetic excursion traffic during the Preston Guild Week, occurring to 'gridlock' proportions every 20 years. Now known as 'West Lancs Goods', the branch terminus had been reduced in status to the level of receiving but a single daily trip working from a nearby yard, this supplying a cattle foods supply depot based in the old station building.

And so it came to pass that, one evening, a friend and I cycled round to the address given on the tour booking form, which turned out to be the home of the secretary of the RCTS (Lancs & North West Branch), to each hand over the £1 or so necessary to purchase tickets.

It was Springs Branch's still-surviving No 49451, which permitted me to achieve both of the afore-ascribed ambitions and I do recall that the loco was sent to Lostock Hall shed a few days prior to the tour, 'for cleaning' – a duty in which my friend and I volunteered to assist. Indeed, for me, that exercise proved to be another personal 'first' and, given what was to transpire in years to come, probably the single major incentive in persuading me that steam should be allowed to die with some dignity – at least in my photographs!

Although the trip had been entitled the 'Mid Lancs Railtour', this was evidently somewhat of a misnomer, for both the itinerary notes and my Ian Allan *Pre-Grouping Atlas & Gazetteer* clearly confirmed that, apart from some ingeniously organised gyrations around Lancashire, we were also to delve deep into the Yorkshire Dales, indeed reaching as far as a place called Grassington & Threshfield, of which I then knew nothing.

Well, on 22 September 1962, we set out on our journey of discovery and, after accomplishing a complete 360-degree circle via Lostock Hall, passed through the 'other' Preston Station, before again diving off the main line almost immediately in order to traverse the entire length of the now long-closed Longridge Branch. Soon to be re-engined with Fleetwood shed's far speedier Hughes-Fowler 'Crab' 2-6-0 No 42844, this capably driven by Lostock Hall's Terry Campbell, we then headed straight for East Lancs territory, via a final trip (for most of us) around the Great Harwood Loop, before No 42844 handed over to Skipton's Standard 2MT No 78036, to transport us down the short branch from Earby to Barnoldswick. Returning to Earby once more, we regained No 42844, to again delve even further eastwards, and towards Skipton, where we ran straight into the Ilkley line platforms.

Forging away from Platform 5, the driver opened the regulator wide to begin the stiff climb towards Embsay Junction, No 42844 barking aggressively as we crossed over the Midland main line to Leeds and we disappeared into the stygian gloom of Haw Bank Tunnel. Swirling clouds of sulphurous smoke darted in and out of the carriage windows in the darkness, before suddenly dissipating as we emerged to survey the stupendous views of the rolling Dales now unfolding. The signalman at Embsay Junction was waiting for us and had already descended his steps in order to hand over the tablet for the single-line beyond.

We were now into North Eastern Region territory and, with double-tracks at that time still

Rylstone Crossing is where once the only intermediate station on the branch, Rylstone (for Cracoe), had stood. Two tall wooden-posted lower quadrant signals protecting the roadway, controlled by a ground-frame in a hut nearby, the gates here have to be operated by the train crew. No 75019 has just arrived and awaits the guard to undertake this task. 1 June 1968. BOB CLARKE

The crew keeping a sharp eye open for straying sheep, Standard 4MT 4-6-0 No 75048 heads towards Skipton, between Rylstone and Embsay Jct in April 1968, with a train-load of ballast ultimately destined for Kirkham & Wesham Yard. IAN KRAUSE

Standard 4MT 4-6-0 No 75048 exits the 219 yards-long Haw Bank Tunnel, on the approach to Skipton, in April 1968. Although trains on the line to Ilkley have ended three years previously, double-track still survives at this stage as far as Embsay Junction. ALAN CASTLE

The grass-covered paving-stones and redundant gas-lamp standards say it all – Ilkley line services no longer depart from Skipton. On 1 June 1968, as a 'Peak'-hauled express from the Settle & Carlisle line sets out on the final leg of its journey to Leeds, Standard 4MT 4-6-0 No 75019 passes through the station, with a load of limestone ballast from Spencers Sidings. ALAN CASTLE

continuing onwards towards Bolton Abbey and Ilkley, we branched-off to the left. The Ilkley and Arthington routes were to witness their final trains some four years later, with last rites being performed by Neville Hill DMUs during a day, as I recall (for I was there), of heavy snow showers. However, today, the set of rails we were on were transporting us the 8¼ miles towards our own destination of Grassington & Threshfield. This former Midland Railway terminus had closed to passengers somewhat earlier, indeed as far back as 22 September 1930, although the occasional excursions for hikers (and, indeed, railway enthusiasts) continued to visit the area until the late 1960s.

Squealing around the tight curves, our five-coach rake of LMS stock made towards the hills, ambling along at a much-reduced pace from that experienced earlier, but it was marvellous to lean out of the window to watch the little farms pass by, with sheep scattering in every direction from our path. Soon we came to Rylstone Crossing, where the gates had to be operated by the train crew. Two tall wooden-posted lower quadrant signals protected the roadway, controlled by a ground-frame in a hut nearby. For the more observant, among the long grass could just be

discerned the remains of where once the only intermediate station on the branch, Rylstone (for Cracoe), had stood.

We were on our way again and it wasn't long before the great mass of Swinden Lime Works came into view. Everything hereabouts was covered in lime dust - even the grass in the fields. We continued ever onwards and upwards, then, suddenly and without warning, Grassington & Threshfield station opened out before us. The terminus had been built some distance away from the centre of the village and consisted of a long single platform housing the original low-roofed, wooden buildings, all of which still existed 32 years after the last tickets had been sold from the booking office. The original signalbox, however, was moved from its original location into the yard, ultimately to serve a very different purpose, that to be a mountain-rescue post.

No 42844 ran round its stock in the goods yard and, after photographs had been taken, we were soon on our way once again. The fun was not yet over, for, beyond Blackburn, our final treat lay in the traversing of the old Lancashire Union line to Chorley – another route from which passenger traffic had long evaporated. However, for me, the

highlight of the tour had been that ride into the Dales. I vowed to return.

And so it was that, the following May, I stepped down as the only passenger from a DMU in Embsay's platform and, working my way through the country lanes, I eventually found Embsay Jct 'box. The ensuing wait at the lineside for an hour or so eventually provided its just desserts. With dieselisation taking hold in parts of Scotland long before it had in much of the rest of the country, I had just missed the magnificent K4s working over the Mallaig Road. Another RCTS railtour was now to provide me with a sighting of one, albeit this example being far from its natural home and in a livery that I never knew. Running about half an hour late, the West Riding Branch's 'Dalesman' tour from Bradford eventually hove into view from the Ilkley direction and bound for Grassington & Threshfield.

Being a supporter of all things LMS and the products of Crewe and Horwich, I, nevertheless, had a penchant for the syncopated Gresley three-cylinder beat, ever since the first time that I had heard this wonderful sound. The recently restored LNER K4 2-6-0 No 3442 *The Great Marquess* (ex-BR No 61994) had been booked to work this special and, as it was also the engine's first outing in preservation, the temptation to see it proved irresistible. Running round its stock at this location (as excursions sometimes did), I was able to gaze upon No 3442 for all of 15 minutes, before it was on its way up the single line. That three-cylinder beat was certainly somewhat alien to the more usual sounds usually emanating hereabouts - whether from sheep or the creations of Henry Fowler!

Although scheduled passenger services had been withdrawn nearly 40 years previously, the branch was to remain steam-worked right until to the end of steam on BR. Coal and cattle-feed were regularly delivered to the goods yard at Grassington, and limestone traffic from the quarries at Threshfield and Swinden was sufficient to ensure a daily pick-up working from Skipton, this always a 'Derby 4' turn from Skipton shed, until the BR Standard Class 4MTs eventually took over. 'Derby 4s', or other short wheelbase engines, had always been used, as a consequence of the very short run-round head-shunt at the buffer-stops at Grassington, and except for the odd excursion, when the appearance of a 'Crab' 2-6-0 was not unknown, the branch had never seen anything else.

With the demise of steam gaining pace at other arguably more exotic locations and so much more to do with so little time in which to achieve this, it was to be almost another five years before I was to return. In the meantime, Skipton shed had closed to steam in April 1967 and the majority of its allocation of Standard 4MT 4-6-0s had then been transferred to Carnforth. It was Rose Grove shed, however, that took over the working - which had now become part of its 'No 94 Target;' the engine leaving shed at 06:00 to shunt in Skipton Up Sidings, before departing at 09:35 for Spencer's Sidings, on the branch. Curiously, but quite evidently because Carnforth could better utilise a fleet of Standard 4MTs than 10F (and 10A already maintained a spares stock), the same engines continued to maintain their monopoly on the branch. Working out of Carnforth, one engine at a time, they ran light to and from Rose Grove - being changed around on a quite frequent basis, with most of the 10A allocation appearing from time to time.

Having traversed the now-closed direct line from Skipton via Earby, Standard 4MT 4-6-0 No 75019 makes a cautious approach to the curving platforms of Accrington station, with a ballast working from Spencers Sidings to West Lancashire on 1 June 1968. The locomotive bears the shedcode '24G' – a misnomer by this date, but actually being a somewhat sentimental reference to its former depot of Skipton, from which it may very well have worked on this very duty! This particular shedplate had, in fact, been affixed by an engine-cleaner at Rose Grove shed the previous night! ALAN CASTLE

On 31 May 1968, the final steam freight working of all ran over part of the Settle & Carlisle line. No 75019 worked a 'ballast' from Spencers Sidings to Appleby, in the event coming to be 'looped' at Settle Jct, Horton-in-Ribblesdale, Ribblehead and Blea Moor, much to the delight of the few car-borne photographers 'in-the-know'. This almost unreported working, quite amazingly, had occurred five months after the closure of Kingmoor shed to steam! Here, the train is seen crossing the viaduct at Gargrave. BOB CLARKE

In the final throes of steam working, visiting enthusiasts became familiar with Nos 75019, 75027 and 75048, the final three survivors of the class. No 94 Target was shown in the timetable books as terminating in Skipton Yard at 10:28 - in theory. However, in practice, the trainloads of ballast from the quarry were required to be delivered forwards to a whole variety of locations. These included Blackburn, Bamber Bridge, Kirkham and, in several instances during May and June, as far afield as Kirkby Stephen or Appleby.

That, indeed, was the case on 31 May 1968, a date which effectively witnessed the final steam freight working of all over the Settle & Carlisle line. No 75019, on its 'ballast' to Appleby, came to be 'looped' at Settle Jct, Horton-in-Ribblesdale, Ribblehead and Blea Moor, much to the delight of the few car-borne photographers 'in-the-know'. This almost unreported working, quite amazingly, had occurred five months after the closure of Kingmoor shed to steam and five months after Britannia Pacific No 70045 had passed that way on the last official steam freight southwards.

Carnforth depot continued to provide Rose Grove with Standard 4MTs almost until the very end of steam. The, by now long-dieselised, goods services on the branch were eventually to be withdrawn from 11 August 1969 and from that point forward, the line came to rely entirely upon the lucrative minerals traffic for its survival.

Although Grassington had lost its passenger services back in 1930, the holiday excursion traffic continued for many years afterwards; however at the same time as the goods traffic ceased, the final passenger-carrying train also ran into Grassington & Threshfield station. This excursion, promoted by the then embryo Yorkshire Dales Railway Society, operated some 67 years after the opening of the line and brought to a conclusion the final chapter in the story of trains to Grassington.

The rails were soon dismantled beyond Swinden, but 40 years on from the end of steam, the truncated section to the limestone quarry still thrives.

No 75019 has started on the 'Long Drag' in earnest and the fireman gives a last glance out of the cab before setting to building up the fire for the climb ahead. Seen approaching Settle Station, it will be noticed that the '24G' shedplate is still affixed! BOB CLARKE

The classic, archetypal Settle & Carlisle view. After being 'looped', No 75019 climbs noisily away from Horton-in-Ribblesdale. It was difficult to comprehend that, after this historically significant photograph had been taken, the so-familiar location would no longer regularly echo to the sounds of seemingly endless processions of steam-hauled freights. BOB CLARKE

On 18 May, the Warwickshire Railway Society operated its 'North Western Steam Tour' from Coventry to Blackpool and Morecambe, the Stockport-Todmorden-Blackburn-Bolton-Preston stage of which was worked in tandem by ex-LMS 'Black Five' No 44949 and Standard 5MT No 73069. The train is seen working up-grade out of Blackburn towards Sough Tunnel, passing Hoddlesden Jct (the former junction of the short single-track branch to Hoddlesden, near Darwen). DAVE RODGERS

Early summer steam specials

For the Preston-Hellifield-Carnforth stage of the WRS 'North Western Steam Tour' of 18 May, No 70013 *Oliver Cromwell* was utilised. Here, the special, with what appears to be a rake of almost entirely ex-LMS stock, approaches the level crossing at the closed Hoghton Station. ALAN CASTLE

On 26 May, the Stephenson Locomotive Society operated a railtour which was steam-hauled in each direction between Stockport and Carnforth behind 'Black Five' No 44949. Shortly after leaving Carnforth on the return leg via Hellifield, the train is seen crossing Capernwray Viaduct near Melling. ALAN CASTLE

On 1 June 1968, British Railways (Scottish Region) ran another of its very successful 'Grand Railtours' from Edinburgh Waverley. Travelling via Beattock, Carlisle, Carnforth, Hellifield, Manchester, Woodhead, Sheffield Victoria, Bolton, Ais Gill, Kilmarnock, Stirling, Alloa and the Forth Bridge. Here, on the steam section from Carnforth to Guide Bridge, No 70013 is seen climbing away from Manchester Victoria. Banking assistance is being provided as far as Miles Platting by the Victoria station pilot, which, on this date, is Newton Heath's 'Black Five' No 44884. BOB CLARKE

On 9 June 1968 it was the turn of the London Midland Region to utilise No 70013 on a railtour. Hauling the 'Midland Line Centenary Special' from St Pancras, on its final stage from Derby to Manchester Victoria via Matlock, the special is seen here leaving Litton Tunnel midway on the 1-in-100 climb from Monsal Dale to Millers Dale. PETE FITTON

The 'Midland Line Centenary Special passes Millers Dale Junction. No 70013 *Oliver Cromwell* was the last steam locomotive to haul a passenger train over the Derby to Manchester route, for, as from 1 July 1968 the route between Matlock and Peak Forest Junction closed completely. The connecting services between Millers Dale and Buxton had ended a year earlier and, as seen here, the south curve onto the Buxton branch had then been disconnected. TIM STEPHENS

Carrying arguably one of the most garish and unsightly headboards ever seen, the LCGB 'Two Cities' railtour of 23 June 1968, from Liverpool Lime Street, traversed no fewer that four separate routes to Manchester during the course of its ambitious itinerary. Seen at Earlestown, awaiting the arrival of 8F No 48033 at the head of the special, is a very presentable Standard 5MT 4-6-0 No 73069. TOM HEAVYSIDE

The return working from Manchester was routed via the Hope Valley line, being hauled again by No 70013 back to Derby. Seen here climbing to Cowburn Tunnel, the locomotive later returned light engine from Derby to Carnforth. PETE FITTON

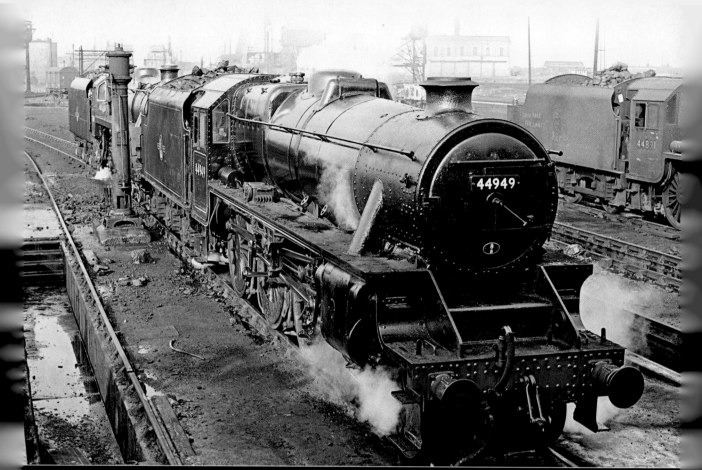

Stanier 'Black Five' 4-6-0 No 44949 stands outside Newton Heath shed on 20 April 1968. Although carrying an 8B Warrington Dallam shedplate, the engine had been a 9D engine for over two years by this time and had never been allocated to 8B. ALAN CASTLE

Closed 30 June 1968

Newton Heath depot opened in 1876 and, with no fewer than 24 roads under its roof, immediately became the largest establishment on the L&Y system. Some 180 engines were on the allocation in 1934 and, in 1955, this still stood at 154. In the final year of steam, the remaining 40 engines consisted entirely of Stanier

On the wet day of 8 June 1968, only some three weeks prior to closure to steam, 'Black Five' No 45096 moves off shed along a strangely empty yard. TOM HEAVYSIDE

 Newton Heath MPD

 Patricroft MPD

 Bolton MPD

Patricroft depot opened in 1904 and served the LNWR routes on the northern side of Manchester. From 120 locos on the allocation at the Grouping, the allocation by 1960 had fallen to around 70, a total maintained virtually to the end. In the same period the shed acquired a large number of Caprotti-fitted BR 5MT 4-6-0s, of which No 73143 is seen here in this 6 April 1968 view. Also recently arrived, from Buxton, is Stanier 8F 2-8-0 No 48775, which will move yet again, to Lostock Hall, when Patricroft closes in June. TOM HEAVYSIDE

A number of conventional Walshaerts valve gear-fitted Standard 5MTs were also on the allocation. Seen here is No 73050 – a former Somerset & Dorset line engine which survived to be preserved today on the Nene Valley Railway. Alongside is the LMS Stanier equivalent in the shape of No 45392. TOM HEAVYSIDE

A gloomy outlook over Bolton shed yard during the last week of steam. In falling rain, a pair of 8Fs face out over a line of withdrawn engines awaiting their final journeys. ALAN CASTLE

Final days at
Bolton shed Stephen Leyland

The engine sheds at Bolton's Crescent Road, Great Lever, were built by the Lancashire & Yorkshire Railway during the 1870s and considerably enlarged to their final form as a 12-road depot in 1888.

Well into the early 1960s, locomotives based at the depot - which was then coded 26C - still manifested strong links with their L&Y ancestry, there being eight elderly engines from those days among several others of more recent design. These 50 to 70-year-old locos were, however, withdrawn for scrap by mid-1963 (at which time the depot code also changed to 9K) and other types moved in to replace them.

The premises had capacity for considerably greater than the 30 that were nominally on the allocation towards the end of 1960 and, to cater for all the traffic that was Bolton's responsibility, far more were actually needed on a day-to-day basis. The allocation was in fact supplemented by an ever-changing 'float' of locos recently overhauled at nearby Horwich workshops and all of which had to undergo running-in 'trials' on Bolton duties before returning to their respective depots. While steam overhauls were in full swing, up to 15 could be 'on trial' at any one time, but when the works ceased to repair engines in May 1964 - and no more 'trials' engines were available - the 'permanent' allocation rose to just over 40.

With the further closure of Bury MPD in April 1965, the level soared again to 57 locos and activity also soared overnight. By April 1966, with advancing dieselisation the allocation had fallen back to just over 40. It was at this time decided to replace about half of the popular and established

Stanier 'Black Fives' with the BR Standard equivalent - a batch of 12 arrived in ones and twos during the late spring and early summer, generally in very poor condition and mostly from store. Some survived for only a few weeks, but others, however, became transformed thanks to the skills of Bolton's fitters, into good working units and quite worthy of the reputation that the depot maintained. Regular passenger duties with steam having ceased just before their arrival, of the work available to them, the Standard 5MTs were most suited to parcels traffic, but they did come to be used on just about anything from heavy freight to the Trinity Street station pilot.

Come the start of 1968, and with the operational area for steam in the North West further contracted, 9K power no longer ventured any further than Healey Mills eastward, Colne and Rawtenstall in the Rossendale direction, Heysham (SO) to the north west, Wigan yards and Astley Green to the west and assorted Manchester yards central to or north of the city, including routes out to Guide Bridge, Bury electric, Oldham and Rochdale and, of course, all immediate lines radiating from Bolton. By April, the active stud had been hovering around the 20 mark for some weeks and, despite an 11th-hour boost due to a revision in north Manchester workings, the writing was on the wall and the shed eventually closed at the end of June.

As teenage steam enthusiasts from Bolton, four friends, Paul, Vernon, Keith and myself adopted the depot almost as a second home during the last few years of its operation. Through our voluntary cleaning of the loco stud (if not our persistent presence), we became generally accepted there.

Those first two weeks of 1968 were also my last as train-register keeper at Bolton East Jct signalbox and I can confirm that all of 9K's engines were seen in action during those nine operational days. In terms of loco availability, this fact alone did confirm just how much more efficiently the shed was working, compared with any previous time between the Bury MPD closure and mid-1967. Now, in early 1968, 14 or 15 locos were required daily, but say 12 months before, when the requirement was around 23, the allocation had stood at nearly twice that.

No 73040, as the 'worst' of our two remaining BR 5MTs, was an extremely regular fixture on Bolton station pilot, right into the spring; whereas No 73069 proved a firm favourite for the 17:45 Colne-Ashton Moss parcels, which was re-engined off shed at Bolton. Its return working, the 03:45 Manchester-Colne newspapers, took the loco throughout and tales of very fast running with this light train sometimes bordered upon the unbelievable!

Sunday cleaning at 9K on 7 January focussed on a lot of No 44802 - the 'new' engine - and the driver's side of No 48504, both being fresh subjects. The week just gone had been wintry enough, with intermittent snow, but that to come proved to be bitterly cold throughout. Working on the 8F was extremely unpleasant, hands having to be held in the nearby brazier's flames, now and then, to maintain any kind of feeling. It didn't clean up all that well either! Next morning, Paul and I went to watch it on Kearsley Pilot, an equally iron grey day of frosty sleeper ends. An old school friend of mine was the fireman.

On 27 January, No 48111 was observed waiting at Manchester Victoria on the Patricroft-

Crumpsall-Astley Green with coal for Crumpsall Power Station and the 04:00 Burnden (Bolton)-Moston trip loco was scheduled to assist the train onwards up the hill to Miles Platting. Saturday 10 February, another day with snow underfoot, it had been decided to start by intercepting 9K's returning Bolton-Bamfurlong job, as this negotiated gradients during the reversal process at De Trafford Jct, Hindley. The train engine, No 45110, banked the Springs Branch Type 2 diesel to that point, where roles weren't the only thing that reversed.

A subsequent occasion did catch No 44802 truly hammering uphill on the 1-in-94 through Westhoughton when commandeered to bring 50 empty vans to a still van-hungry Bolton, but on 10 February it all fell apart after No 45110. Funnily enough, No 44802 played a part in the disastrous sequence of events that were to unfold. This began with a phone call to 'Ossie' Leigh, the only acting 9K shed foreman who still resented us 'interfering'. True to form, he was fairly obstructive and left us hardly the wiser over the running (or not) of the 12:35 Halliwell-Healey Mills empties - which we had favoured catching at Littleborough. An unsuccessful attempt to light a fire in the Hindley waiting room, on this raw day during an almost morning-long dearth of trains stopping there, did nothing to boost morale either!

Getting to Littleborough, it transpired, was quickest by express; first to Todmorden and then coming back, but this caused a fearful row with the stationmaster over incorrectly issued excess tickets. The subsequent wait at Littleborough was to drag on and on, with the signalman telling us that a Type 3-hauled train was the one we were seeking, and me remaining unconvinced. Getting on for an hour after that, it was agreed to phone Bolton shed again and at which time came THE fateful blow of the day, for No 44802 steamed through - while we were all still crammed inside the call-box! Desperately, and quite unrealistically, enquiries were made into any form of transport eastwards, to chase the train, but it was hopeless and I suppose we knew it. Situations in 1968 could become desperate in the search for steam!

The only redeeming feature of 10 February came later with a reasonable run to Preston on the 'Belfast Boat Express' which, at Bolton, did cross 9K's peculiar Saturdays-Only job, the 18:45 Heysham-Ardwick containers, tonight with No 44947. The engine selected for this duty was booked to run light to Heysham for that purpose.

A dozen locos were lying condemned at 9K on 13 February, but at 20:30 that evening, 14 more were fired for service, including Nos 48026 and 48090, very recent transfers from Newton Heath. None were under repair and the missing seven locos made up the current allocation of 22.

Good steam action was still to be had on weekday evenings at Bolton station, with plenty of shunting going on making-up parcels and, to a lesser extent, goods trains with through trains added to the activity. On 22 February, No 73040 was having a rare night off the Pilot job and some of us had a ride out into 'A' Sidings on the stand-in, No 45294. It was probably this which enabled observation of a 9K working rarely seen, ie the 22:15 Burnden Jct-Healey Mills, via Manchester Victoria, which that night left a minute early behind No 45110.

Although its smokebox number plate has mysteriously disappeared in recent weeks, this has not deterred Bolton's unofficial engine-cleaning gang and No 44802 still looks extremely presentable as it takes on coal on 19 June 1968, less than a fortnight before withdrawal. PETER FITTON

While at the station on No 45294, I arranged a footplate run on the 20:20 Bolton-Bedford parcels for the following night, a Friday, with driver, Ronnie 'Sparky' Horrocks. When I turned up, it was to find not the usual Carnforth engine, but our own No 44802. The guard was nowhere about and, as a result, this worthy was given a sound berating in his absence by Mr H in a largely unprintable diatribe concerning tardiness and working practice. Ronnie's driving usually involved excessive pyrotechnics (hence his nickname!) and, tonight, he was furious because of the guard's late arrival. "I hope he's in!" Ronnie cried, as the wheel-slips began, No 44802 then being hammered most of the way to Bury, largely against the grade, but we only took 11¼ minutes! I tape-recorded my own efforts at shunting at Bury and where the load was increased to 25 vehicles. Ronnie let me drive up Broadfield bank, too, and we reached Rochdale just inside the time allowed.

A 9D Newton Heath loco took over the parcels here, with No 44802 proceeding light-engine to Ancoats for the 22:30 Heysham fitted goods. We didn't get away until 23 minutes late and, at that time during the week, the area was littered with goods and parcels traffic, so 5P05, on 19 loaded containers, made uncertain progress all the way from Philips Park to Manchester Victoria. From a halt opposite Exchange station, Ronnie adopted again the tactics for which he was renowned, setting the controls for a noisy journey to Bolton, with the reverser only a couple of turns away from full forward gear and the regulator not quite fully open on the quadrant. We kept well on the right side of 40mph to Moses Gate loop, but we were faster to that point than certain 'Boat Train' runs of the period! No 44802 had steamed well, despite the thrashing and, in the shed office afterwards, 'Sparky' insisted that I play all the recordings to him and his assembled colleagues. Of course, he lapped-up any banter and good humoured criticism! On a subsequent occasion, with the same job, he let me drive all the way back from Ancoats, as reward for keeping an eye on the loco – this while he and his mate went to the pub!

The Buxton, Trafford Park and Northwich MPD closures of 3 March triggered five further transfers to Bolton, but all three of the ex-Buxton 8Fs were condemned almost immediately, going the same way as resident No 45294. However, Nos 44929 and 44965 from Trafford Park at least saw some use. This brief rallying in allocated numbers was very short-lived due to the withdrawal during March of several 8Fs plus No 44965.

Once its remaining regular passenger duties were dieselised in April 1966, Bolton shed came to rely merely upon excursion work and enthusiasts' railtours for any Class 1 work and, by 1968, only the latter still existed. However, word of 9K's good mechanical reputation and often-cleaned locos had clearly got around, ensuring more than its fair share in that field. Nos 45110, 45290, 48652 and 48773 were, in some cases, repeatedly called-upon for such duties and, in No 73069's case, its Bolton maintenance legacy and external smartness brought about its selection in preference to the 'also ran' BR 5MTs at Patricroft.

Even as late as the end of March, word was going round the shed that five BR 5MTs would be coming when Patricroft closed. This only seems surprising in the light of later intelligence which exposed the uncertain nature of the depot closure programme. In reality, the near-opposite prevailed, when our own two BR 5MTs were sent to 9H on, or just before, 9 April, and, as is now well-known, both MPDs closed simultaneously. Quite remarkably too, these locos were the first transferred away from Bolton since December 1966! On the same evening as the discovery that 9K had been reduced to a 2-class only shed, No 45073 from Stockport arrived and, for a month after this, the allocation stood at 20.

Cold nights and beautiful days continued into the new week, which saw me, among other things, taking in the evening eastbound steam worked traffic at Darcy Lever, which featured the hitherto unmentioned 18:05 Bolton (Rose Hill)-Moston behind No 48380 on a good load. 350hp diesels started to creep in on Station Pilot later in April, but on Thursday 11th, No 45104 was treading in No 73040s footsteps. Recently, I'd markedly improved this 'Black Five's' appearance by scratching-off the poor latter-day Crewe paintwork, where this concealed perfectly good cabside lining-out.

Six 9K engines were fired on Good Friday for the Saturday resumption of goods work, contributing to one of the best days for local trips with steam in 1968. Again, we went for the Bamfurlong-Halliwell, but, on the DMU to Hindley, this crossed us heading east! Luckily we caught up with it by bus, while the train shunted at Westhoughton. The driver of No 48026, Wilf Faulkner, was well known to us and, as the train

The work of the Bolton unofficial cleaning gang is also well in evidence in this 26 June picture. Two days later, No 45104 became the last-ever steam locomotive to arrive back on shed, having been on Castleton Pilot duties all day. It was then withdrawn, but No 44888 moved to Lostock Hall for a few further weeks' work. PETER FITTON

carried a brake van at each end, by virtue of its earlier reversal, we were allowed to ride in the leading one onward to Halliwell, only six feet from the smokebox of the tender-first 8F.

So, at 10:06, hauling 23 of loaded-coal and the two brakes, No 48026 was 'right-away' Halliwell with three microphones held towards the smokebox door and Wilf launching into a very powerful restart up the brief remaining 1-in-94, before coasting over Lostock Jct. Upon approaching Astley Bridge Jct, the train was allowed to slow more than normal with only light steam on, but eventually the regulator was thrust open – fully so it seemed. The terrific blast remained rock steady, with speed around 10mph, until a few yards before the junction cabin, where we turned left onto the branch and also where the loco now lost its feet! Ten seconds is a long time to listen to an engine slipping with steam fully on and wheels attempting to grip, but that's how long Wilf left matters before shutting off, with our then losing a lot of momentum. The next few minutes saw a struggle to clear the junction, punctuated by more skidding and momentary adhesion, but we did make it - and what a show it had been - clearly put on especially for the 'guest' passengers! We were dropped off at Burnden Jct, quite elated by the action thus far and without a thought from anyone on the subject of trespass!

After a spectacular show from No 70013 on railtour duty at Spring Vale and a following empty parcels train, I was later positioned on Chorley bank for 9K's No 44947, which scurried uphill with the Heysham-Ardwick containers. The 'Belfast Boat Express' run that night was dire however, and, indeed, Bolton shed had to provide a replacement shovel - for the fireman had lost his own en route from Manchester!

Bolton's allocation had fallen to 18 by the next round of shed closures (Nos 45381 and 48702 being withdrawn), so the 10 locos inherited, six from Stockport, three from Heaton Mersey and one from Edge Hill on 6 May were a big boost and the largest simultaneous influx since the dozen BR 5MTs had arrived two years previously.

Bolton picked up some work from Newton Heath in the traffic and motive power revisions

that the above closures created. The number of Targets, ie non Working Timetabled trip freight turns, had risen from eight to 13, with 9D the apparent loser (but 9D had probably accumulated other turns from elsewhere). Some of those 13 covered a lot of common ground at various times and the majority operated south of Bolton, in a still labyrinthine 'tangle' of short runs between such yards as Rose Hill, Kearsley, Pepper Hill, Agecroft, Brindle Heath, Windsor Bridge, Tank Yard, Moston, Brewery Sdgs, Ashton Moss, Dewsnap and Hartford (Oldham).

Longer trips that were supposedly non-stop, traffic-wise, were Rose Hill-Moston, Horwich-Moston, Agecroft-Dewsnap, Kearsley-Dewsnap, Brindle Heath-Horwich, Brewery-Horwich, Hartford-Dewsnap and Astley Green-Kearsley. In the same district, there was also the Patricroft-Crumpsall, with its associated workings and 'assistings'. On other routes out of Bolton, there was still the Castleton Pilot - which started with an early morning trip from Brewery, Heap Bridge Trips, Rawtenstall Pilot (with trips to Bury), Bolton-Bamfurlong-Halliwell, also 'Continuous Pilot', and not forgetting the Trinity Street Station Pilot and Bolton Ballast. The seven Targets, which ran on Saturdays too, were mostly in the north Manchester area, again chiefly performing cut-down versions of their weekday schedules. Much of this being in the early hours, only four locos

left 9K after 'breakfast', except for the afternoon Heysham loco. This brings us to the next category - non Target work, which was as per the following list as per the table below. To this list should be added the 20:20 Bolton-Bedford parcels 3M13 (to Rochdale only) and the 22:30 Ancoats-Heysham goods (5P05), both worked by the same Bolton crew, but with a Carnforth engine.

The 18:16 Rawtenstall-Rochdale parcels was discontinued from 6 May, but the work acquired from 9D more than compensated and yet another working which clung to steam traction, the 21:45 Bolton-Ashton Moss parcels, was henceforth routed via Castleton curve, still with 9K power, but Newton Heath men.

Where, the reader may ask, were all the diesels that were set to take over all the above work in just a few weeks' time? By and large they remained conspicuous by their absence and no gradual takeover would appear to be occurring. From about the early May changes, the odd Type 2 or so nervously appeared in the shed yard, but tentative appearances on the Ashton Moss parcels and the Halliwell-Healey Mills were all I personally noted, that is, except for the Station Pilot, as mentioned before.

True, diesels were prominent at Bolton on non-9K traffic, but the increasingly popular Broadfield evenings continued to stave off the inevitable absolutely on each occasion, rendering the eastbound procession, with its varied hard-working engine exhausts, all the more of a draw.

That generous early May influx of motive power to 9K enabled the depot not only to cover the additional work, but to select the two least effective engines for withdrawal. These were Nos 44664 and 44829, the former not having steamed for many weeks.

In the light of recent experience, Westhoughton seemed the best bet to catch the Bamfurlong-Halliwell and on 11 May it provided the highlight of another local trip for steam action. At 10:15, and as briefly alluded-to earlier, there came, rising and falling on the fresh westerly, an urgent staccato exhaust, immediately impressive.

Re-arranged that day to bring 50 vans to Bolton, No 44802 thundered past with equal to the weight of a 12-coach express, but on 104 goods wagon bearings. The speed was around 27mph and on a rising 1-in-94 gradient.

No 48380 was laid aside during the coming week, but officially condemned later in May. Loco-hauled traffic at Bolton in general was 50 per cent steam powered on the 13th - still about normal for the time being. Other local evening

FREIGHT:		
00:36	Ashton Moss-Agecroft	8J32 MX
05:17	Ashton Moss-Agecroft	8J24 MSX (04.30 ex Mottram)
05:25	Ardwick-Moses Gate	5J16 MSX
13:35	Ashton Moss-Agecroft	8J33 MO (also runs MX, dep. 14:04)
11:20	Abram-Bolton	8J50 SX
12:35	Halliwell-Healey Mills	7N55 SO (to 25 May only)
14:30	Halliwell-Healey Mills	7N95 SX
22:16	Halliwell-Healey Mills	5N12 SX (formerly ex-Burnden Jct)
03:25	Healey Mills-Bolton	8M05 MX (return working of 5N12)
22:52	Mottram-Philips Park	8J38 SX
18:45	Heysham-Brewery Sidings	5J44 SO (formerly to Ardwick)

PARCELS & EMPTY STOCK:		
21:45	Bolton-Ashton Moss	3J20 SX (17:45 ex Colne, now diesel to Bolton)
03:05	Red Bank-Manchester Vic.	3P97 MX (Worked by Newton Heath MO)
03:45	Manchester-Colne News	1P97 MX (This and 3P97 were return working of 3J20)

Black Five 4-6-0 No 44947 stands outside the shed on 2 March 1968, awaiting its next turn of duty in the company of two classmates. MERVYN LEAH

trips, not necessarily for 9K workings, continued to be undertaken and the painting-in of missing sections of tender lining on No 45110 summed-up the contemporary scene for myself and friends.

Some special Bolton-powered Healey Mills-Brewery coal runs on Saturday 18 May brought about the cleaning, in readiness the night before, of Nos 44947 and 45104, and on the day, at Todmorden, they enlivened the scene, adding to identical merchandise already beginning the climb to Copy Pit, steam banked too, plus a railtour that also went that way. Activity on both lines west of Hall Royd Jct kept us very busy!

The recorded contents of Bolton MPD at 20:20 on Tuesday 21 May were certainly not indicative of a depot heading for closure less than six weeks hence, but we now knew that an end of June date was set for 9K, Newton Heath and Patricroft. Three engines were stopped or spare, 16 were in steam and one newly fired. No 48168 arrived on the ash pit soon afterwards, two were missing and a dozen steam stood withdrawn, as also were half as many diesel-shunters! No 44888 was the next to leave, for the Ashton Moss parcels diagram, but that appears to have been the last time the train was steam-worked. No 48026 was officially still in stock but, in effect, permanently retired and counted here in the 'withdrawn' total. Number plates had also begun to disappear from some of Bolton's serviceable 'Black Fives' in the last month or so that the shed was open. The 'culprits' not being ourselves!

Brewery Sidings and environs were selected for Saturday 1 June's trip, in order to catch some Newton Heath flavour. Local goods-workings and associated light-engine movements prevailed over alternative loco-hauled traffic and proved quite plentiful until early afternoon. Steam outnumbered its rival 2:1 and, while Newton Heath locos played their part in the proceedings, those from the 9K stable were singularly prominent, almost as if they'd turned out in a deliberate show of strength to snub the 9D stud on its very doorstep! Short-lived 9K machine No 48720, for example, wildly and most uncharacteristically out of beat, battled upgrade with 33 of coal for Middleton Jct .

The Castleton-Bolton, with No 45073, was already in Bury at 18:00 on the 5th, as we headed for another Broadfield evening and later the 18:05 Bolton-Moston provided the unusual spectacle of Nos 48692 and 48652 double-heading a 65-wagon train. The day after, we heard that No 48392 had 'had it', but the last withdrawals at 9K, including that loco, were officially in the second half of the month. The heat of Trinity Sunday afternoon (9 June) softened the accumulation of grease and dirt scraped from No 48773's motion at 9K, as I assisted some of the five others who had assembled there and were engaged in similar work.

A busy week of local trips lay ahead, but other than Broadfield again, they were not geared to Bolton workings. The cloudier midweek gave way to five perfect days from the 13th; weather that fitted the traditional view of summer 1968, but it was not ever thus! A number of condemned engine movements within that fine spell made only small inroads into the scrap-line at Bolton, when No 44965 was taken away. Due to a defect rendering it unsafe to be dragged elsewhere, No 44829 was cut up on site.

With only nine days to go, the summery weather had broken and there loomed industrial unrest on BR, which threatened to even further curtail what little steam activity would commemorate not only the fall of Bolton MPD, but also Newton Heath and Patricroft as well. But, through the darkly gathering clouds of full dieselisation and dispute, the last vestiges of ever-receding blue still found the strength to shine through.

During the week just ended, four more 9K locos had been officially condemned – Nos 45046, 48026/392/504. For the last week of its existence, therefore, the allocation stood at 21 steam, but what would have been the last days of normal operation were already over, thanks to the guards' dispute which began on Monday the 24th. During that first day, members of ASLEF voted to join too and, during a long evening at Bolton East, just two light steam engines were seen with a less-reduced diesel-worked traffic.

On Thursday, 27 June, at least the Bedford parcels was able to run that night, 9K men on No 45390 (10A), but the only other steam loco seen was No 45231 (10A), despatched light to 9K in lieu of its cancelled train, the 16:50 Heysham-Moston, because the diagram dictated that this was the following evening's Bedford parcels engine. Carnforth was quite correct in sending the engine, though, in the present circumstances, Bolton would have had lots of spare power, should the Bedford parcels be lucky enough to run on Friday night. If it did, I didn't see it, but the Heysham-Moston managed to put in an appearance, albeit very late, with No 44897 (10A).

It was ascertained that four engines were booked off Bolton Motive Power Depot the next morning, 28 June, for specific regular work, this being about normal for a Saturday in those closing weeks. I was at the shed at 06:35, with the commemorative loco headboard that I had painted for the last day. After No 45269 had turned, 9K's last-ever normal steam locomotive departure was about to take place, itself no mean historic moment. Next to No 45269, stood No 44897 of 10A, in a curious state of limbo. After completing part of its diagram as related, it now straddled the steam-to-diesel transition at 9K, because the other part of its work on Monday belonged to the new era.

No 45104 had gone off with Castleton Pilot, and No 45269's duty was Target 89, the 10:00 Agecroft-Dewsnap. With my headboard (an old bed-head) and with a small Union Jack in place below it, plus Paul and I on the footplate - courtesy of driver Tommy Sammon and fireman Malcolm Frost (the 'Frozen Fish Duo' as they were known), No 45269 negotiated the exit pointwork at 07:05. The occasion was marked by frantic whistling and several exploding detonators, but the 'bobby' and booker at Burnden Jct 'box remained unruffled by the commotion. It was, after all, not a good day for them either.

We made swift progress to Agecroft (54mph max) then sat there for almost two hours, waiting for a guard. No 48652 soon trundled by, light engine back to 9K and into the last eight miles of its 25-year career. Type 4 diesels went by on the Up 'Boat Train' and the Scarborough special from Bolton, conjuring up reminders of a very different holiday train scenario but a year earlier. Eventually, it had to be admitted that the Agecroft-Dewsnap would not run - an unlucky casualty of the current unrest was now detailed to return light to Bolton. Conscious of the acute disappointment over not being able to make a 'go' of the official last working, Tommy got permission at least to do a bit of a tour and return via Manchester Victoria and the Castleton curve.

It took over 1½ hours to regain 9K, inclusive of 10 more stops of varying duration. Maximum exposure of the headboard came during half a minute motionless at Victoria. Over in Exchange, No 45055 (9H) was another 'last'. Our lengthiest halt, in the loop at Middleton Jct, coincided with No 44735 (9D) also slowly heading light for home and, in response to our headboard, its fireman chalked 'Last Day' too, on their tender-side, as the loco drifted by. This was a moving moment. Shortly afterwards we stopped to chase stray cattle, but then it was plain-sailing home with 46mph maximum through Radcliffe Black Lane. No 45104 was still at its post at Castleton, as we passed. Grateful for what we'd been able to salvage from the earlier let-down, No 45269 entered 9K, now to be greeted by about 40 enthusiasts. The cameras clicked and whirred and the time was 10:52.

Half an hour later, No 45104 returned from Castleton, the final 9K turn to arrive. Its ashes were scattered in the pit, prior to a last move to position it next to No 48652 and another 8F, adjacent to the main line -condemned with 11 more at the end. On this special day, most hadn't turned a wheel and I don't think we knew exactly which ones would live on elsewhere for the rest of the summer but, in the event, 10 were given a few weeks reprieve at the three surviving depots.

The Bolton Evening News, which had endeavoured to keep on top of the guards' dispute and its repercussions on the public, had not a single word to say about the demise of the almost 100-year-old Crescent Road locomotive sheds.

Engines, there were to see at 9K for months to come, as the scrap was gradually sold to private cutters. Ironically, the last to be taken away was a 'foreigner', No 48646 (ex 10D), which had its journey to the breaker's yard interrupted in August, remaining almost until the winter.

The site was demolished and cleared during 1969.

Just two steam specials operated immediately before the final weekend, both towards the end of July. On 21 July, the Roch Valley Railway Society organised a tour starting at Manchester Victoria and travelling to/from Southport by four different routes. This view shows Lostock Hall's No 45110 en route between Southport and Burscough Bridge on the ex-L&Y route to Wigan Wallgate, shortly before taking the now-lifted spur onto the Preston-Ormskirk line. DEREK HUNTRISS

Mid-summer specials

Left: Having already run two extremely successful railtours earlier in the year, on 28 July 1968, the Manchester Rail Travel Society, in association with the Severn Valley Railway Society, ran its 'Farewell to BR Steam Tour' from Birmingham New Street. From Stockport to Carnforth via Wigan North Western, motive power was No 70013 *Oliver Cromwell*. This picture, taken from the remains of the old Boars Head Junction station platform (closed in 1949), shows the extremely unusual ex-LNW signal box that used to control the junction of the former Lancashire Union Joint line to Chorley. The signalbox was closed and demolished when the West Coast Main Line was electrified in the early 1970s. ALAN CASTLE

Right: Returning from Carnforth and heading for Skipton with the MRTS/SVRS special of 28 July, the train is seen near Bentham, now headed by Standard 4MT 4-6-0s Nos 75019 and 75027 - by this date these being two of the three remaining working members of the class. Notice the burnished brass cab-window frames and No 75027's lined green livery. PETER FITTON

Having climbed up to Hoghton summit from the Ribble Valley, the distinctive local landmark containing the historic Hoghton Tower provides a dramatic backcloth to *Oliver Cromwell* approaching Pleasington station on the Preston-Blackburn line with the MRTS/SVRS special of 28 July 1968. PETER FITTON

With a reversal in direction at Skipton, the special now takes the section of railway between Skipton and Colne that, although not a target under the Beeching axe and, indeed, a one-time major artery for Yorkshire-Lancashire holiday excursion traffic, closed in January 1970. Seen near Elslack are 'Black Fives' Nos 45073 and 45156. DAVE RODGERS

Having travelled via Wigan and Bolton, during their ambitiously circuitous itinerary around Lancashire, Nos 45073 and 45156 head for Blackburn once more, and working hard up-grade, head out across Entwistle Viaduct. TIM STEPHENS

On the final stage of the tour, from Rose Grove to Stockport, and with evening shadows starting to form, the MRTS/SVRS special of 28 July climbs past Cliviger on the Copy Pit route to Todmorden. No 48773 was originally constructed in 1940 by the North British Locomotive Company and, in 1941, was sent to Persia (Iran), becoming Iranian State Railways No 41-109. In 1954, it was no longer required in the Middle East and was sent to the Longmoor Military Railway, as WD No 500. In 1957, it was taken into British Railways (Scottish Region) stock as No 48773 and eventually arrived at Bolton in September 1964. Right at the end of steam, it was transferred to Rose Grove from Bolton in July 1968, before finally being purchased for use on the Severn Valley Railway. MAURICE BURNS

Having taken the now-lifted West Curve at Todmorden, the MRTS/SVRS special heads up the Calder Valley line towards Manchester. The sun now having set well and truly behind the hills, No 48773 is seen on the last few yards before entering Summit Tunnel on the final leg heading towards Stockport. MIKE POPE

1P58 to Blackpool
Memories of 1968
Peter Fitton

The study of reporting numbers has always proved to be very involved and a book could easily be written on this subject alone. The problem with referring to a specific train by its reporting number was that the working often shared the same number with more than one train. For main-line expresses, this did not usually apply, as, in most instances there were far fewer trains travelling to one specific destination over the whole route (the down 'Royal Scot' was always 1S57, for example), but local services on secondary and commuter lines were too numerous to each warrant its own numerical description. A single number, therefore, was often allocated to each type of train on each particular route. (Manchester-Blackpool South 'all stations' stoppers all used 2P63, Manchester-Blackpool North stoppers all used 2P64, all Blackburn to Blackpool North stoppers used 2P52 – and so on.) Every day there were two 'portions' of main-line expresses from Euston that, having detached their front sections for these to go forward with their train locos to destinations further north, the remaining parts ran as separate trains to Blackpool South. Being expresses, rather than 'stoppers', they both used the code 1P58. Lostock Hall shed provided the motive power.

A very clean Lostock Hall 'Black Five' No 44683 climbs out of Preston station, with 1P58, the 12:44 Preston to Blackpool South on 26 December 1967. PAUL RILEY

'Black Five' No 45345 rounds Ribby Curve, Kirkham with the 12:44 Preston to Blackpool South on 28 March 1968. PETER FITTON

Until Lostock Hall's 'Black Five' No 45305 worked the last lunchtime 1P58 on 17 May 1968, the 12:44 Preston to Blackpool South (the rear portion of the 09:05 ex-Euston) was *the* steam passenger train to photograph in the Fylde. As I was working in Kirkham or Lytham at the time, lunches were spent eating sandwiches, waiting with 'Pentax' at the ready! On the days that she was on time, some fine photos were taken; better still if 8P21, the 8F-hauled 10:52 Burnley to Wyre Dock coal train, also came through. And there was always the chance of a local ballast working, but waiting for 3J03, the 13:50 Blackpool North to Manchester parcels, meant being late back!

Then came June, when days were longer, and the other 1P58 was steam. In my younger days, the 17:05 Euston to Blackpool Central was a star performer, a 1B Camden-shedded Royal Scot roaring by the bedroom window in St Anne's - always the fastest train of the day away from Ansdell station. It was years later that I found out the obvious reason - pubs closed at 22:30 and the crew were thirsty!

In 1968 the 17:05 at least ran steam from Preston to Blackpool South; we could ride it and, hopefully, could just photograph it in the light, as departure was at 20:50 (again, hopefully)!

Having used the last bit of sunlight to photograph No 44971 passing Kirkham on 8 June, flash was used on the same loco at St Anne's the following Saturday. This last one had been a very poor run, with the engine priming badly, and a max speed of only 38mph before Kirkham, which took all of 19 minutes for 7¾ miles! Not bad for seven coaches!

After riding the narrow-gauge trains at Bressingham the following weekend (Alan Bloom's wife Flora was my parents' bridesmaid way back in 1942) and seeing the Keighley & Worth Valley Railway reopen on 29 June (another milestone event), it was back to '1P58' again, 6 July surprisingly producing a Brush Type 4 on the train. How filthy the diesels were in those days!

The now-preserved No 45305 did the honours on 13 July, clocking 55mph max and 14min to the Kirkham stop, and 58mph at Moss Side, arriving at Lytham in 24½ minutes.

'Black Five' No 44971 passes Ribby, Kirkham with the 12:44 Preston to Blackpool South on 8 June 1968. PETER FITTON

'Black Five' No 44950 rolls into Lytham with the 12:44 Preston to Blackpool South on 10 May 1968. Rationalisation of lines in the Fylde is now well-advanced and the platforms look exceedingly bare after many years of being adorned with two fine L&Y canopies. PETER FITTON

'Black Five' No 45212 storms away from the snow-covered platforms of Lytham with the 12:44 Preston to Blackpool South on 9 February 1968. PETER FITTON

On 20 April 1968, 'Black Five' No 44971 waits time at Ansdell & Fairhaven with the 20:50 Preston to Blackpool South. PETER FITTON

20 July 1968 and Lostock Hall's No 45388 has been specially cleaned to work the 20:50 Preston to Blackpool South. Having arrived light from shed, the loco is standing in the holding siding at the north end of Platform 5. The 17:05 from Euston is tonight running about 15 minutes late and so the fireman Mick Halsall is keeping a wary eye open for its arrival. PETER FITTON

My picture that evening was of the train disappearing away from Lytham station, with the signalbox gaslights showing. (1/30th second exposure needed on 50ASA slide film).

And so to 20 July. Driver John Burnett, on an excellent No 45388 plus six coaches, left Preston 15 late and ran well, managing just over 60mph before the Kirkham stop, done in 12min and 68 at Moss Side to arrive in Lytham in 22 minutes. At St Anne's, I even managed to take his photo. However, just think back to that classic steam run made in 1908 on the 17:10 Blackpool Club Train of 11 corridors, 300 tons, when local driver A Traill ran non-stop from Manchester Victoria to Lytham, to arrive eight minutes early on a 60min schedule! The loco was Aspinall L&Y 7ft 3in 4-4-0 No 1098, rebuilt by George Hughes with superheater, Walschaerts valve-gear and piston valves - just like No 45388.

A very clean No 45388 appeared again in Preston station on 27 July. As this was previously thought to be going to be the last day of steam on the 20:50, someone had put a rosebay willowherb wreath on it. I produced a '1P58' board for the occasion, using a square NE Region type that had been 'exchanged' at Blackpool North shed in 1967 - the LMR ones, which hung over the smokebox handrail, covered the loco number, so were disliked! It was just possible to photograph No 45388 on its train in Platform 5 (now 3), run under the subway, and join some 70-plus other enthusiasts in the now-packed seven coaches.

I don't know who the crew were, but they did us proud - 72mph at Spen Lane and, after not stopping at Kirkham, running a fast 74 by Moss Side. Between Ansdell and St Anne's, we got up to 55mph… shades of the old 17:05pm! Acceleration away from St Anne's was electric; to achieve all of 60mph by Squire's Gate (1½ miles) was tremendous. And we had to stop in Blackpool South platform (another ¾ mile only) and not in the carriage sidings! So, the atmosphere was right for a party!

Normally, No 45388 would have left the coaches in the carriage sidings at Blackpool South, turned and watered, and proceeded

Lostock Hall driver, John Burnett and his fireman, Mick Halsall look out for the tip from the guard for the 'rightaway' for 1P58 at St Anne's on 20 July 1968. PETER FITTON

The Euston train having eventually materialised and the front portion gone forward, No 45388 is seen here slowly picking up speed after a cold start out of Platform 5, heading into the sunset towards the imposing spire of St Walburge's Church. DAVE RODGERS

back light engine to Preston. Today, however, arrangements were made to stop en-route near my home, a camera flash being fired to let the crew know exactly where.

The fireman then went to the nearby railway telephone to let the signalman at Moss Side know there was a problem with the loco! ...Quite a few of us enjoyed food and drink that night, at 23:30, including the local Police Constable and Town Councillor. St. Andrews Road South had never seen anything like this! Experimenting with those large PF100 flash bulbs, I even recorded the event on film (see photo).

At around midnight, some of us joined the crew for a ride to Preston, getting a lift home in the unlucky one's car. We had made something out of the occasion.

The last week of steam arrived - many of us spending time rushing like headless chickens around the North West. We then learnt that the 20:50 Blackpool and 21:25 Liverpool would be steam on 3 August after all. Thus, after seeing No 75019 make the last two revenue-earning BR freight workings from Heysham to Carnforth in the afternoon, it was time to ride the very last steam to Blackpool. The train, which was packed solid, was hauled by a poorly steaming No 45212 - reported to be due to blocked tubes, this being her last run, and we set no records. The farewell photos were taken on Blackpool South turntable, using the small PF5 expendable flash bulbs - remember them? What a pity Blackpool Tower wasn't lit! In fact it was not until 1998 that I took a photo of a 'Black Five' with the Tower illuminated.

So ended the saga of 1P58. At least No 45212 is preserved, and the reporting number also hangs in my garage. It has actually been out on the main line again... on No 6233. And there are always the photographs and slides to remind us of those now far-off days.

Those 40 years have passed very quickly... I now must get booked on the 1T57 re-run!

On 27 July 1968, the Barrow portion of the Euston train having been despatched on its way, No 45388 couples onto the rear portion of the train, which, as the Eastern Region reporting number board indicates, will now become 1P58. PETER FITTON

It is now nearly midnight on 27 July 1968 and the return journey of No 45388 light-engine to Preston has not got very far! Here the locomotive is seen standing stationary in the darkness near St Anne's Station, its crew nowhere in sight. In fact an impromptu 'farewell to Fylde Coast steam passengers' party had been arranged, the details of which must remain essentially obscure! It can, however, perhaps be revealed that this event occurred within a few yards of the photographer's home and that the local police constable and town councillor were among those present! PETER FITTON

A view of the north end of the shed. Newton Heath's 'Black Five' 4-6-0 No 44949 has just arrived on a SLS special working and awaits departure time for the return journey, via Hellifield. In the background can be seen several privately owned locomotives, at that time intended for use on a reopened Ulverston-Lakeside branch. These include the last two remaining Fairburn 2-6-4 tanks Nos 42073 and 42085. Ivatt 2MT 2-6-0 No 46441 has been repainted in a controversial non-authentic LMS maroon livery. PETER FITTON

Carnforth MPD
closed 5 August 1968 — Alan Castle

Three separate companies, the London & North Western, the Furness and the Midland Railways all owned routes that ran into the important junction of Carnforth and each initially possessed their own motive power depot. Those of the first two-named were close together on the west side of the extensive yards, while the Midland's roundhouse was sited about half a mile away alongside the Wennington line. Although the latter structure survives to this day, albeit now in non-railway use, all of these establishments eventually came to be combined by the LMS into a brand-new modern depot erected in 1943-4 on the site of the old Furness shed.

The mechanical coaling plant, which also still survives (but, currently not in working order), contains two 75-ton bunkers, each with jigger-feeds to two tracks. Close to this is the, also-surviving, concrete ash-elevating tower. A 70ft vacuum-operated turntable and a 75,000 gallon water-tank completed the picture. Inside the building, alongside a modern repair shop, was a wheel-drop capable of coping with driving wheels of up to 7ft diameter.

Carnforth had been coded 11A since the LMS reorganisation, with the District Motive Power Superintendent, also controlling some five other depots, occupying an office on the premises. The code became 24L in the Accrington district in early 1958, but, in September 1963, due in the main to Carnforth's superior maintenance facilities, the Carnforth District was once more reconstituted, now assuming the code 10A - one which it retained until the very end of steam.

As mentioned elsewhere in this book, by 1932 eight ex-MR Class 4P compound 4-4-0s had been supplied to specially selected crews at the depot in order to haul the Ulster boat trains, which ran both from Morecambe to Crewe non-stop and also to Manchester. Although some 0-6-0s did survive for a few years longer at other sheds further round the coast, most ex-Furness Railway engines had been withdrawn by World War II. Nevertheless, in its heyday from the mid-1930s to the early 1960s, Carnforth still had on offer a quite interesting and varied allocation of LNWR, Midland, LMS and later British Railways types, totalling in all of about 50 engines.

Dieselisation appears to be well advanced in this 15 April 1968 view. Nevertheless, steam will continue to have the upper hand for a few months yet. In the foreground, Standard 4MT 4-6-0 No 75048 and Stanier 'Black Five' 4-6-0 No 45394 have just had their fires banked up ready for their following morning's duties. MIKE TAYLOR

In later days, BR Standard types, 8Fs and 'Black Fives' were of course the mainstay, the ubiquitous Stanier two-cylinder 4-6-0s forming nearly half the locomotive stud by 1954, but, more typically in the mid-1950s, the allocation also included 2-6-2Ts, 2-6-4Ts, 4F 0-6-0s, 3F tanks and ex-LNW 0-8-0s.

Richard Dixon started work as a cleaner in April 1940 at 11A Carnforth LNWR shed. He then became a fireman/relief driver for nine years and a driver for 26½ years, before retiring in September 1988 after 48½ years. *"In 1944 we transferred to the new shed, which was built on the old Furness shed; also the Midland shed closed at the same time. We all changed over and new working links were made: two passenger links, four goods links, shunt link, trip link and one old man's link (no night work) (about 1952). We had the London link and booked off at London, then working the 16:55pm Euston-Heysham 'Ulster Express'. We also worked the 06:10am 'Belfast Boat Train' from Morecambe Promenade to Manchester Victoria, then empty stock to Cheetham Hill, returning with the 09:50am Manchester Victoria to Barrow, changing locos at Carnforth.*

In summer working, we had three extra coaches for Glasgow and, one year, I worked the train for five weeks in a row as relief driver coverage. When the changeover took place, we worked to Leeds which, before, was covered by Midland Shed men. We started to lodge at Stourton, Leeds Holbeck. We also lodged at Edge Hill, Crewe, Warrington and Carlisle."

Carnforth is famous as the location for one of the best railway films of all time - *Brief Encounter*; so much so, in fact, that this has created the basis for a visitor centre on the station platforms. Expanded from a one-act stage-play by Noel Coward, the production is without doubt one of the true masterpieces of British film history. Throw in the superb use of Rachmaninov's swooning Second Piano Concerto and some of the best black-and-white railway photography of its era, particularly of the night shots of the unrebuilt Royal Scot thundering northwards non-stop through the platforms (to the accompaniment of some very non-LMS whistling) and the Stanier 2-6-4T No 2429 that repeatedly arrived at one of the Barrow line platforms at the head of the same rake of two coaches. The result was irresistible.

The external filming of the Milford Junction refreshment room used film 'flats' specially erected on Carnforth station. The set however, bore a very close resemblance to the genuine refreshment room at Carnforth station which has been resuscitated and is open once again today. The interior film scenes took place on a set at Denham studios and, commenting on this, Richard Dixon, recalls that he often used to look over the wall from the shed yard, to watch the filming. In his own words, he succinctly observes: "I knew that it wasn't the real thing… that place was NEVER open at night!"

WC Addy from Leeds was also lodging there as a passed cleaner, when the film was being made, most of which, he says, was done during the hours of darkness. "We worked loose-coupled coal trains and goods from Leeds to Carlisle, Carnforth and Lancaster. On the 22:40pm from Leeds, we could see the bright glow of the filming from the top of Giggleswick. The train the film-makers used was a two-coach set with a tank engine. Each compartment had frosted windows

with a floodlight inside. It was stabled in Carnforth shed and, as we dropped down to fill our tank, so did the film train - much to the annoyance of the yard foreman. "Get out of their way," he told them. "Tell them to clear off to London," shouted my driver."

Although they had known for two years that it was going to happen, notice of the closure of the shed to steam did come as a major blow for the 4200 residents of Carnforth. Many of these were still railway workers and it meant the end of an era and a life for their locos. Ninety-nine of them were immediately given redundancy notices and, in the tediously predictable words of the local press of the time, the headlines read "Railway boom town has reached the end of the line."

On 11 August 1968 - one week after the last day of regular steam activity - Britannia Pacific No 70013 *Oliver Cromwell* and 'Black Fives' Nos 44781 and 44871 were turned out to work the *'Farewell to Steam'* Special, which was run from Liverpool to Carlisle via Ais Gill. Former 10A

fireman, Ian Thistlethwaite recalls that, upon returning with the two 'Black Fives' light-engine from Manchester, he and his brother, Malcolm, the two firemen, were requested not to drop the fires, because, it was explained, the engines were required for filming by the BBC the following day. Having accomplished that final duty, effectively Nos 44781 and 44871 were the last two engines in steam on British Railways standard-gauge.

The shed closed completely as from 31 March 1969, albeit now with merely a diesel allocation. At the time, the press reported that *'over 300 men have been made redundant',* however, in true misreporting tradition, it would appear that this figure must have included the earlier steam-shed redundancies, but the newspaper did, however, graciously add that *'British Rail have promised the men other jobs'.* Doubtless, if that were actually so, in the railway's own inimitable manner, it would invariably have involved uprooting entire families and communities and relocating these to totally alien and remote places.

11A CARNFORTH STEAM LOCOMOTIVE ALLOCATION 1948

Fowler 2P 2-6-2T: 40001/41/103, Fairburn 4P 2-6-4T: 42267, Stanier 4P 2-6-4T: 42428/29/31/2/ 544/601/13/15, Fowler 2F 0-6-0: 43189/237/329/570/7/760, Fowler 4F 0-6-0: 44060/118/ 26/374/5/510, Stanier 5MT 4-6-0: 45039/50/291/306/33/43/92/427, Fowler 3F 0-6-0T: 47317/ 39/406/7/9/10/503/605, LNW 'Super D' 7F 0-8-0: 48934/9109/51/88/269/314, LNW 2F 0-6-0: 58329/34. ` **Total: 48**

24L CARNFORTH STEAM LOCOMOTIVE ALLOCATION 1962

Fowler 2MT 2-6-2T: 40086, Stanier 2MT 2-6-2T: 40206, Stanier 4P 2-6-4T: 42319/59, Stanier 4P 2-6-4T: 42578, Fowler 4F 0-6-0: 43908/4083/399/445/69, Stanier 5MT 4-6-0: 44709/874/92/904/5/5014/54/97/193/230/303/6/26/94, Stanier 'Jubilee' 6P5F 4-6-0: 45582/92/606/33/86/96/714/730, Stanier 'Princess Royal' 8P 4-6-2 No: 46200/3, Fowler 3F 0-6-0T: 47322/75/473/514/668, LNW 'Super D' 7F 0-8-0: 49428/49, Riddles 'Austerity' 8F 2-8-0: 90187. ` **Total: 42**

10A CARNFORTH STEAM LOCOMOTIVE ALLOCATION 01/01/67

Ivatt 4MT 2-6-0: 43004/23/7/66, 43105/19, Stanier 5MT 4-6-0: 44667/709/33/58/78/874/89/ 92/4/905/48/5001/14/7/25/54/72/92/5/134/93/209/27/326/8/42/73/4/90/4/5424/35/45/95, Ivatt 2MT 2-6-0: 46400/31/3/41/86/99/522, Stanier 8F 2-8-0: 48247/384/519/712, BR Standard 9F 2-10-0: 92087/118/28/2212. **Total: 55**

10A STEAM LOCOMOTIVE ALLOCATIONS 31/12/67

Stanier 5MT 4-6-0: 44709/58/874/89/94/7/963/5001/17/25/54/95/134/209/5342/ 90/4/424/35/45, BR Standard 4MT 4-6-0: 75009/20/1/34/41/8/62, BR Standard 9F 2-10-0: 92077/88/118/67/212. **Total: 32**

June 1968 sees the last remaining Standard 5MT 4-6-0 No 73069 in company with the last remaining Britannia No 70013 *Oliver Cromwell.* **Also seen is Stanier 'Black Five' 4-6-0 No 44894 being prepared for the road.** ALAN CASTLE

Rose Grove conversation piece. In this springtime 1968 view, Archie Johnson (left), an ex-24A Accrington driver, and Dennis Holloway, a steam raiser, stand outside the shed office as the early morning sunlight reflects off two Stanier 8F 2-8-0s awaiting their next turns of duty. ALAN CASTLE

Rose Grove MPD

closed to steam 5 August 1968

Mike Taylor

Rose Grove motive power depot, Burnley, was opened in 1899, being one of 32 depots of the Lancashire and Yorkshire Railway. It was allocated depot No 23. Throughout its L&Y days, it was basically a freight loco shed, although it did have a small number of passenger turns, being ranked sixth in importance on the L&Y system.

It was a standard brick-built, straight dead-ended building holding 36 locos on six pit roads inside for maintenance, boiler-washout etc and six pits outside the shed front to take one loco for preparation before going into traffic. There were further roads either side of the shed building, some for stabling wagons of loco coal, a finishing road, a coaling road and a further ramped-road up to the height of the loco tenders, where coal was hand-shovelled by men on continuous duties. Above the ramp was a water-tower that supplied the three L&Y-style water columns on the outside shed roads. A 55ft turntable was situated between the shed and the coaling finishing roads. These three columns, along with the water-tower, survived right up to the end of steam in 1968.

During 1937, facilities were modernised, when a new 90ft coaling plant was built (similar to the one still existing at Carnforth), with two hoppers,

one for low-grade and one for high-grade coal for passenger locos and locos on important freight duties, together with an extra loco-finishing pit and an ash-plant. A modern vacuum-operated 65ft turntable was installed nearer to the coaling plant/ash-pit roads, enabling an extra road to be put in south of and alongside the shed building, referred by the shed staff as the 'new road'. Shortly afterwards, the shed was given a new 'louvre' pattern roof, first proposed in 1933, but not acted upon for some years.

During the 1947 oil-burning conversion of some locos due to the coal strike, a tall brick building was constructed on the approach to the coal tower to service oil-burning 0-8-0s from Wakefield depot. Rose Grove drivers and firemen were even trained in the operation of these, but, with the cessation of the coal strike and resumption of regular supplies of coal, the project was abandoned and the facilities never used. This structure stood as a monument to the scheme until the end of steam in 1968, being finally demolished in the very early 1970s along with the coaling tower.

Following the amalgamation with the LNWR in 1921, many different types of locos came to be relieved by Rose Grove men on the excursions to Blackpool from Yorkshire, these including 'Prince

of Wales' and 'Experiment' classes from Farnley Junction shed. The changeover point was, unusually, at Burnley Manchester Road station and not at Rose Grove.

The importance of Rose Grove in passenger workings is shown by a survey of routes covered by its enginemen (see Table 1), covering regular passenger work and also excursion traffic, especially during the summer months and during the local July 'Wakes Weeks'. Lodging turns on passenger/excursions took Rose Grove men to London Euston via Wigan and Stoke, Glasgow and Edinburgh via Preston and Carlisle and Carlisle itself via Preston or Appleby. Route knowledge was also required on duties to Windermere, Holyhead, Chester, Llandudno, Sheffield, Derby, Nottingham, York, Birmingham, Coventry and Leamington.

The 08:00 and 11:55 Colne-London Euston services were invariably hauled by Rose Grove 'Black Fives', always kept in good external condition, right up to the end of this service in 1965. Regular performers were Nos 44947-51 which had been sent to Rose Grove when brand-new in 1942. No 44949 was the last of this batch to survive into 1968, being withdrawn in the June as a 9D Newton Heath loco.

Ex-L&Y 2-4-2 tanks and, subsequently, Fairburn

and Stanier 2-6-4 tanks, described by Rose Grove men as 'good fast runners' were needed for the local expresses, such as the 16:25 Salford-Colne, which was timed for 49 minutes between Salford and Burnley Barracks, usually loaded to 10 coaches. In late 2007, a 'new' service commenced between Burnley Central and Manchester direct, without the need for the usual change at Blackburn, but this run today takes almost 100 minutes and is just one service each day. Compare that to the 1950s journey time of 49 minutes, as described above – and by steam!

It was, however, the everyday coal and freight workings, and the need for a marshalling/sorting area in East Lancashire, that gave rise to the very existence of Rose Grove as an important halfway point, a place where trains to the Yorkshire coalfields and freight yards could be sorted, to go forward to their various destinations on the opposite side of the Pennines.

Sidings at Rose Grove totalled 43, capable of holding some 2000 wagons. The 'Down Grid' was the starting or change-over point for eastbound trains - mainly coal-empties returning to the Yorkshire coalfields. The 'Up Grid', with its fearsome gradient and 15 sidings, at times, became so heavily congested, that no more wagons could be held until space became available. This, in turn, led to many trains being held in sidings along the route from Yorkshire, via the Calder Valley and Copy Pit. It was not uncommon for a number to wait many hours in the loops between Gannow Junction, Burnley and Rose Grove 'Up Grid'.

Trains ran to all parts of the former L&Y system and included several 'lodging' turns, some as near as Newton Heath, Aintree, Wakefield and Blackpool, together with those others listed in Table 2. There were other lodging turns rostered for a number of years, the percentage of these being among the highest of all the 32 sheds on the L&Y system. However, by 1948 lodging turns had ceased, except for the longer distance trains.

Being a purely L&Y shed up to the amalgamation with the LNWR in 1921, Rose Grove's allocation consisted of Aspinall 0-6-0 tender and saddle tanks used on local freight workings, yard shunting and pilot working, together with small and large-boilered 0-8-0s used on the longer freights, in particular the overnight Carlisle run, the furthest out-and-back working in L&Y days for Rose Grove men.

During the 1930s and early 1940s, the LMS Fowler 7F 0-8-0s began to appear, in the shape of Nos (4)9610 and (4)9668, but they never really replaced the 'Lanky Bombers', as those 0-8-0s had become known, although they did outlive the 'Lanky' locos by some years. A pair of standard 3F 0-6-0 tanks (now known by the name of 'Jinties') had arrived by 1934, namely Nos 16559 and 16665. No 16559 (becoming 7575, and then 47575) was to become a 'regular' for many years.

In 1935, the shed code was changed to 24B. At that time, Rose Grove locomotives had duties to Skipton, Manchester (by four different routes), Crewe, Stockport, Liverpool Exchange, Southport, Blackpool, Fleetwood, Morecambe and Windermere.

L&Y rail-motors were a common sight on the Rose Grove-Colne service, until replaced by the L&Y 'Radial' push-pull fitted 2-4-2Ts. These, the first purely passenger types at Rose Grove, had arrived upon closure of nearby Colne motive power depot in 1936. In 1943, the allocation included Nos 10642, 10812, 10885 and 10921,

TABLE 1 PASSENGER TURNS	
Blackpool Central	via Lytham or Marton
Blackpool North	via Kirkham, Poulton-le-Fylde
Fleetwood	Summer only Isle of Man Boat train
Southport	via Burscough or via Longton Bridge
Liverpool Exchange	via Ormskirk
Wigan Wallgate/North Western	via Chorley
Stockport and Crewe	via Bolton, Manchester
Manchester Victoria	via Bolton, Bury or Rochdale
Carlisle	Summer only - Friday night
Bradford Forster Square	via Skipton, Keighley
Wakefield	via Cleckheaton, return via Brighouse
Hellifield	via Blackburn

The Carlisle summer-only service mentioned above was a Friday night departure at 23:40, worked throughout by Rose Grove men, often using a Newton Heath Hughes 'Dreadnought' 4-6-0.
An example of the intensity of morning services can be shown by the following list as operating in the late 1940s/early 1950s:

05:10	Colne-Manchester	08:50 Colne-Skipton
06:00	Colne-Bolton	08:45 Colne-Bradford express
06:05	Colne-Skipton	8:49 Colne-Manchester express
06:30	Colne-Manchester	09:10 Colne-Manchester express
06:58	Skipton-Manchester express	09:55 Rose Grove-Skipton
07:40	Colne-Blackpool express	09:55 Skipton-Manchester
08:00	Colne-London express	09:55 Rose Grove-Blackpool express
08:08	Colne-Fleetwood (summer only)	
08:18	Skipton-Liverpool express	11:55 Colne-London Euston

TABLE 2 FREIGHT TURNS		
01:25	Aintree	Lodge at Aintree Rail Hostel
01:50	Healey Mills	Lodge at Wakefield Rail Hostel
02:00	Moston, Ashton Moss	Lodge at Newton Heath Rail Hostel
02:15	Carnforth	Lodge at Carnforth, private digs
09:50	Barnsley	Lodge at Barnsley, private digs
10:45	Mytholmroyd-Fleetwood	Lodge at Barnsley, private digs
11:55	Hapton-Carlton	Lodge at Royston, private digs
17:30	Wyre Dock	Lodge at Fleetwood, private digs
21:30	Carlisle	Lodge at Carlisle Rail Hostel
21:55	Clayton West	Lodge at Huddersfield, private digs
21:30	Goole	Lodge at Goole, private digs

Enginemen could claim 3s-6d in private digs, but only 2s-6d in company rail hostels.

with 10653 and 10654, later becoming BR-numbered 50653 and 50654 (which were fitted for push-pull working), lasting until 1957 before being withdrawn and being replaced by BR Standard 2-6-2Ts Nos 84010 and 84011 (also push-pull fitted). The latter lasted only a short period, before the local services were taken over by new diesel multiple-units based at Accrington.

The ex-L&Y types still on Rose Grove's books in the early 1950s, particularly Barton Wright 0-6-0STs Nos 51336 and 51497, were used in the main for the 'Up' and 'Down Grid' shunts. By 1960, the very last L&Y type of all, the Aspinall A class 0-6-0s, were down to three in number, namely Nos 52179, 52290 and 52445; these three vintage locos finally being withdrawn in the November. Nevertheless, just six months later in July 1961, some equally ancient machines arrived, in the form of ex-Midland 0-6-0s, Nos 43436 and 43734, dating from the 1880s, from 82G Templecombe shed on the one-time Somerset & Dorset Joint Railway.

They were thoroughly disliked at Rose Grove and only occasionally used, on local pilot duties at Accrington, Nelson and Colne, spending most of their time stored alongside the shed. No 43734 did, however, venture further afield on 17 July 1961. A photograph of it later appeared in a Bradford-Barton book, stood at Rochdale bay platform on a parcels to Oldham. No 43734,

most likely, had worked light-engine to Skipton at 19:45 to work the 7J34 'vans and fitted' plus loose wagons to Oldham (Glodwick Road), booked to attach and detach at Rose Grove between 22:00 and 22:35. The train was then scheduled to call at Blackburn, before working forward via Bolton and Bury to Rochdale and Oldham, probably reaching either Bolton or Bury shed, where No 43734 was probably used to cover a turn from one of these sheds. Just a year later, both No 43436 and No 43734 had been withdrawn, in June and September 1962 respectively, but lingered-on until the summer of the following year before being towed away for scrap.

Stanier and Fairburn 2-6-4Ts had come to Rose Grove by the early 1940s, Nos 42438/9 being allocated here for some years, still being on the books by 1959 alongside other Staniers, Nos 42474/546/7/55 and Fairburn No 42187. When Accrington depot (24A) closed to steam in 1961, more 2-6-4Ts arrived, with some of the other tanks being allocated elsewhere. By May 1963, just two remained, No 42295 being transferred away and No 42547 being withdrawn that month.

The Hughes 'Crab' 2-6-0s were, perhaps, the first modern types to be allocated to Rose Grove, first arriving in the 1930s, they performed varied duties, such as pilot work, freights, Copy Pit banking, passenger and excursion trains. In 1943,

Three staunch steam men on the Rose Grove staff, left to right, Ken Richardson, Dick Shepherd and Terry Millar, pose in front of Newton Heath's No 44846. The loco was being prepared to work 5J10, the 19:05 Burnley Central-Moston freight on 5 June 1967. JIMMY ELLISON

Nos 2706/16/26/8/32 were shedded here and the last ones to remain, Nos 42716/27/828/41/69/98, all being transferred away in November 1964. However, in January 1965, No 42717 (withdrawn in October 1964) was still present, minus its tender, on the coal-stacking line beyond the turntable.

The 'Jinty' 0-6-0Ts lasted until as late as January 1966, with No 47631 and the now-preserved No 47383 being the last two at the shed. A more unusual allocation for a few months in 1964 was No 47211, fitted with condensing apparatus. It did not last long, however, and was withdrawn by the November. The main duty for these engines was the Burnley Bank Top siding shunt, which required, at times, two locomotives, the second one by this time being the relatively recent 350hp diesel 0-6-0 shunter, of which two were now allocated to Rose Grove, the other working in the 'Up Grid' sidings.

The most powerful locomotives allocated from the mid-1940s were the WD 'Austerity' 2-8-0s, at times accounting for over half of the stud. These rugged machines were powerful enough for any type of working over the Pennines to Yorkshire and to the power stations in Lancashire and the Fylde. Rose Grove enginemen found them good steamers and capable of hauling the heaviest of trains, even though they were described by many as 'rough riders'.

However, the very last had been transferred away by mid-1965, to other depots mainly in Yorkshire, and the last remaining three, Nos 90420/681/725, being withdrawn in August 1965. The Stanier 8F 2-8-0s had started to appear from May of that year, ever increasing in numbers as the WDs gradually disappeared from the scene. It is a great pity that not a lot of photographs appear of WDs in this area, this probably being because more glamorous locomotives were still in existence at the time - even on Rose Grove shed, and I often regret not taking the time the record them on film, particularly as they had served Rose Grove so well and for so many years. A further reason, perhaps, was because they were invariably so filthy and, anyway, not as photogenic as the cleaner Hughes 'Crabs', Fairburn and Stanier 2-6-4Ts and 'Black Fives' that Rose Grove cleaners of the time kept so much more presentable. See Table above.

In 1958/9, with the introduction of new diesel railcars allocated to Accrington taking over many of the local area passenger services, the real decline of steam now started at Rose Grove. Notwithstanding this, two services escaped dieselisation for a few years to come. The first one was the morning Colne-Manchester passenger, the return working of a turn that often brought a Newton Heath Jubilee onto Rose Grove shed the previous evening, although motive power could be anything that Newton Heath could provide, with Scots, unrebuilt Patriots, Britannias, and even a Clan, making their appearance. The other passenger turn was the Colne-London express as far as Stockport, a Rose Grove turn for one of its own very clean 'Black Fives'. In 1963, this service was withdrawn and with it disappeared the last remaining regular steam passenger turn at the shed.

It was then only the remaining excursion traffic (of which there was a considerable amount in the summer months to the Lancashire coastal resorts, along with the 'Wakes Weeks' specials in July and September), that brought in extra passenger work for Rose Grove, this, right up until July 1968.

In the 1960s, Burnley Football Club was in the (then) First Division and on Saturday 5 May 1962 faced Tottenham Hotspur at Wembley in the FA Cup Final. At least five, possibly six, specials ran that day from East Lancashire to Wembley, all with Rose Grove men. Conductors were provided for the main line sections of the journeys, with the following locomotives being noted: See table below.

The Friday prior to the annual July 'Wakes Weeks' holidays brought in a variety of locos for the many specials booked to run from the area on the Friday, Saturday and Sunday. The Friday night was a local spotters' delight, because of the 'namers' that would appear. It was, however, almost impossible to get round the depot on these occasions, as this was the only time a watch was kept on the open entrance to deter visitors. Only if locos were stabled on the first road, known as the 'Lighthouse Road', was it possible to catch a glimpse of what delights the shed was holding.

On Saturday 7 July 1962, in addition to some

IT82	45552 *Silver Jubilee* (5A)	Skipton-Wembley, with 11 coaches
IT82	45552 *Silver Jubilee* (5A)	Skipton-Wembley, with 11 coaches
IT84	45615 *Malay States* (17B)	Accrington-Wembley, with 12 coaches
IT86	45254 (5A) + 45209 (24B)	Burnley-Wembley
IT87	45705 *Seahorse* (24E)	Burnley-Wembley
IT85	44940 (24B) + 45229 (24B)	Colne-Wembley, with 14 coaches.

Specially cleaned for a 'Farewell To Steam' railtour on the final weekend, on 31 July 1968, running shift foreman Fred Watson oversees Rose Grove's 8F No 48666 being turned on the 65ft vacuum-operated turntable. MIKE TAYLOR

of the Newton Heath and Blackpool Jubilees, also present was a grimy No 70050 *Firth of Clyde*, allocated at the time to 66A Polmadie. This went out on a Colne-Llandudno special.

Steam haulage on 'Wakes Weeks' specials lasted right to the very end of steam in July 1968 and, at which time, No 45156 formerly *Ayrshire Yeomanry*, recently transferred to Rose Grove from the closed Patricroft MPD, worked an evening Colne-Newquay holiday special of just four coaches as far as Stockport.

Although No 45156, by this time, bore no nameplates, it was the only 'named' locomotive ever to have been allocated to the depot. An unusual visitor for several days in May and early June 1967 was Britannia Pacific No 70015 *Apollo* (9B), in unlined green livery. It had been 'borrowed' by Rose Grove to work several turns, including coal trains over the Copy Pit route to Yorkshire and to Wyre Dock.

On the evening of Saturday 28 October 1967, a railtour in the area brought, No 70013 *Oliver Cromwell* onto the shed, the engine staying over at Rose Grove all day on the Sunday.

However, the very last Britannia of all known to have visited Rose Grove was No 70045 *Lord Rowallan*. On 30 December 1967, after working the 13:10 Carlisle-Skipton freight (making history in hauling this as the working was the last steam freight from Carlisle over the S&C), it travelled light-engine to Rose Grove for servicing. Spending all day on shed on 31 December, all the other Britannias had been withdrawn at Carlisle Kingmoor by this time. Rose Grove, being oblivious to this, turned it out for a New Year's Day coal special from Rose Grove to Wigan. By the time that it arrived at Wigan, the error has been discovered and it never worked again.

During 1968, the only changes from the usual Stanier presence were the visiting BR Standard 4MTs, still allocated to Carnforth shed but working from Rose Grove to cover the Rylstone Quarry workings up the Grassington Branch. Locos frequently seen in 1968 were Nos 75019, 75027 and 75048.

Initially, quite dirty (No 75027, under its grime, was actually still in BR green), later on in the year they came to receive the attention of enthusiasts during a number of overnight cleaning sessions at the shed. The occasional Standard 5MT, from either Bolton or Patricroft, also appeared in early 1968, but this was very much a rarity and then mostly at the head of railtours passing through.

By this time, the general run-down of steam was well under way, with many of the longstanding trains such as Aintree, Sandhills and Bickershaw being cancelled and specials run, as required, in their place. Instead of working out and back, there would only be a train outbound with the working back being light engine.

Examples of this, from the diary of Terry Millar (ex-Rose Grove fireman), as early as February and March of 1968 being as follows:-

Conditions at the shed during those final few months were gradually worsening, with track in the yard in a poor state of repair, causing many minor derailments and a need to make careful movements.

On 2 August, just days before the end, the derailment near the entrance of No 48666, returning from Todmorden banking duties with driver Rennie Lonsdale, was just such an example. It had been cleaned-up ready for

Less than 24 hours later, disaster befalls No 48666! Upon returning to shed, having worked the 04:10-11:00 Todmorden banker duty with driver Rennie Lonsdale and fireman George Kileen, the loco promptly derails itself on the extremely dubious trackwork entering the depot, thus causing a major obstruction until it is put back onto the rails. Mobile once more, it is not worth the time and trouble to repair any damage sustained, so No 48666 is promptly withdrawn and banished to a siding – its place on the special now being allocated to No 48773, which is, coincidentally, stood close by. DAVE DYSON

Having spent its last regular working day on 'No 19 Target', the Blackburn to Clitheroe tripper, No 45156 (formerly *Ayrshire Yeomanry*) returns to shed. It pauses briefly on the main line alongside the shed's coaling road. Part of the 1937-built twin-hopper coaling plant is visible on the left, to the right of which is the water-tower that supplied the three L&Y-style water columns on the outside shed roads. Before the automatic coaler was erected, this structure originally included a ramped-road up to the height of the loco tenders, where coal was hand-shovelled by men on continuous duties. MIKE TAYLOR

February 8	Rose Grove-Healey Mills	Loco 48448	worked light engine back
February 14	Burnley-Wyre Dock	Loco 45447	light engine to Blackpool North shed, home passenger
February 15	Burnley-Burn Naze	Loco 44690	light engine to Blackpool North shed, home passenger
February 17	Huncoat-Healey Mills	Loco 48384	light engine home

The evening Burnley-Moston suffered a similar lack of return working for the crew in February 1968:

February 26	Burnley-Moston	Loco 44949	returned home passenger
February 27	Burnley-Moston	Loco 44890	returned home passenger
February 28	Burnley-Moston	Loco 45382	returned home passenger.

working an end-of-steam special, but, after re-railing, was withdrawn, never to steam again. No 48773 then stood in, in its place, for the railtour.

Also by now, only Stanier 'Black Fives' and 8Fs remained on the books, with just a handful of the original batch of those transferred there in 1965 still working through to the very end. As locos were withdrawn, further replacements arrived from other sheds that had closed to steam. A number of remaining serviceable engines from

Northwich, Heaton Mersey, Edge Hill, Patricroft, Springs Branch and Bolton appeared for a short while, before eventually being withdrawn.

During the last weeks, very few of Rose Grove's 'Black Fives' were in service; most were stored or withdrawn and only Nos 45156 and 45287 (both transferred here from Patricroft at the end of June) were seen in steam. However, one of Lostock Hall's allocation could be found on shed every weekday afternoon, ready for the 19:14

Left: 3 August 1968 and the specially cleaned No 48773 awaits its final task in BR service; that of working the Blackburn-Carnforth stage of one of the Last Day specials. Following this, the locomotive became the only engine on the allocation to survive the cutting torch, moving to the Severn Valley Railway and preservation. MAURICE BURNS
Right: Awaiting departure off shed at Rose Grove on 3 August 1968, the crew of No 48773, driver Arnold Hodgson and fireman Jim Walker, pose for the camera before travelling to Blackburn to take over the Carnforth via Hellifield leg of the LCGB 'Farewell to Steam Railtour'. HUGH SYKES

Colne-Preston parcels. These 10D visitors, especially during the last weeks, had been cleaned by enthusiasts at their home depot and at least one over-zealous 10D fireman on the turn also regularly painted the smokebox hinges and front buffers white.

Thus, the vast majority of serviceable locomotives were the 8Fs, with virtually every working of these during the final few days receiving the attention of enthusiasts from all over the UK, and from abroad as well.

The Burn Naze and Wyre Dock Power Station coal workings were just about the lengthiest steam-hauled turns, being 8F-worked right up until the final workings of Friday 2 August 1968. On a few days in May and June, the Burnley Bank Top sidings to Burn Naze 21-ton wagon coal trains were worked exclusively by steam… from 'colliery to power station tippler'. The Bank Hall Colliery steam loco, (Andrew Barclay 0-4-0ST 1448 of 1919) named King, would haul three to five wagons from the pit, along the colliery line (by the side of Thompson Park in Burnley) to the weighbridge and then on to the interchange sidings at Burnley Bank Top. Here, a Stanier 8F was waiting to take the made-up full train loads onwards to Wyre Dock and where that power station's fireless locomotives would transport them onwards to the tippler.

A listing of all the known workings during the final few days can be found later in this book, however it might be mentioned that, in particular during Friday 2 August and Saturday 3 August, the shed had resembled more an 'Open Day' atmosphere than a working steam shed, with scores - perhaps even a few hundred - enthusiasts, photographers and 'locals' with their children wandering around, watching and recording on film, cine and sound the locomotives moving around the yard. The small contingent of police, I only counted at the most two, brought in to 'control' the crowds had seemingly given in to it all and were quite bemused at the goings on.

Saturday 3 August 1968 saw just local shunt workings and the last of the Todmorden banking locos arrive back on shed, No 48278 arriving first and then No 48191, with their chalked smokebox and tender inscriptions proclaiming 'Last Steam Copy Pit Banker 3rd August 1968'.

Other locos in steam that day were: 48348/93/519/715/73. The remainder, being either stored or withdrawn, consisted of: 44690/899/5096/350/82/97/447, 48062/115/67/ 257/323/84/400/10/23/48/51/665/6/727/30.

Sunday 4 August was a far quieter day than the few previous ones at Rose Grove, as it was the day of the 'End of Steam' railtours. Locos that had been in steam the previous day were still warm, with just a few pounds of steam pressure remaining, but just two had a full head of steam.

A very clean No 48773 was being prepared by Driver Arnold Hodgson and Fireman Jim Walker for the Blackburn to Carnforth via Hellifield leg of the LCGB 'Farewell to Steam Railtour' and a very grubby No 48519 had also been kept in steam, as standby for No 48773, just in case of any last-minute failure.

No 48773 went off shed, accompanied by running shift Foreman Des Melia to the shed exit, and then proceeded light-engine to Blackburn.

The only other crew booking on at Rose Grove on the Sunday were driver Arthur Green and his fireman Bob Ashworth, this for a pw working in Rose Grove 'Up' sidings, in conjunction with the bridge-renewal work over the station and yards. The turn had been booked for a 350hp diesel shunter (Class 08).

Sensibly, rather than immediately drop the fire in No 48519, which had a full head of steam, it was decided to use the 8F on the pw job, to burn through the already built-up fire. And so it fell to No 48519 and its crew to be the last steam loco to leave Rose Grove shed… and to No 48773 to be the last steam loco to arrive on shed in the evening upon its return light engine from Carnforth.

So that was it, the end of 79 years of steam locomotives at Rose Grove motive power depot, the end of an era; for the men of Rose Grove, the end of a lifetime on steam. Some retired or took redundancy, but, as the railway continued to be decimated over the course of the next few years, many more were leaving for more secure jobs.

From 5 August 1968, the only sounds then to be heard at Rose Grove shed were those of diesel horns and even this was only to continue for a few more months, until the servicing point was

transferred from the shed site to adjacent to the station.

There was one seldom-reported steaming four days after the official end of steam.

On Thursday 8 August 1968, No 48773 was lit-up again and moved around the yard for watering and coaling, by driver Winston Hartley, in preparation for a light-engine journey to Bescot and then to Bridgnorth, Severn Valley Railway. However, the engine never got beyond the shed limits. Preston Control had stopped the movement, reminding Rose Grove that there was now a ban in place preventing any further steam locomotives operating over BR tracks (apart from, that is, the following weekend's 15-Guinea Special). So No 48773 was placed back inside the shed, with the instruction that its connecting rods were to be removed, to prevent any further recurrences. Some time later, it did move again, and to the SVR, but now being towed by a diesel.

The steam-fitters had one last duty to perform over the next few days, that of dismantling all the connecting rods and tying them onto the running plates. (Most sheds had merely cut them through and thrown them into the tenders.) This prevented lubrication problems arising when being towed out-of-steam.

Engines seemed to be shuffled around the shed yard for a few weeks more, in readiness for their final journeys in convoys to the scrapyards. This occurred over a period of several months, with No 44899 having the honour of being the very last locomotive to depart, being added to a convoy already en-route from Lostock Hall to Hull in March 1969.

The shed building, after lying derelict for a while, was demolished in 1973 to make way for the M65 motorway.

Nothing now remains at Rose Grove; the 'Down Grid' lies under the M65 and a car-sales area, the 'Up Grid' has commercial units in the sidings, but the station platforms still exist with the usual 'bus shelter' for protection against the elements and the 'down' loop just about visible under the weeds. A walk down Lower Rosegrove Lane today will take you to where the shed entrance used to be, the perimeter retaining-wall still being visible, but the only sounds emanating now from over this are those of the incessant road traffic.

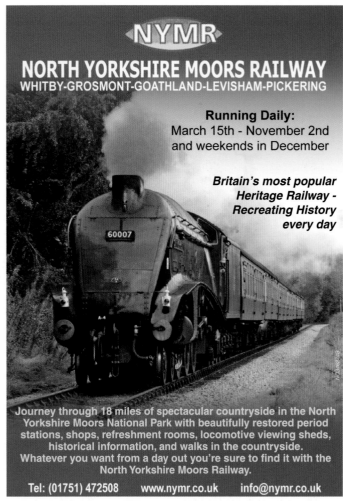
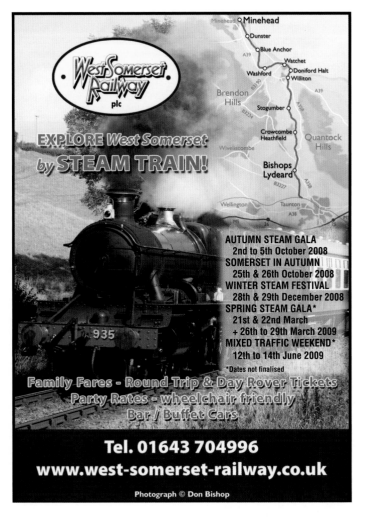

A Sunday afternoon line-up on 31 March 1968, of all 10D-allocated motive power, includes Nos 48646, 43019, 43106 and 48476. The 1954-rebuilt section of the shed roof contrasts most sharply here with the remaining part of the original 1882 L&Y 'northlight' structure on the left. PETER FITTON

Lostock Hall MPD
closed 5 August 1968

Alan Castle

The Lancashire & Yorkshire Railway originally stabled its locomotives arriving at Preston in a very cramped and primitive five-road depot situated in the fork (later to be converted into carriage sidings) created by the LNWR main line and East Lancashire line platforms at the station. By 1877, the situation had become so intolerable that investigations were instigated into sourcing an alternative location. A suitable site was eventually found about three miles to the south, in Lostock Hall, and construction soon commenced of a conventional L&Y-design brick-built eight-track straight single-ended building. This was opened in 1882 and contained typical standard features evidenced elsewhere on the system, these including the shedmaster's bay window overlooking the loco yard.

Lostock Hall was one of 32 depots at that time on the Lancashire and Yorkshire Railway, being allocated No 27, which it kept until January 1935 when it became 23E – under the parent depot of Bank Hall, Liverpool. In May 1946, now under Accrington, it became 24C; finally, in Sept 1963, under Carnforth, becoming 10D.

Its 40 or so locomotives were provided for workings over the L&Y lines in the Preston area, these including local freight and passenger turns, in addition to shunting duties and a few long-distance goods workings. The shed was also responsible for a number of passenger jobs to Blackpool, Fleetwood, Liverpool and Manchester and had one trip in the 1880s through to Leeds via Burnley.

In the years after 1900, 0-6-0s of Barton-Wright design, later followed by newer Aspinall and Hughes versions, constituted over half of the allocation. There were also over a dozen 'Radial Tank' 2-4-2Ts, which worked local passenger

turns, particularly on the West Lancs line to Southport. Numbers grew after the Grouping, attaining a total of nearly 60 in the 1930s. Now with also a growing number of Hughes and Fowler 0-8-0s, 'Crab' 2-6-0s and 4F 0-6-0s made up the numbers. New coaling and ash disposal plants were erected in 1937 and in 1938 a 60ft vacuum-operated turntable was also installed nearby. At the end of World War II, the total allocation fell to 42 engines, with Fowler 7Fs outnumbering other types, all of the L&Y versions having been dispensed with. A re-roofing of the building was completed by 1954, with other than over the offices and workshops areas, the old north-light pattern roof being cut back in length and replaced by a more modern steel-framed design, which remained until closure.

After Nationalisation, the LMS 0-8-0s came to be gradually replaced by WD 2-8-0s as from about 1950 and arrivals of new Stanier and Fairburn 2-6-4Ts made further inroads into the stock of 'Radial' tanks. The 2-6-4Ts became immediate favourites with crews, at least one, No 42158, being on the allocation for all of its working life! A couple of others almost achieved a similar distinction, one example being No 42296, which arrived from Low Moor in 1950. This engine had the honour of being specially cleaned by the shed staff (by that date, an uncommon occurrence) on 6 September 1964 in order to work the final train of all between Southport and Preston.

The pattern of work from the date of the depot's opening, in servicing all the ex-L&Y routes and yards in the Preston area, continued throughout, very much unchanged, until the early 1960s. The ex-LNW shed at Preston, traditionally, had provided the power on all the LNW routes, that is, until a disastrous fire occurred on 28 June 1960 which destroyed the shed roof and damaged a large

number of locomotives. Former driver, Andy Hall, recalls that a number of footplatemen went up to the top of the coaling plant to watch the blaze and the pall of black smoke engulfing the town!

Although the now roofless building at 24K struggled on for another 15 months, it finally succumbed on 12 September 1961 and part of the remaining allocation and duties were then passed to Lostock Hall. Effectively, this meant the end of the last LNWR locos in the Preston area and those that did not get withdrawn were moved to Carnforth and elsewhere. Some Ivatt and BR 2MT 2-6-0s and seven 'Jinty' 3F 0-6-0Ts, however, were transferred from 24K to 24C. At this time ex-MR examples, Nos 47201 and 47211, also arrived in the area – the latter still being fitted with condensing pipes from its days in the London area. Another 'Jinty', No 47314, which arrived from Springs Branch in 1966, was actually a former Somerset & Dorset Joint Railway loco, being introduced in 1929 as that company's No 23. No 47564, arrived from Barrow in 1963 and, upon withdrawal from service later, was converted at Darlington Works into stationary boiler No 2022 - essentially by removal of its side-tanks. Upon completion of those duties (at Newton Heath MPD), the remains were purchased for preservation at the Midland Railway Centre. Currently used as a source of supplies for the three other examples at the MRC, it may well still be restored to working order in the future.

One of the more positive aspects arising from the transfer of work to 10D was the increase in the number of passenger diagrams for the shed and, with the Preston station pilot turns also coming to be assumed by Lostock Hall, there was a commensurate increase in light engine movements. Among these were now the daily journeys of one or other of the two unique LMS 0P

0-4-0STs, Nos 47002/8, also transferred from Preston, but being the only engines capable of shunting the very sharply curved coal-yard at Greenbank Sidings - adjacent to the West Coast Main Line, about a mile north of Preston station. Having to travel each day from Lostock Hall to their place of work, their short wheelbase meant that they could not be relied upon to operate the track circuits en-route and, consequently, had to be hauled by one the station pilots (invariably a 'Jinty') in each direction.

As time passed, the variety of motive power thinned-out considerably. The pre-grouping L&Y locos were all gone by 1963, as well as a number of tank engines with the withdrawal or dieselisation of local services. Some Ivatt 4MT 2-6-0s arrived in 1966, but do not appear to have been universally accepted, although the final example survived until June 1968, by which time it was the last member of the class in service. The WD 8F 2-8-0s on the allocation at their peak had numbered some 16 examples, but with the displacement of Stanier 8Fs from depots in the Midlands, the latter started to arrive in considerable numbers in 1964. By the end of 1965, all the WDs had gone.

Enthusiast, Bob Gregson once asked an engineman: "Why were there so few Standard engines based at Lostock Hall?" "The 9Fs aren't bad," the driver replied, "but they aren't needed round these parts – and the others haven't got the guts! Put it this way, a 'Black Five' in bad nick can still handle a heavy load; a Standard in bad nick is a non-starter." I would add to this by observing that the Standard 2MT 2-6-0s (the only Standard class to be shedded here) were also not that

"Bowden's Gap". In early 1967, 'Black Five' No 45339, the last in a line of locos being shunted by driver Mick Bowden, jumped the stops at the end of No 2 Road and continues on its wayward journey straight through the rear wall of the depot! This part of the shed was rebuilt in 1954 in such a way that, should an accident like this occur, due to the insertion of large lintels and vertical gaps in the brickwork, only one section of wall would be demolished. The picture was taken within minutes of the incident occurring and clearly shows a now rather bent and battered brand-new radiator, only just delivered for one of the shed's Yorkshire Engine Co 0-4-0 diesel-shunters, leaning against the wall. Within a short time afterwards, a neatly-painted slogan appeared alongside the hole. This exclaimed, "BOWDEN'S GAP" and it wasn't too long before some wag had appended this with the words, "....THE SHAPE OF SHEDS TO COME!" BILL ASHCROFT

popular with crews having to use them (from the mid-1960s) on station-pilot duties, especially at night, due to the draughty nature of their cabs. However, slightly earlier in time, when they were extensively used on local passenger turns, turn-and-turn-about with larger locomotives, there were fewer complaints. On the last day of services on the Preston-Southport branch, I had the opportunity to drive both Nos 78040 and

78041 and can report that these two were an absolute delight to handle, even with the numerous station stops and starts.

Former Lostock Hall loco-fitter Charles Findlay says that, at the end of steam, there was a mechanical foreman and leading fitter and approximately 26 to 30 maintenance staff. These comprised of fitters, electricians, boilersmiths, fitters' mates and labourers. On the running side, he says that there was a shedmaster, three foremen and their assistants, storemen and three clerks and, of course, along with these were all the drivers, firemen, cleaners and shedmen.

The last shedmaster was the late Harold Sedgbeer. Harold was a Somerset man who served his apprenticeship at Highbridge on the Somerset and Dorset Joint. He came to Lostock Hall via some Midland Division depots and then from Skipton. He was alleged to be antagonistic to enthusiasts but, in fact, if they followed the normal courtesies and asked first, and they seemed reasonably responsible in their approach, he would permit shed visits - if he had a member of staff able to spare the time to go round with them. Anyone else, particularly those who 'sneaked in' without asking were quite firmly shown the exit!

The running shift foremen were usually former drivers who had chosen to move over to the supervisory grades, and their deputies were also drivers, but who could be replaced on the footplate roster to stand in as RSF when required. The RSFs and deputies were of many types. The more successful (and usually more popular) were almost amateur psychologists! They had to know their men, upon whom they could call when faced with a problem to solve or an unexpected job to fil1. Some never got co-operation, because they adopted the wrong approach, but others were successful beyond expectations. The fact that they kept the job running, often in the most trying circumstances, illustrates that in most of us there is usually a hidden talent of which some of are unaware.

Former fireman John 'Fingers' Fletcher calculated that, at the end of steam there were still 200-250 footplatemen, of whom, he felt, five per cent were dedicated steam men - an unfortunate fact, when bearing in mind that although a lot of

---

LOSTOCK HALL MPD LOCOMOTIVE ALLOCATION 1948

Stanier 3P 2-6-2T: 40190/1/2/4/8/9, Stanier 4P 2-6-4T: 42434/5/6/7/80/81/556, Stanier 8F 2-8-0: 48526/7/8/9/719/20, Fowler 7F 0-8-0: 49502/3/23/4/34/85/611/2/4/5/6/7/40/9, Barton Wright 2F 0-6-0ST: 51345/526, Aspinall 3F 0-6-0: 52160/71/244/96/317/34/6/68/99/460/7/522/41.

Total: 50

LOSTOCK HALL MPD LOCOMOTIVE ALLOCATION 1960

Stanier 3P 2-6-2T: 40183/92, Fairburn 4P 2-6-4T: 42158/87/286/96/8, Stanier 4P 2-6-4T: 42433/4/76/81/634/61/80/1, Aspinall 2F 0-6-0: 52290/429/45/56, Riddles 'WD' 8F 2-8-0: 90258/66/77/95/331/5/67/413/541/56/658/75/81/9/720.

Total: 34

LOSTOCK HALL MPD LOCOMOTIVE ALLOCATION 1962 (Following closure of Preston shed)

Fairburn 4MT 2-6-4T: 42158/87/286/96/8, Stanier 4MT 2-6-4T: 42433/4/76/80/1/634/61, Ivatt 2MT 2-6-0: 46449, Kitson 0P 0-4-0ST: 47002/8, Fowler 3F 0-6-0T: 47293/319/60/86/413/72/572, BR 2MT 2-6-0: 78036/7, Riddles 'WD' 8F 2-8-0: 90258/66/77/95/335/541/84/658/75/81/ 9/713/20.

Total: 38

LOSTOCK HALL MPD LOCOMOTIVE ALLOCATION 31/12/1966

Fairburn 4MT 2-6-4T: 42187/224/97, Stanier 4MT 2-6-4T: 42546, Ivatt 4MT 2-6-0: 43019/41/6/118, Stanier 5MT 4-6-0: 44915/58/5107/97/226/347/402/21/44/50, Fowler 3F 0-6-0T: 47531, Stanier 8F 2-8-0: 48062/77/164/266/307/20/93/438/45/68/70/510/618/37/66/707/ 30/9, BR 2MT 2-6-0: 78020/1/37/41.

Total: 41

LOSTOCK HALL MPD LOCOMOTIVE ALLOCATION 04/08/1968

Stanier 5MT 4-6-0: 44713/806/888/910/971/5055/073/110/260/305/318/386/407/44, Stanier 8F 2-8-0: 48253/294/476/723/765.

Total: 19

LOSTOCK HALL MPD LOCOMOTIVE ALLOCATION 11/08/1968

Stanier 5MT 4-6-0: 45110.

Total: 1

Lostock Hall survived until the end of steam on BR and was an active and much-visited centre of steam operation throughout the final years. 8Fs and 'Black Fives' now comprised the bulk of the allocation and in December 1966, for example, over 50 engines could often be seen in steam at the shed. On Christmas Day 1966, former Lostock Hall Engine Shed Junction signalman, David Hardman, recorded the following present: 42096/2105/87/224/97, 42546/611/65, 43019/41/6, 44665/832/4/7/915/5069/107/41/97/402/44, 47314/26/472,48000/2/46/62/77/ 201/307/20/393/438/41/5/68/550/618/66/79/707, 70014, 73128, 75058, 78020/1/37/41/58, 92027, D2862, D3005/210/368/71/4/530/1/81/782/846/7/4114

Total: 65

With the closure of Lower Darwen MPD in February 1966, a number of Ivatt Class 4MT 2-6-0s were transferred to Lostock Hall. These gradually began to replace the Stanier and Fairburn 2-6-4 tanks that had been a mainstay on the allocation for a great many years. The design was noted for its American looks – with the running-plate at high level and a gap left ahead of the cylinders, many considering it to be an ugly design. However, the locomotives incorporated new mechanical features, such as rocker-grates, intended to reduce maintenance costs and were well-liked by many Lostock Hall crews. Here, in early 1968, No 43027, a relatively recent transfer from Workington depot, is receiving attention to its superheater elements. DICK MANTON

passenger work had been lost, 75 per cent of the work was still with steam. Nevertheless, John makes pains to add that, in his experience, he felt that 10D was a friendly place to work at.

According to former fireman, Paul Tuson, there were eight links:

No 1 Link provided mainly passenger work and consisted of about 8-10 sets of men.

No 2 Link consisted of passenger work and parcels turns, with some goods work, and consisted of 10-12 sets of men.

No 3 Link consisted essentially of goods work, again consisting of 10-12 sets of men.

No 4 Link was another goods link, again consisting of 10-12 sets of men.

No 5 (or Spare) Link covered all jobs and rest days, etc, consisting of 10-12 sets of men.

Disposal (and Preparation) Link possibly consisted of about eight sets of men. There was also a Trip Link, which provided work for men who were on restricted duties, due to ill-health, eyesight problems etc.

Finally, there was the Shed Link, which consisted of three sets of men with fixed booking-on times of 00:01, 08:00 and 16:00.

Former fireman, Joseph Booth, adds to the above by mentioning the summer 'London Link', when Lostock Hall men, although mainly ex-Preston drivers, worked the 'Lakes Express', lodging in London, with either an unrebuilt Patriot, or more often a Britannia, and returning, if he remembers correctly, with a parcels train on alternative days and often with a Duchess.

Here is one example of 'how to make friends and influence people', as the saying goes. The disposal link consisted of a number of sets of men whose job was to coal, clean the fire and grate, turn, fill the tank and move any incoming locos onto the shed for their next turn of duty. When they had done six, that was their quota, and if it took less than eight hours, they could go home. In the latter days at Lostock, driver (the late) Charlie Stewart was on his regular disposal tasks in the evening and needed to deal with just two more engines to complete his turn of duty. Charlie was

an aggressive character, who was off main line duties because, it was said, he could not face main line work after a loco he was in charge of had been hit by a passing train and turned on its side, some years earlier. He was quick-tempered and easily 'set off' by the younger men, who were always up for a bit of 'micky-taking'.

One dark winter night, a 'Black Five' was sent down to Preston to work 1F51 to Liverpool, because the rostered engine (which worked to Heysham earlier that day) was stuck behind the train from Glasgow which it was scheduled to work onwards. Control had ordered another loco and the spare crew had got the fire ready on the replacement, as the main train rolled in. Immediately behind it came the rostered loco, and crew, who decided to stick with the engine they had had all afternoon and so the replacement was sent back to the shed. The driver reported to the deputy foreman (the late) Barney Campbell, suggesting that there was still a good fire on the engine and common sense suggested that it should be found another job, rather than throw this all out. Barney agreed. Now comes the psychology!

Barney sent a cleaner to find Charlie Stewart, who was told that, if he would dispose of that loco, he could call it a day - even though he still had two to do (supposedly). As Charlie left the office, Barney started counting. He had reached 76 when the door flew open with a bang, followed by Charlie, with a bright red face and murder in his eyes!! You can imagine his words. "Who the hell brought that ******* engine on shed with all that ******* fire in it?"

Barney feigned surprise, looked at the books and faintly hinted that it might have been Rose Grove men! Barney then suggested, "Damp it down, fill the tank and put on the front of the shed - I'll find a job for it!" before finally adding, "I'll count it as one and you can go home." Charlie retired to the mess room, telling everyone "Barney is the best foreman we have, he looks after me, I'd work for him any day!" Mission accomplished!

Lostock Hall worked passenger turns to

Blackpool North/South, Liverpool Lime Street/Exchange, Crewe, Wigan, Windermere, Barrow, Morecambe and (until 1964) Southport. Parcels workings included Colne, Heysham and Skipton. Goods workings extended to Rose Grove, Burnley Central, Warrington, Crewe, Blackpool, Aintree, Carlisle, Appleby, Hellifield, Heysham, Southport and elsewhere. Trip jobs went to Courtauld's at Ribbleton and Deepdale Sidings on the Longridge branch, Horwich, Chorley, Euxton ROF, Garstang and shuttled between the various yards and sidings in the Farington and Preston areas.

At one stage, it had been planned that a large new diesel depot be erected on the site, but changes in traffic patterns inevitably led to the abandonment of this idea well prior to the end of steam.

And so it was that a large proportion of the footplate personnel received a disgustingly brief, impersonal and curt letter from the office of the Preston Divisional Manager, this advising them that, as from 5 August 1968, their services would no longer be required by the British Railway Board. In that 'brave new age of dieselisation, automation and speed', the faceless bureaucrat who had prepared these missives could not find it in his heart to add a single word, from either himself or his superiors, as a token of appreciation and gratitude for the years of unstinting service that had been rendered to the Railway. Totally unacknowledged went any recognition of that art developed by these men in producing efficient locomotive performance and consistently reliable steam motive power, in often impossible situations. That much was, indeed, a hymn to old-fashioned skills, craftsmanship, loyalty and camaraderie between fellow workmen that formed part of an unbroken tradition going back a century and more, but which would now vanish forever, replaced by and the eternal quest for bland, boring, cost-saving efficiency. The often back-breaking work, particularly for firemen, had been an art born of years of training and experience and, at Lostock Hall, there were several young lads straight from school with avowed intentions of pursuing a lifetime on the railway and now effectively abandoned with no other training and precious little in the way of career prospects. The learned skills of a fireman extended far beyond simply shovelling coal all day. Indeed, the back-breaking work was an art born of years of training and experience. The author having wielded a shovel himself on many a main line run, he can conclusively confirm just how difficult it was to maintain that steam pressure-gauge needle at just below the red line, while at the same time making sure that there was always still enough water in the boiler to make the steam in the first place! When discussing the job, many a driver retorted: "Any idiot can start a locomotive; it's stopping it in the right place that matters!"

Staff were often expected to start work at 04:00, clearing pits of the burnt ashes from yesterday's engines, crawling through the bowels of the locomotive to oil inaccessible points and to check and repair boiler tubes. On cold winter mornings and humid summer days alike, several hours' hard preparation was needed in order to raise steam.

As has been observed in more than one place earlier in this book, the downhill slide in standards had been proceeding apace for many years. Engines in quiet appalling condition came to be mechanically patched-up using parts from other withdrawn locomotives and, although each shed usually still had engine cleaners, such personnel had stopped cleaning engines long before the end of steam. As more and more staff became discarded, they had far too much work to do in other areas.

Joseph Booth recalls a slightly earlier time, in fact on his own first day as a cleaner (7 May 1962), when he was one of eight assigned to clean unrebuilt Patriot No 45543 *Home Guard* with another eight on No 45550. These two engines had been temporarily transferred here following the Preston shed fire. He adds that there were no fewer 42 cleaners at this time and the rest being given either 9Fs or tanks to clean. The following day, both of the Patriots were steamed ready for diagrams, being based at Lostock for three months, before being moved again to Carnforth - where they only lasted for a short while.

Everywhere, the lack of spare components from BR workshops had reached chronic proportions, a situation resulting in otherwise good engines being taken out of service merely for the most minor fault or even because of a sheer lack of parts. I am aware, for example, of at least one very reliable and free-running 'Black Five' being consigned for scrap merely because it had been 'failed' with no more than a few broken floorboards on the footplate! No 44800, another really good engine, went the same way, because of a few leaking tubes – which in other circumstances would have been rectified by a few minutes of re-expanding – or even removing and replacing them. No 43027 had a piston gland-packing problem, blowing it on its first trip after renewal, (possibly a poor fitting), but that was the end of that. No 45444 was withdrawn because some of the rivets that securely held the cab in place had failed, causing the cab to rock forwards and backwards when in motion. No 45107 was withdrawn for a far more serious fault - a 13inch-long fracture from the corner of one of the axle-box guides in the mainframe.

Lostock Hall's 'Black Five' No 45345 waits permission to back off shed on Sunday 25 February 1968. It will run light to Preston Station, where it will work the 16:53 (SuO) Preston to Liverpool Exchange – a through portion of a service from Glasgow and Edinburgh. Because of the perfect lined-out livery discovered under its latest poor Crewe repaint (the latter easily being removed with the serrated edge of a half-crown piece!), this is one of a few engines that were kept in reasonably presentable condition by the regular (SuO) amateur cleaning gang. PETER FITTON

Drivers at Lostock Hall remarked that they had waited for years for really good engines to arrive, but that when their wishes did come to be granted, this only occurred right at the very end of the depot's existence! It was all so desperately sad for anyone who had an interest in steam, and the unfortunate thing for the preservation movement, still then really only in its infancy, was that, maybe, better engines than those actually saved were available earlier, but these had perished through some very minor fault and an acute lack of funds to invest in attempting to save them.

Nevertheless, 'refugees' did arrive from other recently closed depots and many of these remained in service at 10D until the bitter end and, by doing so, one or two became 'legends in their own lifetime'. Nos 44806, 45305, 45386, 45388, 45407 and 48476 (three of which passed into preservation) came from Speke Junction; Nos 45055, 48294 and 48765 from Edge Hill; Nos 43106, 44878 and 45212 from Kingmoor; No 45353 from Chester; No 48723 from Heaton Mersey and Nos 45110, 45260 and 45318 from Bolton, to mention just a few. These locomotives came in the last few weeks of steam, when sheds had been struggling to manage with 'camels', to use a popular description of the day for a poor locomotive. One such 'camel' was No 44878, which had a bit of a reputation and one driver recalls the struggle he had with it on a freight over Ais Gill in late 1967. He adds that it never did work a passenger train during the whole of its time at 10D, spending most of this on 'trippers'.

Dwelling for a moment longer in discussion on individual engines, former driver John Burnett, who still lives within a stone's-throw of the old shed, turns back the clock to the summer of 1967 to indulge in just a little reminiscing. There was a Glasgow-Manchester and Liverpool express, which split at Preston in the afternoon. He says that he used to work the seven or eight coaches onwards to Manchester with a 'Black Five', maybe No 44800, 45149 or 45450, which were regulars on this turn. Encouraged by enthusiastic firemen and remarks from the guard, as John confirms, some really worthwhile performances were enjoyed by all concerned on these trains!

No 44800 was fresh out of shops when she came to Lostock Hall and, he says, this was almost too good to be true! On the other hand, No 45149 was a 'rough old bird', but had an extremely sharp exhaust note, and, John being something of a GWR enthusiast, he dares to mention that, when ascending Chorley Bank, the sound was the equal of a Hall 4-6-0! With No

45450, he recalls being brought almost to a stand by signals at Leyland, then, when the road was cleared, its acceleration was an unforgettable and most rousing prelude to a fast run, which he knows was not only a delight to the crew but also to several passengers! Albeit some of the steam sanding gear came adrift, as they rocked and waddled over Lostock Junction at 60mph-ish! They did stop, however, to pick up the bits and pieces as they came back light-engine. The signalman handed them over… along with one or two choice remarks!! No 44950 was a 'disgraceful rust bucket', but, John reckons, could 'fairly fly'. On one of the Glasgow-Liverpools, if the train hadn't had to stop at Ormskirk, he would have done Preston to Liverpool in half an hour, which, he adds, 'is close to the optimum on the Liverpool line'!

This potted history draws to a close in recording that, as from Monday 5 August 1968, all the remaining footplate crews still required for work were officially transferred to the signing-on point nearby at Preston Station. Although Lostock Hall had taken over the provision of most motive power since 1961, the old office at Preston shed had eventually been transferred over to a room on the station's platforms and had continued to supply crews. The last shedmaster retired at this time and the first Area Managers' organisation became responsible for traffic arrangements in the Preston area.

For some time, diesel locomotives had already been stabled in the open on sidings either side of the main line north of Preston station, but there was naturally still a requirement for maintenance and refuelling – facilities that were only available at Lostock Hall. For this reason, part of the maintenance staff remained at the shed to provide such a service. Fred Swindells came from Carlisle to Lostock Hall to take over from former shedmaster Harold Sedgebeer in the role of Traction Inspector. Lostock Hall carried on until 1971, servicing diesels, but when the new Springs Branch Traction & Maintenance Depot gradually came to assume that function, four of the fitters then went onto Preston station and the remainder transferred to Springs Branch and elsewhere, or followed their footplate brethren into inevitable redundancy.

After closure, the shed building at Lostock Hall was taken over and used for the work that had previously been carried out at Lostock Hall C&W works, the latter now being demolished. Its continued presence, albeit with the removal of many previous sidings and, inevitably, the demolition of the coaling and ash disposal plants, continued to provide a silent memorial to a bygone era. Even this, however, was destined eventually to disappear and some 20 years after the last steam locoman had booked off duty, the remaining staff departed. Having lain empty, derelict and partially roofless since 1988, the building was finally demolished in January 1990. The only access to the site being in a particularly difficult location between two hump-backed bridges, planning permission for any development requiring road access was unlikely to receive approval and today, the filled-in pit roads of Lostock Hall Motive Power Depot still bear silent witness to the age of steam, albeit now through a rapidly advancing forest of ever-encroaching vegetation.

As at the other 'final three' depots, several locomotives ending their days on Lostock Hall's allocation, survived to tell the tale. These were: 43106, 44806, 45000, 45110, 45212, 45305, 45407, 47564 and 78019.

Nos 45407 and 44806 were removed from 10D on the evening of 7 January 1969, being towed to Carnforth by D5242 and into the preservation era. The clearout of the remaining steam locomotives continued at a somewhat pedantic pace; at the beginning of March, the shed still contained 12 engines. However, 10 March saw D5238 remove Nos 44713, 44950, 45073 & 45269 to Drapers, Hull, while 16 days later, D5262 followed with Nos 44874, 45318, 45386 & 45444. The last machines there, Nos 44894, 45017 & 45388 remained until late April, when they also moved on to Drapers, Hull, the move of No 44894 being the last of any non-preserved standard-gauge steam engine to leave a BR shed.

The late Bill Wilson, driver of No 45017 on one of the SLS specials on the final weekend, reckoned that the residents of Lostock Hall and nearby Tardy Gate didn't want to see the end of the steam locomotive at their local shed, but, on the other hand, they were glad to see the last of the Sunday night smoke, a pall of which covered the village when engines were being lit up in readiness for the following week's work. It wasn't only the shed that was closing, however, but Lostock Hall wagon works, goods yards and carriage sidings as well. Bill added that most of those made redundant were offered jobs elsewhere, but many saw sense and took the money instead.

The story of the last weeks of 10D only plays a very minor role in the 66-year history of Lostock Hall MPD and, in any event, much of this is related elsewhere within these pages. Officially, no plans had been made to mark the closure. Ernie Heyes, driver of No 45318 – the last regular steam passenger of all – wasn't even aware that he had been selected with the honour until the very last minute. All that week he had been working over the Long Drag on the 'Herbranston Tanks' and, on the Saturday night, 1F51 – the Liverpool passenger – should have been hauled by a Class 40, until some strings had been pulled at a very local level.

We have space for three or four final anecdotes, however, and the first is one related by local enthusiast, Bill Ashcroft, following his conversation with a friend, who was a deputy running shed foreman back in 1968. For a period towards the end, a Type 2 diesel, No D5238, had been stationed at 10D for crew-training. The instruction was that, only in very exceptional circumstances, was this locomotive to be used for normal rostered turns and it really was kept in immaculate condition. The funny side of our first story relates to the fact that the same number series was used at the time for both Type 2 diesels and the Stanier 'Black Five' 4-6-0s! Each evening, 1P92, the Barrow-Huddersfield parcels train was rostered for Type 2 haulage onwards from Preston and, when booking-on for work, the Preston-based drivers on this job meticulously checked their locomotives for faults. One night, the phone rang at Lostock Hall shed. It was a Preston driver, asking for a fresh engine, because he had discovered that his locomotive had a fault. No doubt he was seeking another diesel. Bill's pal offered him 'Fifty-fifty five'. Down the line, the driver sardonically asked if this was 'one with a fruit machine.' He was using the engineman's nickname for the diesel's control box, which had a number of handles with circular knobs, (sometimes known as 'toffee-apples') fitted in the cabs of some of the early Class 24 diesels. "No! It's one with a bloody great fire and a shovel!" was the reply from the shed! "I'll ring you back!" said our driver, and put the phone down. That call never came!

Another amusing tale that Bill recounts is of the Sunday morning in early 1967, when he was walking along Watkin Lane, pushing a pram containing a small child, past the back of the shed, but without his camera. The shed yard was being shunted at the time, as was normal in order to get locos into the right positions for their Monday morning duties, and Mick Bowden was the shed shunt driver. He was propelling a line of locos right down the empty No 2 Road, when the member of the shed staff, who was acting as shunter, shouted, "RIGHT!"… when, strictly speaking, he should have shouted, "STOP!" Naturally, the line of locos kept moving… with the furthermost loco, recently transferred 'Black Five' No 45339, soon jumping the triangular stops at the end of No 2 Road and continuing on its wayward journey through the rear wall of the shed!

Now, the shed was built in such a way that, should an accident like this occur, only one section of wall would be demolished. As will be observed in the accompanying photograph, each road had a large lintel and vertical gaps in the brickwork, and, as a result, a large loco-sized doorway appeared, totally unplanned, in the place of the personnel access door which had formerly been in the same position.

The tale is not yet quite over, for there were yet other encumbrances still marring the path of No 45339's wayward progress. Immediately outside the door was parked the pride-and-joy of fitter's mate, Billy Moat, namely his glass fibre-bodied 'Reliant Robin' and, alongside this, also stood a brand-new radiator, only just delivered, for one of the shed's Yorkshire Engine Co 0-4-0 diesel-shunters.

By the time that Bill had hurried home to collect his camera, the Reliant (now in what he describes as 'a sorry state'!) had been removed, but the radiator was now leaning, rather bent and battered, against the wall alongside. Bill adds that, within a short time, a neatly painted slogan appeared alongside the hole. This exclaimed 'BOWDEN'S GAP'. Former fireman, Paul Tuson, also recalls that it wasn't long before some wag had appended this caption with the words, '...THE SHAPE OF SHEDS TO COME!' That wall was never rebuilt and, during quieter spells, at night, it is said that boards appeared over No 2 Road pit… with staff cars being driven into the shed to be serviced. It was only in later years that the Outdoor Machinery section put large doors over the gap, to keep the wind out!

There are many other stories associated with unplanned 'demolitions' at 10D, for example, the not uncommon occurrences of locos being moved while the 'bag' was still in the tender and with the unfortunate but predictable consequences arising. One tale, however, stands out above all others as a demonstration of

The LMS Standard No 2 coaling plant, erected at Lostock Hall in 1937 (being identical to that at Rose Grove), has just been visited by 'Black Five' No 45017 on 4 August 1968 and the engine, driven by fireman, Billy Bamber, now runs off the 60ft vacuum-operated turntable (also installed in the same year).
MIKE POPE

A colourful scene on 27 July 1968. No 70013 *Oliver Cromwell* is being stabled here overnight before working a MRTS/SVR railtour from Stockport to Carnforth the following day. English-Electric diesel D403 is temporarily on loan to the shed for crew-training (the class is still being constructed at this time) and No 45407 has been out of steam since its last booked turn on 'No 78 Target' two days previously and has presumably been undergoing a boiler washout. PETER FITTON

initiative arising form the misfortunes of others. One night during the winter of 1966, while negotiating the hump-backed bridge of Watkin Lane at the rear of the shed, an articulated lorry skidded on the icy surface and collided with the wooden Lostock Hall station booking office - this being located at the bridge's peak - half demolishing it. (As an aside, although unsubstantiated, there are rumours that, as fate would have it, yet another Reliant was parked in a similarly unfortunate location at the moment that a considerable amount of maroon and cream-painted timber cascaded down into the shed yard below!)

Joseph Booth, by now passed-out as a fireman, arrived at the shed shortly before midnight in order to book-on at 01:25 to prepare the engine rostered for the 06:10 Blackpool North-Euston as far as Crewe. Although he could not but help noticing the consequences of the accident, he at first thought nothing of it as he had an engine to prepare and, although early, he did usually spend this time in cleaning the loco. Having a 'brew' in the mess, as always, Joseph looked at the Shedman's Engine Board to see what locos were on shed. He noticed that No 70010 *Owen Glendower* was marked down as 'spare' and decided to ask running foreman Alf Carnegie if Alf would agree to exchange for the 'Black Five' rostered. Alf was sympathetic, but stressed that the 'Brit' would take far too long to raise steam.

Joseph thought about this for a moment, and then a thought struck him. Was there not a ready supply of combustible material right outside the door - the remains of the booking office? So, Joseph asked Alf if he would roster the 'Brit' should he be able to raise enough pressure in time. Although obviously believing that this could not be done, Alf agreed! Joseph hurried quickly to

the scene of the accident and to the pile of combustible material awaiting him on the ground. What an appropriate solution to everyone's problem, indeed, and he proceeded to carry as much as he could over to the awaiting No 70010 in the shed.

After managing a couple of trips unobserved, it was only a matter of time before he came to be approached by the police officer attending the incident. What on earth did he think he was doing, he was asked? Joseph replied that the wood was needed for an engine needing to be steamed quickly – which was a quite truthful statement, of course! The officer countered this by advising that Joseph was removing evidence from the scene. However, Joseph adds that the officer was then obviously distracted enough with matters up above on the roadway for him to continue in the darkness until he had obtained all that he needed. Needless to say, the wood burned really well, with 150lb easily being raised. Alf, true to his word, then agreed to the change and off went No 70010 light to Blackpool.

Joseph also remembers that, at this time, No 70010 carried painted-on nameplates to replace those originals which had been removed, officially or otherwise. One side bore the name *Owen Glendower* in English and the other side was in Welsh, as *Owain Glyndwr*. The author admits to more than an element of involvement in that particular exercise, recalling a necessity to cycle home to discover the correct spelling in his Ian Allan 'ABC'! The matter did later cause much amusement to those involved, particularly when correspondents to the various railway periodicals of the time could not agree on the actual name being carried – evidently being totally unaware that this varied from side to side! (It is thought that, between 1965 and 1967, no fewer that 16

Britannias were renamed at Lostock Hall, with one or two more being treated in a similar clandestine manner at Bolton and Stockport.)

Bill Lea was a driver who served his entire railway career with steam, based at 24C Lostock Hall depot. Bill made his first application for a job on the footplate shortly after leaving school in 1949 and was advised that he must first undertake and pass a medical examination. An appointment was made for him and he was told to report to Manchester Victoria station, where this would occur. At the station bufferstops, in one of the bay platforms, stood two former coaches, each converted and fitted-out for that specific purpose. An eye-test was part of the examination. Some weeks later, Bill received his results from his medical and was extremely surprised to learn that, in the opinion of the medical officer, Bill was in fact colour-blind and, therefore, that he had been rejected for employment by British Railways.

Bill, of course, went out to source alternative employment, and it was to be almost 12 months later before he was surprised to receive, through the post, notice that the railway would like him to attend yet a further medical in Manchester. The explanation offered was that the previous test had been cast into some doubt, as it had since been discovered that the examining officer concerned was, himself, colour blind!

There are quite a lot of other enginemen's tales relating to the shed over a period of 50 years, some of which are equally amusing, but this is surely one of the funniest! Barney Campbell, another acting shed foreman at the very end of steam, became friendly with one of the young female engine-cleaners during the War. Ironically – perhaps all the more so in light of the three shed closures of 4 Aug 1968 - her name was Rose Grove!

Arch Street, Burnley, 31 July 1968. In the opinion of the author, this is one of the finest 'steam in the landscape' images ever produced. Typifying everything that was synonymous with Lancashire cotton mill country of the 1950s and 1960s, women in slippers and wearing head-squares over hair still in rollers, gossip in this back-street cameo outside their smoke-blackened terraced cottages, while children play on flagstone pathways totally unhindered by parked cars and moving traffic. Apart from the viaduct itself (and perhaps some of the younger observers), everything in this view is no more – indeed even the Bowling Green Hotel has gone. At the rear of the train pictured opposite, with Rose Grove fireman David Hill surveying the scene, No 45388 can be seen slowly banking 8P21 up the hill to Gannow Junction. IAN KRAUSE

Last month of steam

...and now there are only three... Alan Castle

I f the reader is seeking fanciful tales or images in any way akin to the glamour and romance of the 'Glorious Years of Steam', then this chapter will almost certainly disappoint. Indeed, for both professional railwaymen and enthusiasts alike, there really was little that was either eminently outstanding or memorable about those agonising last few weeks.

As with any bereavement, it was all merely a particularly painful period that one just had to endure and, in retrospect, I do recall having written elsewhere in the past that one of my greatest wishes in life would have been NOT to have witnessed the end of steam on British Railways. I guess that many more, if faced with a

similar fanciful option, would have echoed such sentiments.

But, unlike some who were content to remember happier times and to be able to 'leave it at that', I actually resided within easy walking distance of one of the 'last three' and, I suppose, that gave me little option but to permit myself to be involved to some degree in the poignant death throes. With the assistance of my old pal of very many years, Bob Downham - who had the remarkable foresight to record each detail of every single loco movement that he observed for probably at least ten years before steam ended - let us all now travel back 40 years in time.

In July 1968, the locations of these three final outposts, with the dubious honour thrust upon

During a pause in shunting, Lostock Hall driver, Tony 'Yogi Bear' Gillett oils round 'Black Five' No 45407, while standing in Garstang & Catterall Yard with Target 67 on 26 July 1968. TOM HEAVYSIDE

them of completing the last chapter in the history books, are certainly not celebrity top-ranking names inextricably associated with express passenger locomotives and famous titled trains. Indeed, just about as far from this as it is possible to get, the 'bread-and-butter' duties of Carnforth, Lostock Hall and Rose Grove centre – as they always have done – strictly upon the efficient operation of freight traffic, with the very occasional passenger working thrown-in for good measure. Such moments in the limelight will be brief enough, for even these establishments are officially scheduled to close to steam as from midnight on Sunday 4 August, and, at which time, the curtain will be brought down on steam traction on the British Railways standard gauge.

Yes, currently some of us do seem to be spending most of our weekends engaged in illicit pursuits mainly avoiding the notice of management, while simultaneously attempting to restore a sense of respectability to a fast-disappearing collection of unkempt and rusting relics of a bygone age - still functioning often only on a wing and a prayer, merely because there still are not enough new diesels available to replace them!

Again, yes, we will get the occasional good shot, if the train runs to time and if the sun shines (particularly if it also falls on the single side of the engine that we usually only have had time to clean). Some success is achieved, as the photographs in the following pages will confirm.

However, all of this is merely a drop in the ocean in the general scheme of things… and we know it! The time has come for steam and no-one at all can change decisions that have already been made by that bunch of faceless bureaucrats sitting at desks over 200 miles away in their ivory tower of 222 Marylebone Road.

All we really can do now is to savour the familiar sights, sounds and atmosphere for as long as is possible. The final month proves to be a frenetic one for those privileged to witness the last rites; indeed, it is a mad dash to get to as many locations as possible in order to record as much as one can. That is easier said than done, for few of us can afford our own transport and, on weekdays - when most steam action obviously occurs, there is the added encumbrance of being compelled to go out to work, if only to finance the basic essentials in life - such as adequate film stock for the following weekend's activities. Furthermore, as 'the time' draws ever closer, the ensuing waits at the lineside grow longer and longer – even when one does actually know where to look and at what time of day! Although we try to ignore these, such blatant, facts, steam's life-blood is rapidly ebbing away.

Perhaps the one single positive aspect of this contraction of steam manifests itself in the inevitable coming-together of a large number of individuals from every walk of life and from just about every corner of the country, merely in order to share in such a unique experience. The remarkable fact today, 40 years on, is that the camaraderie that ensued in those final days created lasting friendships that, in the majority of cases, have survived the intervening years. Between us all, we did manage to record a great deal and, for myself, this has nowhere become more apparent than during the course of the researching for this book, where, almost entirely through the offices of my many longstanding

Although much reduced in quantity, steam continued to operate over the Calder Valley line via the Copy Pit route. Here, Rose Grove's 8F No 48410 climbs past Cornholme with a coal working from the Yorkshire coalfields bound for the Lancashire power stations.
ALAN CASTLE

On 31 July, No 48340 heads 8P21, the heavily laden 10:50 Burnley Central to Wyre Dock, across Burnley Viaduct. Out of sight in this view is 'Black Five' No 45388, providing banking assistance at the rear as far as Gannow Jct. IAN KRAUSE

No 48423 passes Rose Grove West on the 13:40 Burnley-Burn Naze on 3 August 1968. In attempting to precisely identify the once numerous coal workings towards Preston and the Fylde, it was easiest to remember that the two-door 22-ton wagons went to Burn Naze only and the single door 16-ton wagons to Wyre Dock. Both destinations were power stations - at Burn Naze, the ICI works coal tippler could accommodate the two-door wagons, but at Wyre Dock, the CEGB Power Station could only accommodate 16-ton wagons. MIKE TAYLOR

On 1 August 1968, No 45110 is on 3P20 and is seen near Rose Grove West. The front-end embellishments had been done by the fireman, Joe Booth, who was on the turn for most of the week, and on this occasion the driver was John Burnett. PETER FITTON

On 15 June 1968, Rose Grove's No 45350 passes Chaffers Sidings 'box in Nelson with 3J83. PETER FITTON

friends, I have come to amass well in excess of a thousand photographs - all of which were taken merely in the early 1968 period! Each one of those images is important in its own right, but, clearly, in singling-out a mere fraction to use in the pitifully few pages available here, this feature can but present a mere flavour of what occurred. Notwithstanding that, I sincerely hope the reader will find them sufficiently absorbing without any real necessity to provide lengthy captions and superfluous detail. Images like these speak for themselves and need no tall stories to enhance their impact. This is 1968 as it really was, 'warts and all', and, for me, foolish or fictional embellishments to any such account seem redundant.

By the beginning of July, only five locomotive types remain in service; the bulk of these being the ubiquitous Stanier Class 5MT 4-6-0s and Class 8F 2-8-0s, along with five Standard 4MT 4-6-0s and a solitary example each of the Standard 5MT 4-6-0s and Britannia Pacifics. All, bar one, of the regular steam passenger workings have disappeared and, apart from a tiny handful of parcels trains, all steam action is (at least, on paper), supposedly restricted to freight and station pilot duties and the, by now, inevitably quite frequent enthusiasts' specials.

According to official loco diagrams, the final regular steam-hauled passenger is supposed to be the 1P58 (Saturdays Only) 20:50 Preston to Blackpool South (a portion of a through train from London Euston) rostered for a Lostock Hall Stanier 5MT.

After completion of its duties in stabling the stock, the loco is then booked to return light from Blackpool to Preston, to officiate as station pilot – or, more specifically, to provide steam heat for the two sleeping cars that it will attach (along with a BG) to the rear of the 20:30 Windermere-London at around 22:30. Although little-recognised as such, technically, this too, is a 'passenger' working, albeit merely for a matter of a few hundred yards and only between the platforms at Preston. It is not the only example, either. A similar task involves another 10D loco, in the removal at 03:46 of two more sleeping cars plus a BG from 1P54, the 23:15 Euston-Windermere. The BG later going forward at 04:10 attached to a Manchester-Blackpool parcels, these vehicles are stabled in a bay platform with the loco steam-heating them until around 08:00.

Despite the official edict, for a variety of reasons, other steam passenger workings still do occur, even if somewhat sporadically and, at times, not even to the knowledge of the 'grapevine', until after it is all over.

On parcels traffic, there are now only four regular turns. The first is an 'out-and-home' working, booked for a Lostock Hall 'Black Five', namely 3P00, the 02:50 Preston to Colne and 3P20 19:14 (MX) Colne to Preston. On the main line, there is 3P24, the (MSO) Preston to Barrow (also a Lostock Hall 'Black Five') and 1P92, the 20:28 Barrow to Preston (a Carnforth 'Black Five').

On the freight side, workings are equally elusive and, working timetables for these appear to have been published more as a 'guide' than for any other ulterior motive.

In the Preston area on weekdays, about 20 or so steam freights still pass by (but not all necessarily through Preston station itself). These include local trip workings between the various yards in the area with those at Garstang, Horwich, Chorley, Deepdale and Courtaulds – the latter two being on the truncated former Longridge branch. Ballast trains also run, as required, between the Preston and Lancaster areas, and longer-distance general-merchandise traffic traverses the various routes between Carnforth, Warrington (Arpley), Bolton (Burnden Jct), Manchester (Ancoats) and Liverpool Edge Hill. Block-train oil-tanker traffic also runs on three days a week between Heysham and Darwen.

However, by far the majority of the remainder of the traffic consists of coal trains between the Bickershaw and Parkside Collieries (in the Wigan area) and Whitebirk Power Station (just beyond Blackburn), this complemented by additional workings between Rose Grove or Burnley Central and Wyre Dock or Burn Naze (Fleetwood). There are also two or three workings over the Copy Pit route, usually as far as Healey Mills Yard, near Wakefield in Yorkshire.

Most of the routes that this freight traffic uses pass through rugged and hilly terrain in or at the edge of the Pennines. Consequently, several are heavily graded in places and feature impressive engineering works. The Bolton-Blackburn line, for instance, provides hard work for trains in both directions towards a summit near Sough Tunnel, but particularly so northbound on the gradients of at mainly 1-in-73 for the first six miles out of Bolton. In these final days, the actual tracking-down of steam workings during daylight hours on the route is far more problematical!

On the line over into Yorkshire via Copy Pit, there are similar gradients for five miles from Gannow Jct to Copy Pit Summit and, in the opposite direction, the route is even steeper, with westbound trains being faced with almost four miles of 1-in-65 on a very winding set of tracks all the way up from Stansfield Hall Jct, Todmorden. In order to provide the rear-end assistance that most trains need, there are usually at least two 8F banking engines regularly out-stationed from Rose Grove at Todmorden. Additional bonuses for the photographer in East Lancashire are the eye-catching urban viaducts providing such significant landmarks both in Burnley and also in Accrington, where they tower over much of the surrounding townscapes.

Situated close to the gateway to the Lake District and the Cumberland Coast ('Cumbria' is a word that will not be coined for another six years!), the remaining steam turns from Carnforth shed continue to penetrate deep into similarly highly scenic regions. With the Lakeland mountains rising sharply from the coastal plain on the right and breathtaking sea-views to the left, a small handful of workings pass over two spectacular estuary viaducts and, for those workings continuing onwards to Barrow, there are also ascents in each direction of the notorious Lindal Bank.

Away from the coast, steam still visits various other goods yards on a daily basis; these including Kendal and Windermere. Yet other occasional workings penetrate into the Dales as far as Giggleswick and even to Skipton.

Listed opposite are the known regular workings from each depot and, although it is accepted that these may well be far from complete (and, almost certainly, they will not be totally accurate), they do assist in conveying a fairly reasonable impression of the sphere of operation of what little steam action does remain.

10A CARNFORTH STEAM DIAGRAMS - JULY 1968

Rep. No	Dep.	Day	From		To	Other details	Loco
1P92	20.28	(SX)	Barrow	-	Preston	Parcels (to Huddersfield)	5MT
3P24	09.58	(SO)	Preston	-	Barrow	Parcels	5MT
3P25	09.25	(MSX)	Lancaster Castle	-	Heysham	Parcels	5MT
4P20	18.12	(FO)	Heysham Moss Sdgs	-	Darwen	Oil tankers	5MT/8F
4P21	18.40	(TThO)	Darwen	-	Heysham Moss	Oil tankers	5MT
4P21	13.35	(SO)	Darwen	-	Heysham Moss	Oil tankers	5MT
4P25	16.40	(TO)	Heysham Moss Sdgs	-	Plumpton Jct	Oil tankers	5MT
5F16	04.15	(Dly)	Carnforth	-	Edge Hill	General merchandise	8F
5F24	15.05	(SX)	Heysham Harbour	-	Warrington Arpley	General merchandise	5MT/8F
5J32	17.13	(SX)	Morecambe	-	Moston	General merchandise	5MT
5P05	22.30	(SX)	Ancoats	-	Heysham Harbour	General merchandise	5MT
5P23	11.45	(SX)	Ribble Sidings	-	Carnforth	General merchandise	5MT
6P42	06.25	(Dly)	Carnforth F&M Yard	-	Barrow	General merchandise	5MT
6P52	14.55	(SO)	Heysham Harbour	-	Carnforth MPD	General merchandise	5MT
7J32	16.50	(SX)	Heysham Harbour	-	Morecambe	General merchandise	5MT
8P27	19.25	(SO)	Heysham Harbour	-	Carnforth	General merchandise	5MT
8P76	08.55	MSX	Barrow	-	Carnforth F&M	Soda ash empties, general merchadise and ballast, running via Sandside as required	5MT
Target 46	12.35	(SX)	Carnforth Yard	-	Kendal	Trips between Kendal & Burnside	5MT
Target 47	07.00	(SX)	Carnforth Yard	-	Windermere	Trips between Kendal & Milnthorpe	Std 4MT
Target 47	09.15	(SO)	Carnforth Yard	-	Kendal	Mainly household coal	Std 4MT
Target 48	06.10	(SX)	Carnforth Yard	-	Ulverston	Shunts A/R	Std 4MT
Target 49	07.50	(SX)	Carnforth Yard	-	Heysham Hbr - Giggleswick - Lancaster Quay - Carnforth - Heysham Hbr		5MT
Target 49	07.10	(SO)	Carnforth Yard	-	Heysham Moss Sdgs - Heysham Harbour - Heysham Moss Sdgs		4MT/5MT
Target 50	06.25	(SX)	Carnforth Yard	-	Heysham Moss Sdgs - Harbour - Moss - Carnforth - Moss Sdgs		5MT
Target 61	07.00	(SX)	Carnforth F&M Yard	-	Waterslack Quarry - Arnside - Grange - Sandside		5MT
Target 61	07.00	(SO)	Carnforth F&M Yard	-	Waterslack Quarry - Grange - Carnforth (Shunt until 13.35)		5MT
Ballast	08.15	(FSX)	Lancaster Castle	-	To work A/R in Morecambe, Carnforth & Skipton area		5MT

10D LOSTOCK HALL STEAM DIAGRAMS - JULY 1968

Rep. No	Dep.	Day	From		To	Other details	Loco
1F51	21.25	(Dly)*	Preston	-	Liverpool Exchange	TC from Glasow/Edinburgh separates from Manchester portion at Preston	5MT
1P58	20.50	(SO)	Preston	-	Blackpool South	TC from London Euston separates from Windermere portion at Preston	5MT
1P92	20.28	(SX)	Barrow	-	Preston	Parcels to Huddersfield	5MT
3P00	02.50	(Dly)	Preston	-	Colne	Parcels	5MT
3P11	08.15	(SX)	Rose Grove	-	Colne	Parcels & to shunt	5MT
3P20	19.14	(SX)	Colne	-	Preston	Parcels	5MT
3P24	07.50	(MO)	Wigan	-	Barrow	Parcels	5MT
5J82	22.30	(SX)	Carnforth	-	Ribble Sidings	General merchandise	5MT
6P16	19.10	(SX)	Ribble Sdgs	-	Carnforth	General merchandise	5MT
6P52	14.30	(SX)	Heysham	-	Preston N.U.	General merchandise	5MT
7P11	10.50	(SX)	Ribble Sdgs	-	Heysham	General merchandise	5MT
7P65	11.00	(SX)	Preston N.U.	-	Rose Grove	Empty coal	5MT
8P20	15.40	(ThFO)	Burnley Central	-	Burn Naze	Coal	5MT
8P32	13.40	(SX)	Rose Grove Up Grid	-	Ribble Sidings	Coal	5MT
Ballast	08.00	(Dly)	Lostock Hall MPD	-	Miscellaneous ballast workings in Preston / Lancaster areas		5MT
Stn. Pilot	19.45	(MX)	Lostock Hall MPD	-	Preston Station (to steam-heat sleeping cars off 1P54 until 08.00)		5MT
Target 63	06.00	(SX)	Farington Jct	-	Deepdale Sdgs - Courtaulds Sdgs - Farington Jct - EL Goods - Ribble Sdgs - NU Yard		8F
Target 63	07.00	(SO)	Farington Jct	-	Deepdale Sdgs - Courtaulds Sdgs - Farington Jct		8F
Target 67	08.15	(SX)	Farington Jct	-	Horwich Works - Ribble Sdgs - Dock St - Oxheys - Maudland -Farington - Garstang - Oxheys - NU Yard		5MT
Target 66	07.30	(SX)	Farington Jct	-	Shunts yard & trips locally A/R		5MT
Target 70	07.30	(SX)*	Farington Jct	-	Chorley - Ribble Sidings		5MT
Target 78	06.45	(SX)	Farington Jct	-	Preston E.L. Goods - Garstang A/R - Maudland Jct - Farington Jct		5MT
Target 78	07.50	(SO)	Farington Jct	-	Preston Dock St - to shunt		5MT

10F ROSE GROVE STEAM DIAGRAMS - JULY 1968

Rep. No	Dep.	Day	From		To	Other details	Loco
3J83	13.25	(SX)	Colne	-	Red Bank C.S.	Parcels ECS	5MT/8F
5J10	19.05	(SX)	Burnley Central	-	Moston	General merchandise	8F
5P02	07.35	(MSX)	Preston N.U.	-	Farington Jct	General merchandise	8F
6P03	06.05	(MX)	Bamfurlong	-	Carnforth	General merchandise	8F
6P25	18.30	(SX)	Preston E.L Goods.	-	Ribble Sidings	General merchandise	8F
6P31	00.40	(MX)	Rose Grove Up Grid	-	Farington Jct	Coal	8F
6P32	13.10	(SX)	Rose Grove Up Grid	-	Wyre Dock	Coal	8F
6P69	23.28	(SX)	Brewery Sidings	-	Blackburn	General merchandise	8F
6P77	00.55	(MX)	Carnforth	-	Burnley Central	To Rose Grove (MSX)	8F
7N61	18.20	(SX)	Farington Jct	-	Healey Mills	Empty coal	8F
7N68	21.45	(SX)	Preston N.U.	-	Rose Grove	Empty coal (to Cudworth)	8F
7N78	08.35	(Dly)	Wyre Dock	-	Healey Mills	Empty coal	8F
7N79	10.45	(Dly)	Wyre Dock	-	Healey Mills	Empty coal	8F
7N82	06.53	(MX)	Farington Jct	-	Rose Grove	Empty coal (to Cudworth)	8F
7N87	10.50	(SO)	Preston N.U.	-	Rose Grove	Empty coal (to Carlton)	8F
7N99	18.40	(SX)	Preston N.U.	-	Healey Mills	General merchandise (Change engines at Rose Grove)	8F
7P04	02.15	(MSX)	Rose Grove Up Grid	-	Ribble Sidings	General merchandise	8F
7P33	16.40	(SX)	Wyre Dock	-	Preston N.U.	Empty coal and general merchandise (works 7N99)	8F
7P80	14.35	(SX)	Wyre Dock	-	Burnley Central	Empty coal	8F
8F43	08.55	(Dly)	Whitebirk Power Stn.	-	Bickershaw Coll'y	Empty coal	8F
8P11	08.15	(Dly)	Parkside Coll'y	-	Whitebirk Power Stn.	Coal	8F
8P12	11.30	(Dly)	Bickershaw Coll'y	-	Whitebirk Power Stn.	Coal	8F
8P19	12.00	(SX)	Burnley Central	-	Burn Naze	Coal	5MT
8P20	15.40	(ThFO)	Burnley Central	-	Burn Naze	Coal	8F
8P21	10.50	(SX)	Burnley Central	-	Wyre Dock	Coal	8F
Target 10	08.30	(ThSX)	Blackburn Darwen St.	-	Clitheroe	Shunt	8F
Target 19	04.20	(SX)	Blackburn Darwen St.	-	Clitheroe	Shunt	8F
Target 22	07.30	(Dly)	Rose Grove Up Grid	-	Blackburn	Shunt Blackburn & Huncoat	8F
Target 83	11.00	(SX)	Rose Grove Up Grid	-	Whitebirk Power Stn.	- Rose Grove Down Grid	8F
Target 86	05.55	(Dly)	Rose Grove	-	SHUNT	Trip A/R to Burnley Cen, Huncoat & Padiham	8F
Target 90	05.50	(Dly)	Stansfield Hall	-	Copy Pit	Bank as required until 11.25	8F
Target 91	03.55	(Dly)	Stansfield Hall	-	Copy Pit	Bank as required until 14.25	8F
Target 91	15.30	(SX)	Stansfield Hall	-	Copy Pit	Bank as required until 22.30	8F
Target 92	06.25	(SX)	Rose Grove	-	Burnley Central	Trip as required to Huncoat & Padiham	8F
Target 92	06.25	(SX)	Rose Grove	-	Burnley Central	Shunt & Trip between Burnley & Rose Grove	8F
Target 94	09.00	(Dly)	Skipton Up Sidings	-	Spencers Sidings	Trip as required on return to Skipton	Std 4MT

* = Occasionally steam-worked A/R = As required (Dly) = Monday to Saturday

On parcels traffic at the end of steam, there are now only four regular turns. Two of these consist of a 'out-and-home' working, booked for a Lostock Hall 'Black Five', 3P00, the 02:50 Preston to Colne and 3P20 19:14 (MX) Colne to Preston. On 31 July 1968, No 45388 is seen leaving Accrington with 3P20. To minimise disruption to other traffic, the business of loading/unloading of parcels was regularly conducted in the former Bury line platform, from whence the train has just backed out.
JOSEPH BOOTH COLLECTION

The Blackburn to Bolton line is one of the most scenic of those still available to steam in 1968 but, with the recent closing of the Manchester Division sheds, daytime workings have now become extremely scarce. It is because of this that a favourite (if not the only) subject for photography has been, for some time previously, 3J83, the 13:35 (SO) Colne to Manchester Red Bank empty parcels train. At the summit of the climb, No 45350 exits Sough Tunnel on 3J83 on 15 June 1968. ALAN CASTLE

3J83 became a Rose Grove turn after the closure of Newton Heath and could turn up with just about any class of motive power at its head. On 1 June 1968, motive power is 8F No 48257 and the train is seen passing through Church & Oswaldtwistle station. DAVE RODGERS

We shall concentrate our review on the calendar month between 4 July and 4 August 1968 and commence this by looking at a day of the week when steam activity might normally be considered to be at its peak. A national 'work-to-rule' has, however, been in place for several days now and the detrimental effect of this upon operations is becoming increasingly apparent. The country's rail network had already been thrown into disarray from 24 June by this dispute of the NUR, before ASLEF then joined in the affray soon afterwards. The situation is to endure for 12 days, with chaos worsening, particularly when the quite incredulous fact is considered that, at this period in the 1960s, more than 20 per cent of day-to-day railway work is currently being conducted during 'overtime'.

These final weeks for steam have, equally unfortunately, also coincided with the annual holidays (or 'Wakes Weeks') in several East Lancashire towns, with the knock-on effect from further (planned) cancellations to other freight workings. Most noticeable will be the absence of the otherwise quite frequent Parkside and Bickershaw to Whitebirk coal workings – which, traditionally, provide much of Rose Grove's work.

Nevertheless, some trains do appear to have been unaffected. During the small hours of this Thursday morning, at Preston station, the Euston sleepers have arrived on time at 03:46 and 'Black Five' No 45110 is there waiting to remove them from the main train (which will now proceed northwards behind its usual diesel) and to place them first into Platform 3 and then into Platform 5 Bay, remaining coupled-up until 08:00 to keep any occupants warm in their bunks.

Further north, at Carnforth, the sole-surviving Standard 5MT No 73069 (10A) – a recent transfer from Bolton – also soon sets out at 06:30 with 'No 50 Target', for a planned itinerary largely centred upon shunting the extensive sidings in the Heysham Harbour area. Within minutes of this departure, the yard is also to see 'No 48 Target' depart for Ulverston behind No 44758 (10A), followed by 6P45, the 06:25 Carnforth-Barrow, with No 75048 (10A) - one of the five surviving

The very last steam-worked 7P80, the 14:35 Wyre Dock to Burnley Central coal empties, passes Weeton signalbox on 2 August 1968. PETER FITTON

(but not all necessarily active) Standard 4MT 4-6-0s. After a short lull, it is soon the turn of No 44963 (10A) to set out on Target 61, with four loaded ballast wagons, heading for Sandside (on the former branch to Hincaster Jct) and then onwards to Grange-over-Sands. Finally, 'Target 46' sets out at 12:35, with No 45134 (10A) and loaded domestic coal wagons, on the Kendal tripper. No sooner has this departed than No 44758 returns to base at around 12:45 with 8P76, the 09:30 Barrow-Carnforth, conveying 12 empty soda-ash wagons, which it now proceeds to deposit in the yards to await onwards despatch to the Northwich area.

Over at Heysham Harbour, Lostock Hall's No 45318 is shunting alongside No 73069 in the yards, having arrived on 7P11, the 10:50 Preston Ribble Sidings-Heysham and delivering no fewer than 52 loaded wagons, the contents of most of which are undoubtedly destined for Ulster. Having completed this task, No 45318 prepares to

depart again with 6P52, the 14:30 to Preston NU. Also patiently waiting close by is No 44874 (10A), ready to follow 6P52 down the main line to Preston with 5F24, the 15:05 to Warrington Arpley, conveying another load of general merchandise from across the water. It being a perfect example of the numerous uneconomic workings that recent removals of steam servicing facilities at destinations around the ever-contracting periphery of steam operation has created, No 44874 will return later that evening light-engine all the way back to Carnforth shed. To round-off this, our first day of observations, the 18:40 (TThO) Darwen-Heysham oil tankers is running and this arrives at its destination on time at around 21:00 behind No 44735 (10A), which has run-round its train at Morecambe.

The following morning, having observed both No 44709 (10A) passing through Preston somewhat late, at 07:45, with 5F16, the 04:15 Carnforth-Edge Hill and then No 45269 (10D)

running back to shed from the station at 08:15 following its sleeping-car steam-heat duty, we head off towards East Lancashire in order to witness operations based on the steam hub of Rose Grove.

En route, at Wilpshire, No 45096 (10F) is seen topping the bank at 08:50, unusually running very early with 'Target 19', the 09:12 Blackburn (Darwen St) to Clitheroe trip working, with which it will return to Blackburn shortly before 14:00 after some hours of shunting. In sidings at Blackburn's Whitebirk Power Station, sits No 48247 (10F), which has arrived at 10:16 on Rose Grove's Target 83. After shunting until noon, the 8F will return with a load of empty wagons to Rose Grove. Meanwhile, over at Padiham Power Station (situated at the stub-end of the erstwhile Great Harwood Loop which is now only connected at the Rose Grove end), No 48666 (10F) has arrived at 10:30 with 'Target 86', which is another local duty, this one tripping as required between Burnley Central Yard and both Padiham and Huncoat power stations.

Moving onwards to Rose Grove itself, a longer-distance working soon appears shortly after our arrival. Struggling on the steep gradient up from Burnley Central, No 48400 (10F) passes Gannow Jct on time, with 8P21, the 10:50 Burnley Central-Wyre Dock coal train. Given the weight of this visibly well-loaded working, its pace appears unusually brisk until the reason for this soon makes itself apparent. Bystanders in the street stop to watch as the huge train thrashes its way off the lofty viaduct up the hill towards Barracks Station with No 45394 (10A) noisily assisting from the rear. The two locomotives soon disappearing from view, their audible progress continues to be heard for many more minutes until the banker eases off in the vicinity of Rose Grove station in order to retire to the shed. This process is a regular duty, but it is unusual to see a Carnforth engine involved, especially as this 'Black Five' has arrived in the area today on 3P00, the 02:50 Preston-Colne parcels – a turn otherwise consistently worked by Lostock Hall. There is another aspect of No 45394 that is noticed to be unusual; it is

Hoghton Summit on the Blackburn-Preston line. On 6 July 1968, 'Black Five' No 45025 passes at the head of 4P21, the 13:35 (SO) Darwen to Heysham Moss empty oil tanks. DAVE RODGERS

A regular turn until the very end was 7N99, the 18:40 Preston Northern Union Yard to Healey Mills (with an engine-change at Rose Grove). As part of the diagram, the loco has earlier worked another freight from Wyre Dock to Preston. This picture of 8F No 48665 is taken on 17 July 1968 within a mile of the train's departure point. Seen on the Up Slow line at Skew Bridge, within a few hundred yards 7N99 will turn off the main line to climb the notorious Farington Curve, en route for Blackburn via Lostock Hall. ALAN CASTLE

A Royal Mail train that also continued with steam right until the very end. 1P92, the 20:28 Barrow to Huddersfield parcels was regularly hauled by a Carnforth 'Black Five' as far as Preston. Here, on 2 August, at a platform bestrewn with mailbags, 'BRUTE' trolleys and miscellaneous barrows, No 44781 has just arrived with 1P92's final steam working and is preparing to come off the train. ALAN CASTLE

Having moved off the train, No 44781 waits for further instructions in Platform 5 bay. Being required for the weekend's last day specials, rather than returning to Carnforth, the engine will shortly travel to Lostock Hall depot for stabling. ALAN CASTLE

Also taken on 17 July 1968, this view shows No 48665, the final Brighton-built locomotive in BR service nearing the top of the climb to Lostock Hall Engine Shed Junction. Within a minute or so, 7N99 will cross over the West Coast Main Line from which it has diverged only a few minutes previously. At the time this photograph was taken, most trains between Preston and East Lancashire used a more direct and more easily graded route via Todd Lane Junction, but, with rationalisation as part of the resignalling when Preston Power Box came 'on-line' in 1972, the whole of the former East Lancashire side of Preston station was closed. PETER FITTON

probably now the only remaining locomotive still bearing the distinctive larger 'Scottish Region-type' cab-side numerals and full lining-out, all clearly resulting from a visit to St Rollox Works some years earlier.

The inevitable repercussions of the 'work-to-rule' are evident and the consequent lull of just under an hour is eventually, but noisily, brought to an conclusion with the arrival of No 48062 (10F) thrashing over the junction off the Padiham line with 'Target 92' to draw its load of power station empties into the 'Down Grid' sidings. Some minutes afterwards, No 48247 (10F) also struggles into the yard, returning with yet another load of empties from Whitebirk. With a further load of coal now behind the tender, it is not long before the insatiable No 48062 sets off for another trip down to Padiham.

It is, indeed, a busy day for Padiham, but this is not untypical. Targets 86 & 83 have arrived separately in the 'Up Grid' sidings and No 48666 (10F) and No 48247 (10F) now combine forces to work forward down the branch with yet more coal. At 13:53, and running a ½ hour late, No 48348 (10F) also draws out of the 'Up Grid' with 6P32, the 13:10 coal to Wyre Dock. Ten minutes later, No 48340 (10F) follows it out onto the main line with 8P32, the 13:40 Rose Grove-Ribble Sidings.

Another lull in traffic occurs, so there is time for a shed visit, during which No 44899 (10F) arrives light from the Preston direction at around 16:00, having previously worked a special ballast train to an unidentified destination. Exactly another hour later, No 48348, which has evidently disposed of its train at Wyre Dock in extra-rapid time and, there being no further work for it, also arrives back on shed light-engine at around 17:00. Not far behind No 48348, follows No 48400 (10F) with 7P80, the 14:35 Wyre Dock-Burney Central coal empties.

For No 48666 there is now a chance to round off its day of mundane Padiham trip workings with a longer-distance foray at the head of 5J10, the 19:05 Burnley Central-Moston general merchandise.

The yellow-stripe celebrity 8F No 48773 has, this evening, been earmarked for a special carriage-shunting duty and is being prepared for this. Leaving shed at about 18:00, it sets out for Colne. At this period in time, a supply of passenger stock is still stored in the carriage shed at Colne and, it being the start of that town's 'Wakes Week', there are several additional trains leaving Colne this evening for various holiday destinations. To augment the available resources (which won't amount to very much in 1968) an 11-coach ECS special, powered by No 48247 (10F), arrived last night from the Manchester direction to provide the balance of the necessary requirements. Sorting all of this into the required formations will take a while, but the task no sooner completed, the engine is back on shed by 22:00 – allowing the crew a final pint before closing time!

Five special trains are booked to depart from Colne between 19:30 and 23:55; two of these - to Heysham and to Liverpool – will consist of four-car DMUs and two more - to Paignton and to Euston – will be diesel-hauled. Rose Grove shed, however, has the honour of providing No 45156 (formerly *Ayrshire Yeomanry*) as motive power for 1T55, the 19:30 Colne to Newquay. Admittedly the train is only to be three coaches in length, but for those 'in the know', this will provide the unique chance to travel behind steam, as far as Stockport, up the notorious Baxenden Bank with its first two miles at about 1-in-40 from Accrington – a very rare opportunity with steam by this time. (At Stockport, the train will combine with a main portion that has most likely started its own journey at Manchester Piccadilly.)

Leaving all of these operations to continue in our absence, we move over to the Preston area now, just in time to witness an hour or so of relatively intense activity. At shortly before 19:00, the wheel flanges of its load of bogie oil tankers squealing around the sharp curves, No 48393

While all this has been going on, the only other steam-hauled parcels working has arrived at the adjacent platform behind No 45407. Here, standing in Platform 5 a week previously, is No 45388 at the head of 3P20, the 19:15 Colne-Preston parcels. DAVE RODGERS

(10F) slowly passes through Preston's East Lancs line platforms with 4P20, the 18:12 (FO) Heysham Moss-Darwen and at 19:02 No 48765 (10D) climbs Farington Curve with 7N61, the 18:20 Farington Jct to Healey Mills, which, due to the dispute, very unusually has today started from Preston NU yard and which will be terminated at Rose Grove as no guard is available tonight beyond that point. Equally curiously, No 45394 (10A) arrives light at Lostock Hall shed from Rose Grove. It will be recalled that we had observed it earlier in the day on the 10D diagram which should have brought it back to Preston on the 3P20 19:14 Colne-Preston parcels. Its place on that duty has tonight been taken by a Type 2 diesel – which is also very unusual. Why this should have occurred is unclear, as No 45394 is to remain based at 10D for another week, being used on local trip workings and even back on 3P00/3P20 the following Monday!

On the main line south of Preston, clearly

having spent some time re-marshalling in Ribble Sidings Yard, No 45200 (10A) is seen at 20:02, pulling slowly out of the Up Through onto the Up Slow at Skew Bridge 'box, with 5F24, the 15:05 Heysham to Warrington Arpley. As soon as the points are set back, No 44806 (10D) arrives from the opposite direction on the down slow, running light from Lostock Hall shed to Preston station, in order to take up its allotted nocturnal task as station pilot. Meanwhile, No 45200 on 5F24 gets no further than Farington Jct, where it arrives at 20:10 and proceeds to sit here on the main line until 20:59. Having allowed some 12 trains to pass by, it now sets its train backwards over the fast lines into the up yard. It remains here until 21:46, when, quite amazingly, No 45394 shows up again to exchange places with No 45200; the latter immediately disappearing onto shed, by now probably short on coal and water. 5F24 eventually sets off again, some 5½ hours after its booked time.

Saturday, 6 July, and although the 'work-to-rule' has at long last been settled, it is too late to alter the workings and rosters, so many trains are still not running. Local trips, however, appear to have escaped relatively unscathed and we start our day back at Farington Jct at 06:35 to discover No 45444 (10D) already hard at work in the yard preparing its load for 'Target 63', the Deepdale and Courtaulds turn up the old Longridge branch.

At shortly before 07:00, the Down Fast signals are pulled off and No 44877 (10A) soon appears, running at speed light-engine back to its home shed. All the depots in the Liverpool area having already been closed to steam for two months by this time, 5F16, the 04:15 Carnforth- Edge Hill, is one of those examples of 'unbalanced workings' where steam still works into areas from which it is otherwise banned. If this had been a weekday, part of the diagram would usually have included 5P23, the 11:45 (SX) Ribble Sidings-Carnforth.

As an indication of the confusion that knock-on effects of the 'work-to-rule' are still creating, at 09:25 our old friend No 45394 is still making valiant attempts to get back to its rightful home, now coming off shed running light to Preston station ready to work the 09:58 (SO) Preston-Barrow parcels.

Inter-departmental communications are clearly in a flux, for that train had already been cancelled by Control, causing No 45394 later to return back

Stanier 8F No 48340, a former Northwich engine until that shed closed, passes Poulton-le-Fylde No 5 cabin, with 8P19, the 12:00 Burnley Central-Burn Naze coal train. The tracks to the right, known as Poulton curve, are those of the direct line from Fleetwood to Blackpool North, over which there was a passenger service until the 1960s. PETER FITTON

'Target 47', the daily trip working serving Windermere and Kendal, unloads wagonloads of coal in Windermere goods yard, while Carnforth's 'Black Five' No 45134 patiently waits. MAURICE BURNS

Another five-minute cosmetic make-over commences in Kendal goods yard on 1 August 1968. While the crew look on in absolute amazement, No 44894, the engine working 'Target 47' today, has its front number plate repainted by Mike Collins, while Alan Castle applies a 24K shedplate from his stock. 'Supervising' the work are photographers Neville Stead and Ian Krause. DEREK HUNTRISS

to 10D. It may be of interest to note that, of the 19 reliefs, specials and ECS workings scheduled to pass through Preston today, nearly half appear to have been cancelled. Indeed, the one regular steam passenger turn of the week, the 20:50 to Blackpool South, is worked by D1618, as 1P79, the main portion of the train to Windermere, is another casualty of the dispute and the remaining Blackpool portion is worked by the rostered 1P79 loco. The sleeping car heating duty also having been cancelled, the only other steam working to be observed is No 45025 (10A) on 4P21, the 13:35 Darwen-Heysham Moss oil tankers and even that only gets on its way a full hour after its booked time.

By the following week, matters are slowly beginning to return to normal and, after a reasonably quiet day steam-wise, on the Monday nearly all booked diagrams are back in business.

Wednesday, 10 July could be considered a typical day, for both steam and photography. With torrential downpours lashing many parts of the country, the sun manages to shine through in the North West and the following regular workings are observed in the Preston area. In order of appearance (use the reporting numbers to refer to the previous tables for train details): 3P00-45073 (10D), steam-heating sleeping cars off previous night's 1P54 and then shunting ballast wagons in Dock St Sidings-44806 (10D), Target 66-45394 (10A), 5P02-44781 (10A), 7P11-44971 (10D), 6P52-45407 (10D), 8P21-48062 (10F), 5P23-45025 (10A), 10-coach ECS to Pitt St Sidings (north of station) arriving at 12:40-45200 (10A), Target 78-45318 (10D), Target 63-45110 (10D), 8P19-48340 (10F), conveying track-laying unit to NU Yard-75019 (10A), 6P32-48493 (10F), 6P52-44971 (10D), 5F24-44874 (10A), 6P16-45305 (10D), Target 70-45055 (10D), another 10-coach ECS - off the East Lancs line arriving at 19:30-45200 (10A), 7N99-48493 (10F), steam-heating sleeping cars off 1P54-44806 (10D), 3P20-45073 (10D) and finally 1P92-44897 (10A). No 48340 (10F), as noted above, arriving at Blackpool North shed off 8P19 is soon appropriated to work a special Blackpool North to Morecambe train of empty stock and it will return to Preston even later on with more empty stock which, curiously, must have come from Morecambe.

On Friday, 12 July, observations in the Rose Grove area reveal a similar typical pattern of work: 7N78-48666 (10F), 8P21-48773 (10F), westbound special coal empties from Burnley Central (probably to Parkside or Bickershaw)-45073 (10D), unidentified westbound coal-48400 (10F), Target 86-48393 (10F), Target 92-48730 (10F), 7N78-48666 (10F), 8P19-48062 (10F), Target 86-48393 (10F), light to 10D then to work 6P16-75027 (10A), 6P32-48493 (10D), 7P65-44781 (10A), 8P32-43893 (10F), 8P20-48765 (10D) and 7P80-48773 (10F).

Among the 20 additional or altered trains for the Preston and Accrington town holidays are two on 19 July which are steam powered, the 1T55 22:20 Preston-Manchester Victoria, which forms part of the 23:34 Manchester Victoria-Paignton, being powered by No 44781 (10A), with the engine penetrating an area nominally banned to steam, since it has started out from Blackpool North at 21:20 with its empty stock and regular steam also no longer travels through to Manchester. Meanwhile, likewise 1H11, the 23:35 Accrington-Stockport works through to Stockport, this time via Bolton, with No 45156 (10F) to attach its five coaches to the 01:10

Manchester Piccadilly-Euston. Obviously, these essentially nocturnal operations provide little in the way of opportunity for photography, but certainly No 45156 produces much in the way of fireworks for those interested in loco performance, particularly on the climb up to Sough Tunnel over the Blackburn to Bolton line, achieving 65mph downhill to Bolton.

The latter route is, of course, one of the most scenic of those still available to steam in 1968 but, with the recent closing of the Manchester Division sheds, daytime workings have now become extremely scarce. It is because of this that a favourite (if not the only) subject for photography for some time previously has been the 13:35 (SO) Colne to Manchester Red Bank empty parcels train. This became a Rose Grove turn after the closure of Newton Heath and can now turn up with just about any class of motive power at its head. In July, however, it will see steam haulage on the 13th only, when No 44781 (10A) appears.

Over at Carnforth on 15 July, Britannia No 70013 *Oliver Cromwell* has departed in steam to Crewe for boiler attention and, while in Works, it is planned for the paintwork to be touched up and re-varnished in preparation for the final railtour duties, which it will resume on 21 July. On 18 July, an unusual sight hereabouts is No 44874 (10A) working a ten-coach 13:55 Barrow - Morecambe relief. Another working out of Barrow during the evening of 23 July, presumably replacement for a failed DMU, saw No 45017 heading three Mk1 coaches towards Carnforth, this in fact constituting the last steam-hauled passenger train on the Furness line.

The main part of the 'Belfast Boat Express' diagram having gone diesel at the beginning of May, the short leg as far as Morecambe with the Sunday morning 06:55 departure from Heysham occasionally still saw steam haulage, an old boat train favourite, No 45342 for example, finding use on 21 July.

Although, previously on 22 June, No 44758 (10A) had been seen in Harrison's Sidings, north of Shap, at 11:00 ready to leave for the south with loaded hopper-wagons, that was thought to have been the last time that a steam-working of any type behind a BR loco in regular service occurred so far north. Nevertheless, on 20 July, No 45017 (10A) reaches Tebay from Carnforth with ballast and two further steam engines are believed to have also got this far on 27 July, although no details are to hand for these,

Before the remainder of the engine can be cleaned properly; No 44894 needs to make a call at Windermere and is seen here making a very smoky departure from Windermere back to Kendal. MAURICE BURNS

the last steam workings through the Lune Gorge.

At this, the very end of steam at Carnforth, the policy with regard to laying-off engines is to not coal them after they return from their penultimate trip, regardless of where the final turn might go to, and the instruction is that the remaining contents of the tender are to be used up on the last working. This potentially dangerous edict does not appear to have been issued at either 10D or 10F! Nevertheless, on 26 July, No 45394 (10A) works the 13:05 (SX) Carnforth-Skipton freight, being noted with the words 'not to be coaled' chalked on its tender, its final trip being made on Target 46, the 12:35 (SX) Carnforth-Kendal and 18:20 return on the following day, duties which it

later appears to have accomplished without embarrassment.

All passenger workings down the Windermere branch having been made diesel duties some time previously, the turntable and water column were removed from Windermere station yard on Saturday 27 July. It is a fact that they have seen little use in recent times, as the Carnforth engine on the daily trip working, 'Target 47', works down the branch tender-first and only takes water in Kendal goods yard when necessary. No 45134 (10A) is on this duty on 22 July, 45025 (10A) on 23 July, 44735 (10A) on 24/25 July and 44894 (10A) on 31 July/1 August.

This is not the end of the story of steam to Windermere, however. Even during this, the final countdown, there are a number of footplatemen who will always prefer working with steam. To them, the realisation that they are within days of a momentous change that is going to affect their lives, it goes without saying that one or two will actively seek opportunities to have a 'last final fling'. On Monday 29 July, Driver Peter Norris books on duty at Lostock Hall in order to collect the loco rostered to work 2P83, the 08:15 Preston to Windermere passenger and its balanced return at the head of 1P27, the 11:00 Windermere-Crewe. Somehow, the rostered Brush Type 4, D1855, has mysteriously managed to 'fail' on shed – although the reasons surrounding this remain unclear - and the other three or four Class 25s close by, allegedly, already all have booked duties. Some fairly reliable sources suggest that a certain 'steam enthusiast' employed in Preston Control just possibly might have been involved in more than an element of collusion in permitting 'Black Five' No 45110 to be prepared for the job.

Back in Kendal yard, the cleaning is completed and more shunting takes place. DAVE RODGERS

Indeed, there are also suggestions circulating that it is now intended to use steam on the duty for the whole of the remaining week. Sadly, for reasons about to be revealed, the latter consideration just will not occur.

All goes well, No 45110 is in good mechanical order and the five-coach train runs to time throughout its northbound journey. However, things do start to go awry immediately upon arrival at the Windermere terminus. Today, forty years on, Driver Norris openly acknowledges that he had obviously not read any of the Notices at shed properly and that his enthusiasm had paved the way to become unstuck, facing him with an uncomfortable dilemma. Upon looking for the turntable in order to turn his engine, Pete is horrified to discover that there is just a gaping hole in the ground where this really ought to have been. Not only that, but the water column has also disappeared from its own familiar location! Both items have been removed for scrap a mere two days previously!

A tender-first return, although unsatisfactory, is not impossible – indeed, it is the only real option. An abortive attempt is made to replenish the tender during the stopover from a hosepipe linked to the station toilet water tap, but clearly this is going to take too long and departure time is fast approaching. There is believed still to be a working column in the goods yard at Kendal, but this will not solve the problem of turning the loco. Pete's choice now is either to run to Carnforth MPD to turn and run back light engine, but thereby delay his return train (which would require some explaining to the powers-that-be!), or he can take a chance and run tender-first! Although, by this date, much of the trip work for the remaining 'Black Fives' does involve an element of tender-first running at slow speed, the major issue here is that No 45110's return job is at the head of a Class 1 express passenger and, not only that, but with a first booked stop not scheduled until Lancaster! So, 1P27 sets out regardless for Preston, but, with little water remaining in the tender, there is no alternative but to halt at the column on the platform-end at Carnforth. In order then to make up time, some exhilarating running ensues, especially on the straight, fast stretches between Lancaster and Preston (some say 74mph is reached!) and with

Its day's work on the branch is over and No 44894 sets off back to Carnforth with a load of empty coal wagons in tow. Seen climbing up the final few yards to Oxenholme station. DAVE RODGERS

One final shot of 'Target 47' shows No 44894 in between the Anglo-Scottish expresses coasting down the West Coast Main Line near Milnthorpe. PETER FITTON

A diesel working during previous weeks, with Morecambe Bay as a backcloth, on 27 July 1968, No 45025 unexpectedly materialises with 3P24, the 09:58 (SO) Preston to Barrow parcels and is observed skirting the coastline near Kents Bank. MAURICE BURNS

only a minimal delay… all things considered!

Clearly, these matters never seem to be isolated ones and, come the following day, steam returns yet again to passenger work on the branch! This time, however, no-one has planned what does occur. Shortly after leaving Windermere, the 09:00 DMU to Morecambe fails with a burnt-out starter motor. The 'Thunderbird' that eventually arrives to the rescue is 'Black Five' No 44894 (10A), which, more than likely, is 'Target 47' loco today and probably already in the Kendal area anyway.

During this, the final week for steam, an excess of empty wagons at Whitebirk Power Station is probably the cause of the first appearance of the Whitebirk-Bickershaw train for a while, with No 48665 (10F) being used on 27/29 July and No 48340 (10F) on 30 July. Most minerals turns are to Padiham power station, and on the Preston line, where the daytime trains are 8P21/7P80, 6P32/7P33/7N99, 7N87/7N68. No 48493 is on 7N87 on 30 July. On 31 July, No 48340 (10F) is on 8P21, (banked by No 45388 (10D) from Burnley Central to Gannow Jct), No 48665 (10F) on 6P32 and No 48393 (10F) on a special Class 8 Burnley Central to Burn Naze, returning on 7N68. Apart from the two workings described above, steam over the Copy Pit route into Yorkshire is scarce.

On Thursday 1 August, fireman John Fletcher and his driver Cliff Nelson book-on at Lostock Hall ready to collect the engine booked to work 7P11, the 10:50 Ribble Sidings-Heysham – a regular 10D duty and with No 45407 chalked-up on the roster-board for them. They are told to wear clean overalls, as 'somebody from the press' will be accompanying them. Eventually it transpires that this 'somebody' is to be a junior reporter from the *Sunday Times* who, they are told, is writing a feature on the end of steam. What they are not prepared for, however, is that the reporter turns out to be an attractive young woman clad in a particularly short mini-skirt! What John recalls most vividly of that day (apart from the mini-skirt, that is) is the fact that the journey is to be extensively delayed, due to a tanker train having derailed itself in Morecambe, causing No 45407 to spend a considerable time 'inside' at Oubeck Loop – in the middle of nowhere! For the record, we do have the name of that cub-reporter – one Anne Robinson! John today wonders what her 'Points of View' may have been about this particular assignment!

In spite of being the second week of Preston Town Holidays, steam engines are very active on local shunts in the Preston area during the first two days of August. On 1 Aug, 'Target 63' has 48775 (10D), Target 66-48723 (10D), Target 67-45260 (10D), Target 70-44806 (10D) and Target 78-45212 (10D); 45110 (10D) has worked 3P00/3P20. The last remaining Ivatt 4MT 2-6-0 No 43106 is also steamed on this date and at 14:00 leaves the shed for the last time, heading initially towards Bescot and then towards a new life on the Severn Valley Railway.

At Rose Grove, No 45287 (10F) is provided to work 3T41, a 15-coach special empty stock working from East Lancs to Blackpool North, passing Preston at 11:15 before then retiring light to Lostock Hall shed. Nos 48400 and 48493 are on Rose Grove to Padiham coal trip workings. No 48519 is on Copy Pit banking duties. No 48665 runs light engine from Rose Grove to Ribble Sidings to head 5P23. Sister engine No 48666 has already been cleaned up on Rose Grove shed in preparation for the depot's very last passenger working – one of the 4 August specials. Meanwhile, it has headed 6P31, the 04:05 Rose Grove-Wyre Dock, before running light back to shed. No 48727 (10F) works 6P32 and the regular follow-on turns, 7P33 and 7N99, as far as Rose Grove. No 48730 has an equally hectic day, working 8P21, then 7P80 as far as Lostock Hall, where it is replaced by another loco, to permit it to visit Lostock Hall shed before returning to Ribble Sidings to work 7N68 as far as Rose Grove. On this date, No 48773 has arrived on shed at 02:45 from Healey Mills, and then works its final freight turn of all at the head of 5J10 to Moston.

Friday 2 August is the last day of full-scale steam freight working anywhere. At Carnforth, No 45025 (10A) is travelling about the region on the inspection saloon. No 44709 departs from Windermere with the very last steam departure of all with the princely sum of two empty coal wagons in tow. On both 8P76, the 08:55 Barrow-Carnforth and the 13:05 to Skipton, these have 45390 (10A), Target 46-48665 (10A), Target 47-44709 (10A), Target 48-75048 (10A), Target 49-

An absolutely spotless Carnforth 'Black Five' No 45390 heads out of Barrow with 8P76, the 08:55 Barrow to Carnforth, on 2 August 1968. This is almost certainly the final eastbound freight working from Barrow. DICK MANTON

The same working – with the same locomotive. Seen a couple of days earlier, on 1 August, No 45390 climbs Lindal Bank from the west and is about to enter Dalton Tunnel. The train on this date seems to be composed entirely of empty coal wagons. DAVID RODGERS

75019 (10A), Target 61-45231 (10A), 5F24-48493 (10F). On 1P92, the final steam working on all of the Barrow-Huddersfield parcels, No 44781 (10A), with Carnforth's legendary Ted Fothergill at the helm, admittedly with a light weight load, is reputed to have touched around 90mph at one point on its dash to Preston.

In the Preston area, we have 3P00/3P20-45407 (10D), Target 70-45318 (10D), 'Target 78'-45212 (10D), 7P11, returning light to 10D-45287 (10F). The last steam freight out of the Fylde is 7P33-48423 (10F), which then goes on to work 7N99, and the last one into the Fylde is 8P20-48727 (10F), which returns light. The 21:25 Preston-

Liverpool, by now normally a diesel turn, is to see steam again twice during this final week and tonight, No 45260 (10D) does the honours.

Rose Grove locos are equally active today, on the following duties: Target 19-45156, 05:20 Preston NU-Healey Mills-48723 (10F), 8P21/7P80-48278 (10F), 5J10-probably 48167 (10F) (no front number plate), 8F43-48400 (10F) returning engine and brake van to Rose Grove, 6P32/7P33/7N99-48423 (10F), 5F24-48493 (10F), 8P20/7N68-48727 (10F). No 48519 (10F) is also noted on a westbound freight and No 48393 (10F) arrives even later on a ballast.

No 48666 is on Copy Pit banking duties and,

upon returning from Todmorden, it enters the depot yard and promptly derails itself on the extremely dubious trackwork hereabouts, thus causing a major obstruction until it is put back onto the rails. Mobile once more, it is not worth the time and trouble to repair any damage sustained, and is promptly banished to a siding – its place on the special now being allocated to No 48773, which is coincidentally stood close by. Although No 48666 does not appear to need much work to put it right, it joins the end of a line of other withdrawn locomotives which already consist of: 44690/899/5096/350/82/97/447, 48062/115/247/57/323/84/410/48/51. The following are observed in steam here today: 45156,48167/91/340/8/93/423/519/666/715/27/30/73 (all 10F) also 45407 (10D).

Saturday 3 August is a much quieter day, Carnforth depot appearing to provide most of the action. The first movement off shed is with No 45342 (10A) on 6P42, followed 2½ hours later by the early-running Target 47 with No 44709. Upon arrival at Kendal, driver Watson Sowerby (formerly of Kirkby Stephen depot) watches on in amazement as his steed is groomed in the goods yard for its final departure. It is now the turn of No 45134 (10A) to make a trip to Lancaster Castle Yard, where it will shunt until 11:00 before returning with a brake van to 10A. No 45231 (10A) works a Class 9 special ballast from Waterslack Quarry to Farington Jct (arriving at 11:54) then, after taking coal and water, runs light back from Lostock Hall shed to Carnforth at 12:22, via Farington Curve. This working may well have been an extension to Canforth's (SO) Target 61 (see table).

On the (SO) itinerary for 'Target 49', No 75019 is observed mid-morning on the first of a couple of Carnforth-Heysham trip workings that it will undertake today. The very last working member of its class, it is later observed passing through Hest Bank tender-first at 16:00 with a heavy train of

Upon arrival at Ulverston on 2 August, Standard 4MT No 75048 shunts wagonloads of domestic coal around the yard. Such is the high level of traffic at this date, that the yard is serviced by 'Target 48' every weekday. DICK MANTON

vans from Heysham, on what is believed to be the last steam-worked freight train on BR. Of the other class members so very recently active, No 75027, with its chimney sacked, has joined the preserved locomotives lined up near the turntable and No 75048 has gravitated to the dump at the north end of the yard. Apart from the workings itemised above, only two other engines are observed to be in steam on shed today – these being Nos 45025 and 45390; Indeed, most of the other working Class Fives have gone to Lostock Hall for the following day's railtours and few will ever return.

Over in East Lancashire, but a single special freight is observed. No 48715 (10F) has been

provided for an additional Rose Grove to Ribble Sidings turn (which passes Lostock Hall at 12:29), the loco then runs light to Moss Lane Jct to reverse direction, permitting it to return to Rose Grove shed chimney-first. In the absence of any other observations, this working may well be the last-ever steam freight into Preston off the East Lancs line. Nevertheless, two engines have been out at Stansfield Hall on banking duties for most of the day; eventually returning to shed, No 48278 arriving first and then No 48191, both with chalked smokebox and tender inscriptions proclaiming 'Last Steam Copy Pit Banker 3rd August 1968'.

Other locos in steam on shed today are: 45156,

On 9 July, 'Target 48' is seen with a slightly less clean No 75048, returning to Carnforth along the sea wall at Grange-over-Sands. Notice the camping coaches stabled in the sidings opposite the signalbox. DAVID RODGERS

On 2 August 1968, No 75048, at the head of the very last steam-worked trip working from Ulverston, passes over Arnside Viaduct, proceeding on its way entirely un-noticed by daytrippers sunbathing on the beach. They would, perhaps, not act in quite the same way had 'Target 48' passed by 40 years in the future! IAN KRAUSE

48348/93/519/715 with No 48773 (10F) being prepared for its railtour duty the following day and No 48519 (10F) being the standby engine.

In the Preston area, No 45318 (10D) starts its very busy final day at the head of 'Target 66'. It is seen in Farington Yard at 12:11 and then arriving back on Lostock Hall shed from the Bamber Bridge direction at 12:45 with diesel fuel tanks and coal wagons in tow.

Seen in steam on shed at various times today are: 44806/88/5073/110/212/60/305/18/88/407, 48476/723 (all 10D), 45156 *Ayrshire Yeomanry*, 45287, 48340/493 (all 10F), and 44781/871/4/94/5017, 70013 *Oliver Cromwell*, 73069 (all 10A). All the Carnforth engines and also Nos 45156, 45305 and 48476 are being prepared for railtours tomorrow. No 45156 has run light from Rose Grove, arriving at 17:15. No 44806 (10D) has earlier worked a ballast train to/from an unidentified destination, and now arrives back on shed at 15:48. Its day's work is not complete, however, as it is required to go off shed again shortly before 19:30, light-engine to Preston station to present itself for station pilot/1A00 sleeping car heating duties. Half an hour later, No 45212 (10D) also slowly departs at 20:00, again light engine, to Preston station and will work 1P58, the 20:50 to Blackpool South - this being the penultimate steam passenger working of all. The large complement of enthusiasts in the seven coaches are to have a poor run due to a succession of signal checks and, with stops being made at all stations from Kirkham, Blackpool South will be reached some 15 minutes late. Doubtless, the usually totally uninformed local press present will, in their inimitable manner, have a field day in apportioning the blame squarely on the steam locomotive.

An even larger number, however, has assembled for 1F51, the 21:25 to Liverpool Exchange, which is to be provided with No 45318 (10D) (which, it will be recalled, had earlier been shunting for most of the day on far more menial duties); the engine leaving shed again, coaled, watered and with a fresh crew, at 20:30 for Preston station. Word has somehow got around and a huge contingent of supporters has

The other Standard 4MT out working on 2 August is No 75019, which is on Target 49, which includes Lancaster Quay siding in its itinerary. Here it is seen shunting at Lady's Walk on the surviving remnant of the former Midland route through Green Ayre station. PETER FITTON

Saturday 3 August 1968. By now the last working member of the class, No 75019 is on 'Target 49' and spends its day working a couple of Carnforth-Heysham trip workings, the final one of which is a heavy train of vans from Heysham back to Carnforth, and what is believed to be the last steam-worked freight train on BR. PETER FITTON

With only days to go before closure, Rose Grove shed had resembled more an 'Open Day' atmosphere than a working steam shed, with scores - perhaps even a few hundred - enthusiasts, photographers and 'locals' wandering around the yard. Here, infants from a nearby children's crèche have their first (and last) glimpses of steam locomotives. ALAN CASTLE

On 2 August two engines have been out at Stansfield Hall on banking duties for most of the day; eventually returning to shed, No 48278 (seen here) arriving first and then No 48191, both with chalked smokebox and tender inscriptions proclaiming 'Last Steam Copy Pit Banker 3rd August 1968'. MIKE TAYLOR

travelled to Preston to participate in this historic journey, which will be the very last ordinary passenger train to be provided with steam haulage. The train itself is soon packed to capacity, the normally small number of ordinary passengers naturally wondering what on earth is going on. At the front end, driver Ernie Heyes and fireman Tony Smith soon provide some spirited running commensurate with the occasion and the journey is completed in a highly commendable time. What Ernie does not realise, until this is pointed out to him by fitter Pete Whalen upon the loco's return to the shed, is that, during the latter stages of the rapid dash across the South Lancashire plain, a hot box was sustained on one of the tender axles at probably some two miles out from Exchange station. It was fortunate indeed that this did not occur earlier in this historically very significant journey!

A more detailed account of the journeys of 1P58 and 1F51 is related elsewhere, but one the most significant aspects of these workings, for local enthusiasts, was in the actual selection of locomotives on the roster. Quite coincidentally, both engines had been 'local' (indeed, Fylde-based) engines for most of their existence. Very aptly, No 45212 was a Fleetwood engine from 1948 until 1963 and No 45318 a Blackpool Central engine from 1955 to 1963.

Both trains carry headboards declaring 'The End' – the one on No 45318 being perhaps the most graphic in its impact. Upon return to Preston from Blackpool South – to date, the last steam engine ever to do so – No 45212 shunts the sleeping cars off the 23:45 Euston-Preston into the bay at Preston and this is very definitely the last occasion upon which passengers will be steam-hauled by a BR engine in normal service, albeit only during part of a shunt move!

Freight traffic everywhere being almost non-existent at weekends, Sunday 4 August 1968 is a far quieter day at all three depots, but particularly so at Carnforth and Rose Grove. Locos that had been in steam the previous day are still warm, with just a few pounds of steam pressure remaining, but, at Rose Grove, just two had a full head of steam. A very clean No 48773 is being prepared by Driver Arnold Hodgson and Fireman Jim Walker ready for the Blackburn to Carnforth, via Hellifield, leg of the LCGB 'Farewell to Steam Railtour' and a very grubby No 48519 had also been kept in steam, as standby for No 48773, just in case of any last minute failure. Perhaps not immediately apparant too many, No 48519 is the last LNER-built locomotive in BR service, constructed at Doncaster in 1944.

In 1958, Jim used to visit Rose Grove as a trainspotter and, in those less Health & Safety conscious days, often used to help the steam-raisers light up locos. On one particular occasion, he turned up to witness the incredulous sight of Arnold dressed in a suit and placing fires in locomotives himself! The steam-raiser had not turned-up for duty. Obviously Jim offered to help and Arnold asked if he knew what to do? Jim answered, 'Yes', so Arnold took him over to the stores and told him to get what he needed, for himself. Between the two of them, they each took half of the shed - lighting up all the engines. That is what one might describe as a real enthusiast!

It is, therefore, all the more remarkable that today, all of ten years on, these two are once again sharing duties, now with the honour of crewing the very last Rose Grove steam engine to work a train. No 48773 eventually departs, accompanied

'Sunset of Steam 1'. In the very last light of a glorious day, an unidentified Rose Grove 8F crosses over the West Coast Main Line at Farington with 7N68, the 21:45 Preston NU Yard to Cudworth, which it will work as far as Rose Grove. ALAN CASTLE

by running shift Foreman Des Melia to the shed exit, and then proceeds light-engine towards Blackburn.

The only other crew booking on at Rose Grove on this Sunday are driver Alan Entwistle and his fireman Bob Ashworth, ready for a pw working in Rose Grove 'Up Grid' sidings in conjunction with the road bridge-renewal work over the station and yards. The turn has been booked for a 350hp diesel shunter (Class 08). Sensibly, rather than immediately drop the fire in No 48519, which has a full head of steam, it is decided to use the 8F on the pw job, to burn through the already very large fire. And so it falls to No 48519 and its crew to be the last steam loco to leave Rose Grove shed… and to No 48773 to be the last steam loco to arrive on shed in the evening, upon its return light engine from Carnforth via Preston.

Over at Lostock Hall, No 48493 (10F) has found itself on shed with no further booked work on the Saturday evening. It will not return to Rose Grove, but is kept in steam until the following morning, as there is one final duty for it to undertake. Being seen in Farington Junction yard quietly shunting ballast wagons at 09:00 on the Sunday morning, this almost un-noticed and un-documented working is the very last non-passenger steam working on BR.

All the glory of the occasion obviously centres upon the various 'Farewell to Steam' specials; indeed, there has probably never before been such a concentration of workings of this nature in a single area, since there are no fewer than six steam-hauled trains touring Lancashire today. At Lostock Hall shed, the engine cleaners of the MNA have been busy. Indeed, this is their swansong too – for after today there will be no more! Overnight, no less than an all-time record of 13 engines have been groomed in one session.

Replacement self-adhesive smokebox numerals or shed-plates have been applied and bufferbeams painted and the final curtain-call for steam stands in the yard in all its majesty, reflecting the early morning sunlight. For those who have laboured tirelessly through the night, before

the very last steam chase begins, there is now time to cogitate on various successes achieved over the years. "Where will we be going tomorrow? What engines will we be cleaning?" is the question we would all love to be asking each other, for realisation still has to hit most of us. But, there is no escaping the inevitable… there is nothing beyond The End. Groups mill around aimlessly, perhaps looking for The Answer in each other, but there is none.

In ones and twos, throughout the morning the last men and machines gradually depart to their allocated rendezvous points, leaving a shed yard eerily empty and silent – for even the enthusiasts have now deserted their 'Mecca'.

Everyone has different recollections of that day and it is, perhaps, best to let the photographs in the following chapters tell their own stories. However, with the onset of evening, very few observers remain to witness the bitter end. By 22:00, there are 16 engines on shed in steam (not all, of course, having been used today) and with

only Nos 70013 and 45156 still awaited back from specials' duty. *Oliver Cromwell* does finally materialise at some time after midnight, but No 45156 is, by far, the last engine of all to return. It is around 04:00 on the Monday morning when Driver Andy Hall backs his 'Black Five' onto a totally deserted shed. There is not another soul to be seen, so Andy's claim today to have been the very last steam footplateman on British Railways (11 August special events aside) appears to be justified.

Walking with his fireman in the eerie half-light down the serried ranks of now withdrawn engines, many still exuding their last ebbing signs of life, Andy proceeds into the engineman's lobby in order to sign-off duty, only to discover that the foreman's office has been ransacked, with even the two shed telephones having been ripped off the wall. The bodies of our dearly departed are not yet cold, but the vultures are already striking! Long live steam, for steam is dead!

'Sunset of Steam 2'. Nightfall at Rose Grove. Chimneys, cooling towers, steam locomotives – everything visible in this evocative view has now disappeared forever. Indeed, a motorway now passes right through the middle of the picture, leaving but two sets of track leading towards Accrington. DEREK HUNTRISS

3 August 1968

Preston's last steam passenger workings

Tom Heavyside

The months leading up to what really was the last day of normal steam activity on British Railways, Saturday 3 August 1968, were for me, as for many other like-minded individuals, a period of intense activity on the steam front. It was a period during which I literally grasped at every available opportunity to imbibe and record what then appeared to be the last dying embers of the steam locomotive, a machine that had served the nation with such distinction over many decades. In this respect I have always counted myself fortunate to have been born and reared in Lancashire, for this was where the last vestiges of the iron horse were played out, in effect not far from my own doorstep.

In those days, much of my travelling had perforce to be by public transport, or alternatively astride my trusty 'Dawes Dalesman' bike, the latter clocking up a prodigious amount of mileage in my quest for steam. Favourite haunts, during the early months of 1968, were the two Stockport sheds, Edgeley and Heaton Mersey, along with those at Patricroft and Newton Heath, while numerous trips were made from my Westhoughton home (between Bolton and Wigan) in the opposite direction to Preston and Carnforth.

And so dawned that fateful Saturday, a day anticipated with dread, for this was the final curtain-call for steam, certainly as far as normal

day-to-day activity on BR was concerned. There would be no repeats. During the 1960s, for many people, a five-and-a-half-day working week was the norm and while the banking world did not require my services every Saturday, it just so happened that on this particular auspicious occasion I was required on duty. Thus it was after lunch before I was able to stow my Ross Ensign 120 roll film camera, along with a plentiful supply of sandwiches, biscuits and cake, into the saddlebag in preparation for the trip to Preston.

Over the years I had travelled the 15 miles or so along the A6 trunk road to this steam Mecca countless times, such being my familiarity with the route that I was aware of almost every pothole and other potential hazard that might be lying in wait ready to trap the unwary, the journey usually taking about an hour depending on the strength and direction of the wind. On previous visits I would probably have made my way first to Fowler Lane, where the road bridge conveniently overlooks Farington Junction, or maybe to Flag Lane or Bee Lane, either side of Farington Curve Junction, all excellent photographic vantage spots on the West Coast main line. But, not on this occasion, for with little if at all any steam activity expected until the evening, I decided my best plan was to head straight to Lostock Hall shed.

As I approached the entrance to the shed along Watkin Lane, I was greeted by the amazing sight

of dozens of camera-toting enthusiasts stood chatting on the pavement, somewhat reminiscent of a gathering outside a church prior to a funeral. The mood, too, was similar, in that there was a definite sombre undertone among the crowd, but yet the majority were obviously trying to remain cheerful, with much of the usual banter and gossip being exchanged.

Normally, from my experience, the shed authorities at Lostock Hall had always turned a blind eye to the casual visitor, but this day they had been overwhelmed by the sheer numbers of those who chose to wander around the confines of the depot, many of whom had travelled quite some distance. The upshot was the local Transport Police had been summoned to clear the yard, so the staff could prepare unhindered a couple of 'Black Fives' that were required for the evening services to Blackpool and Liverpool, as well as a number of other engines needed for one or other of the six specials scheduled to run the next day.

As the afternoon progressed, the pavement became more and more congested and after spending quite some time chatting with friends and acquaintances, I eventually moved off. Initially, I decided to wait by the bridge that carries Coote Lane over the long curve that leads from Engine Shed Junction down to Farington Curve Junction, to observe No 45212 pass light engine on its way to Preston station in readiness for its evening assignment to Blackpool. It coasted by with little fuss and once it had disappeared from sight, I set off in pursuit to the station.

Just inside the station concourse, I was met by an unusually long queue, certainly for a Saturday night, that had formed outside the booking office. The clerk behind the window was busy issuing tickets, mainly for two destinations, either Blackpool South or Liverpool Exchange, for travel by what would be the last two ordinary service trains on British Railways standard-gauge metals to be hauled by steam.

Having negotiated the ticket barrier, I trundled the bike down the slope towards Platform 5. In front of me appeared a seething mass of humanity, with virtually everyone keenly awaiting the arrival of the 17:05 from London Euston, the rear coaches of which would form the 20:50 to Blackpool South. Meanwhile No 45212 was tucked away in the short dock siding under Fishergate Bridge. More or less to time, the London train glided into Platform 5 behind a Brush Type 4 diesel, whereupon two bearded gentlemen, appropriately clad in top hats and tailcoats and carrying at shoulder height a mock coffin draped with slogans on the impending

20:15 on the evening of Saturday 3 August 1968 and Stanier 'Black Five' No 45212 approaches the south end of Preston station, running light engine from Lostock Hall shed, in order to work 1P58, the 20:50 to Blackpool South. This being the penultimate steam passenger working of all, and on a day when but one other steam locomotive had passed through the platforms (that on a ballast working), some considerable interest is being shown in its arrival. ALAN CASTLE

Left: 21:34. Upon arrival at Blackpool South, with the last-ever regular steam-hauled passenger train into the resort, Lostock Hall driver Bob Barker and his fireman Ray Duckworth are inundated with requests for autographs by the dozens of youngsters present! BOB CLARKE

Right: 21:46. After lumps of coal from the tender had been presented to many of the enthusiasts present, No 45212 prepares to take the empty stock out of the platform to deposit in the carriage sidings. Blackpool South once boasted four platforms, all with canopies (one of which can be seen here), a very busy goods yard, and full passenger facilities. However, in November 1964, the true terminus of the line, Blackpool Central, was closed with South taking over its role. The senseless demise of Central also marked the start of a steady decline to this section of the Fylde's rail system, although a very basic service still survives today. PETER FITTON

demise of steam, marched in a suitably dignified manner the full length of the platform. Soon the diesel and its shortened train were on their way north towards Carlisle.

I crossed the footbridge to Platform 4 for a better view of proceedings, as driver Bob Barker (a former Kirkby Stephen man who transferred south upon closure of that shed) slowly reversed No 45212 up to the leading coach of the Blackpool-bound stock and fireman Ray Duckworth coupled up. In similar situations in the past, I would have been busy with the camera mounted on a tripod, taking a few time exposures. No chance on this occasion, there were simply far too many people milling about to even contemplate the idea.

With the coaches packed to the gunnels, I followed the progress of this soon-to-be-immortalised 'Black Five' as it confidently lifted the train away from the platforms in the direction

of Maudlands Junction, the last of a great pageant of steam locomotives that had carried millions to the Fylde Coast down the years.

Attention was then focussed on the south end of the station, where sister 'Black Five' No 45318 was waiting patiently for its share of the glory in bay Platform 5A, pending the arrival of the 17:25 from Glasgow Central, conveying through carriages for both Manchester and Liverpool. Once the Manchester portion had left behind the diesel that had brought it south, No 45318, without much ado, took up its position about the middle of Platform 6 at the head of the remaining section destined for Liverpool Exchange.

A large gallery quickly formed up across the platform, as a member of the station staff, along with another well-heeled gentleman, came striding purposely towards us shouting in an authoritative voice, "Make way for the press!" A certain well-known Prestonian steam

photographer, standing just to my left, was heard to exclaim, in no uncertain terms, "Oh b***** the Press!" To a man, everyone stood firm and the local newspaper cameraman, despite whatever credentials he might have possessed, was forced to take his chance with the rest of the excited gathering!

As fireman Tony Smith scrambled down behind the tender onto the ballast, in order to couple-up, it was time to think about looking for a suitable position in one of the carriages, although first I had to put the bike in the guard's compartment at the back of the train. By this time, the front two vehicles were already somewhat overcrowded, so I settled to travel in the third coach. I was lucky enough to find an empty space along the side-corridor, by an opening window, not minding the fact I would have to stand throughout the 27-mile journey.

Once wheel-tapper, James Bagshaw, had done his examination of the stock, the 'right away' was given and with the relevant semaphore signals in the off position, No 45318 eased out from under the lofty station roof against a battery of flash guns and crossed over to the up slow line by Preston No 1 signalbox. As if in defiance of its impending doom, the exhaust from No 45318 noisily rang out for all to hear, as we crossed the wide expanse of the Ribble and climbed steadily up the West Coast Main Line towards Farington Curve Junction, isolated flashes of blue light periodically relieving the gathering gloom. A few interested bystanders were noted on Skew Bridge, another regular vantage point in past years.

We slowed for the junction prior to taking the Liverpool line, a rather poignant moment for me as this was the spot where I had spent many summer days contentedly sitting on the grassy slopes overlooking the line, briefly remembering the days when Princess Coronations, Royal Scots, Jubilees, Britannias and a host of other well-loved classes had all been quite common. I was jerked back to the here and now as No 45318 began to blast its way up the short, sharp incline to Moss Lane Junction, where we joined what was then a direct line from Blackburn, as well as providing

The empty stock having been stabled in Bloomfield Road Carriage Sidings, No 45212 backs onto the turntable, ready to turn, before proceeding light back to Preston. At one time there were 34 parallel lines near this point and no fewer than 22 miles of sidings between here and Central Station. PETER FITTON

Having turned on the turntable, with the floodlights of Blackpool Football Club and the adjacent coach park clearly visible in the background, No 45212 awaits departure back towards Preston Station, where it is scheduled to undertake its final task in British Railways' service – to officiate as station pilot. During the early hours of 4 August 1968, it will remove two sleeping cars from 1P54, the 23:15 Euston-Windermere and shunt them, complete with occupants, into a bay platform with the loco steam-heating them until around 08:00. PETER FITTON

Preston Station, 21:25 on 3 August 1968 and Lostock Hall's No 45318 with driver Ernie Heyes and fireman Tony Smith are coupled-up and ready for the 'right-away' with the very last steam passenger working, the 21:25 Preston to Liverpool Exchange. MAURICE BURNS

Liverpool Exchange Station, 22:00 on 3 August 1968. After a rousing run from Preston, completing the journey in 33min 48sec, No 45318 stands at the bufferstops. A throng of enthusiasts gather to pay homage to this particular 'Black Five', now with a revered, if largely unsung place in the annals of history. Very shortly the locomotive will run light back to Lostock Hall shed where the end of its career awaits.
ALAN CASTLE

an alternative route out of Preston via Todd Lane Junction.

Once the junction had been cleared, we quickly gathered momentum, as driver, Ernie Heyes, appeared to be urging his charge on, in an endeavour to give the passengers something to remember. As we dashed across the arable flat landscape of West Lancashire, Croston, Rufford, Burscough, Ormskirk, all flashed by in a blur, a member of the stopwatch fraternity claiming we had touched 80mph at one point. We had certainly touched 78 through Maghull and previously 61 through Ormskirk and topping Aughton Bank at 57!

All too soon we were threading our way through the built-up suburbs of Liverpool past Aintree, where the outline of the closed engine shed, its coaling plant still towering into the sky, appeared as a silent tribute to the golden age of steam. Three miles further on, and hardly a trace of the former shed at Bank Hall could be discerned - a stark reminder that the final death throes of the steam age was near at hand.

A few minutes later, No 45318 triumphantly edged its way slowly towards the buffer-stops under the overall roof of Liverpool Exchange station. We had made the journey in 33min 48sec from Preston. A job well done!

By the time I had retrieved my bike, a throng of enthusiasts had gathered to pay homage to this particular 'Black Five', now with a revered, if largely unsung place in the annals of history. As a few ordinary passengers filed past, not really aware of the significance of it all, there was a rousing chorus of *"Auld Lang Syne"* and *"Three cheers for the steam locomotive!"* Outwardly, there was a carnival atmosphere, yet, at the same time, the occasion was tinged with sadness.

I was only able to stop and partake in the proceedings for a minute or two, for I had to go and buy a ticket and board a waiting diesel multiple-unit for the journey back to Westhoughton. Something of an anticlimax I suppose, but over the next hour I did have time to reflect on the day's events, although I am not sure I was really fully aware of the implications, for one of the foremost things on my mind were the specials that would be touring the area the following day. Where would I head, to see at least some of these? That be another tale!

Postscript: Two weeks later, I decided to go back to Preston, although on this August Saturday there was no need to rush, and it was about 15:30 before I started out on the ride north. I called in at Lostock Hall shed, where a number of engines silently awaited their final destiny, the place appearing cold and lifeless, before touring a number of familiar locations to the south of the town as it then was, the most noticeable difference being the fact that there was not another soul in sight with whom to share any thoughts. I didn't linger long before I was on my way home. What was clearly obvious, not only had the iron horse disappeared from the tracks, but so too had the people who until so recently had regularly congregated by the lineside.

It was as if a whole way of life had suddenly gone. Yes, in retrospect, Saturday 3 August 1968 was a sad day, but life goes on and I must confess to now having thoroughly enjoyed a further 40 years of linesiding, if, perhaps, with a little difference in emphasis! Just as importantly, friendships have been maintained, as well as numerous others made over the intervening years.

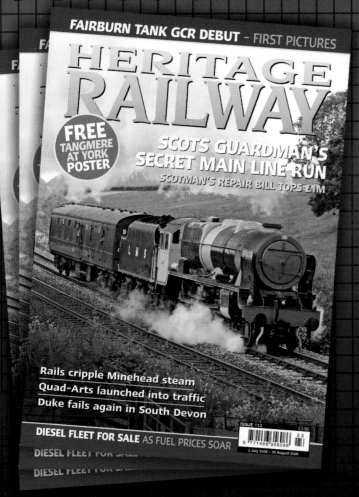

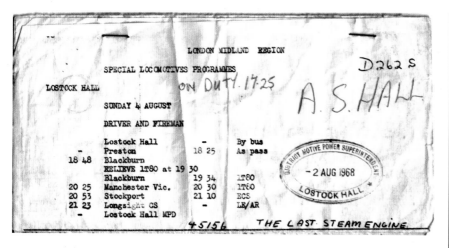

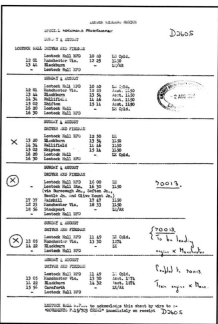

The final steam rosters

4 AUGUST 1968

Alan Castle

The complete list of known motive power movements on this, the final day of steam, was as below:

10A Carnforth

48773 (10F) Light-engine 10A to 10F, after servicing off 1L50.
45390 (10A) & 45025 (10A) Light-engines 10D to 10A via WCML.

10D Lostock Hall

48493 (10F) 10D to Farington Jct Yard to shunt ballast wagons [09:00] and then back to 10D.
45156 (10F) Light-engine 10D to Longsight carriage sidings to collect stock for 1T80 and then return light Stockport (Edgeley) to 10D.
44871 (10A) & 44894 (10A) Light-engines 10D to Manchester (Vic) for 1Z78 [dep 10:37], then return light to 10D.
45390 (10A) & 45025 (10A) Light-engines 10D to Manchester (Vic) for 1Z74, then return light to 10A, via WCML.
44874 (10A) & 45017 (10A) Light-engines 10D to Manchester (Vic) for 1Z79 [dep 11:00], then return light to 10D.
48476 (10D) & 73069 (10A) Light-engines 10D to Manchester (Vic) for 1L50 [dep 10:40], then return light to 10D.
44781 (10A) & 70013 (10A) Light-engines 10D to Manchester (Vic) for 1Z74/1L50 [dep 11:49], then return to 10D.
45305 (10D) Light-engine 10D to Manchester (Vic) for 1T85, [dep 11:49] then return light to 10D.
45407 (10D) Light-engine 10D to Blackburn for 1L50 [dep 12:50], then return light to 10D.
70013 (10A) Light-engine 10D to Manchester (Vic) for 1Z74 [dep 11:49] and light engine Blackburn to Lostock Hall for 1L50, return light to 10D.

10F Rose Grove

48519 (10F) Permanent way train shunt in Rose Grove 'Up' Sidings and then back to 10F.
48773 (10F) Light-engine Rose Grove MPD to Blackburn for 1L50, then return light 10A to 10F, after servicing.

The six railtours were as below:

(1T80) GC Enterprises 'Farewell to Steam Railtour'

(Starting/finishing point: Stockport (Edgeley) 8-coaches Route: Stockport (Edgeley)-Denton-Droylesden-Manchester (Vic)-Bolton-Blackburn-Hellifield-Carnforth (rev)-Hellifield-Blackburn-Bolton-Manchester (Vic)-Droylesden-Denton-Stockport (Edgeley)
Motive power: Class 5MT 4-6-0 No 45156 *Ayrshire Yeomanry* (10D) throughout
Stockport to Blackburn: Driver Ronnie Clough (10D) / Fireman Joseph Booth (10D); Blackburn to Carnforth and return to Blackburn: Driver Colin Hacking / Fireman: Dennis Robinson; Blackburn to Stockport and LE to Lostock Hall: Driver Andy Hall (10D)

(1T85) British Railways 'Last Days of Steam' tour

(Starting/finishing point: Manchester (Vic)) 8-coaches Route: Manchester (Vic)-Eccles-Olive Mount-Bootle Branch-Birkdale-Southport avoiding line-Wigan (Wallgate)-Manchester (Vic)
Motive power: Class 5MT 4-6-0 No 45305 (10D) throughout
Man. Vic to Southport: Driver Vinny Commons (10D) / Fireman Paul Tuson (10D).

(1L50) Railway Correspondence & Travel Society 'End of Steam Commemorative Railtour'

(Starting/finishing point: London Euston) 13-coaches
Stage 1: Manchester (Vic)-Thorpes Bridge Jct-Oldham (Mumps)-Milnrow-Rochdale-Bury (Knowsley St)-Bolton-Blackburn
Motive power: Class 8F 2-8-0 No 48476 (10D) & Standard Class 5MT 4-6-0 No 73069 (10A) – double-headed
48476 Driver: Harry Bolton (10D) / Fireman: Jim Marlor (10D);
73069 Driver: John Burnett (10D) / Fireman: John Roach (10D)
Stage 2: Blackburn-Clitheroe-Hellifield (rev)-Skipton (reverse)-Colne-Accrington-Blackburn-Farington Jct.
Motive power: Class 5MT 4-6-0 No 45407 (10D) & Standard Class 5MT 4-6-0 No 73069 (10A) – double-headed
73069 Driver John Burnett (10D) / Fireman John Roach (10D);
45407 Driver: Fred Barron (10D)
Stage 3: Lostock Hall-Chorley-Bolton-Manchester (Vic)-Miles Platting-Denton-Stockport (Edgeley) (Train scheduled to run via Burscough, Southport and Olive Mount, but diverted due to very late-running.
Motive power: Class 7MT 4-6-2 No 70013 *Oliver Cromwell* (10A)
Driver: Brian McFadden (10D) / Footplate Inspector: Frank Watson

(1Z74) Locomotive Club of Great Britain 'Farewell to Steam Railtour'

(Starting from London St Pancras and returning to London Euston) 12-coaches
Stage 1: Manchester (Vic)-Bolton (Trinity St)-Blackburn
Motive power: Class 7MT 4-6-2 No. 70013 *Oliver Cromwell* (10A) & Class 5MT 4-6-0 No 44781 (10A) – double-headed.
44781 Driver: Frank Herdman (10D) / Fireman: Eric Ashton (10D);
70013 Footplate Inspector: Frank Watson
Stage 2: Blackburn-Hellifield-Carnforth (rev)
Motive power: Class 8F 2-8-0 No 48773 (10F) & Class 5MT 4-6-0 No 44781 (10A) – double-headed
48773 Driver Arnold Hodgson / Fireman Jim Walker (10F)
Stage 3: Carnforth-Hellifield-Blackburn-Farington Jct
Motive power: Class 5MT 4-6-0 No. 45390 (10A) & Class 5MT 4-6-0 No. 45025 (10A) – double-headed.

(1Z78) Stephenson Locomotive Society 'Farewell to Steam Railtour' - No 1

(Starting/finishing point: Birmingham New St) 10-coaches
Manchester (Vic)-Stalybridge-Huddersfield-Sowerby Bridge-Copy Pit-Blackburn-Bolton avoiding line-Wigan (Wallgate)-Kirkby-Bootle branch-Stanley-Rainhill-Eccles-Manchester (Vic)-Droylesden-Stockport (Edgeley)
Motive power: Class 5MT 4-6-0 No 44871 (10A) & Class 5MT 4-6-0 No 44894 (10A) – double-headed.
44871 Driver: Cliff Nelson (10D) / Fireman: John Fletcher (10D);
44894 Driver: Ronnie Hall (10D) / Fireman: Tom Jones (10D)

(1Z79) Stephenson Locomotive Society 'Farewell to Steam Railtour' - No 2

(Starting/finishing point: Birmingham New Street) 10-coaches
Manchester (Vic)-Stalybridge-Huddersfield-Sowerby Bridge-Copy Pit-Blackburn-Bolton avoiding line-Wigan (Wallgate)-Kirkby-Bootle branch-Stanley-Rainhill-Eccles-Manchester (Vic)-Droylesden-Stockport (Edgeley)
Motive power: Class 5MT 4-6-0 No 44874 (10A) & Class 5MT 4-6-0 No 45017 (10A) – double-headed.
44874 Driver: John Commons (10D) / Fireman: Roy Haythornthwaite (10D); 45017 Driver: Bill Wilson (10D)

Farewell to Steam
4 August 1968

by Acting Footplate Inspector Frank Watson (British Railways 1951-1970)

Steam enthusiasts had a field day on Sunday 4 August 1968, as six special train workings had been arranged to be steam-hauled within the boundaries of the Manchester and Preston Divisional Areas.

The Stephenson Locomotive Society organised two separate trains, 1Z78 and 1Z79, to run from Birmingham, via Manchester Victoria, to Huddersfield, returning via Copy Pit, Rose Grove, Blackburn, Bolton, Wigan and Rainford, where they were booked a 10-minute stop prior to the both of them returning to Manchester, via Earlestown and Kenyon Junction. The first special, 1Z78, departed Birmingham at 08:20, followed by 1Z79 at 09:05, and each was allowed time at Rose Grove so that passengers could look around the motive power depot. If everything ran smoothly and the trains to time, it would still be almost 11 hours before they would arrive back at Birmingham (New Street).

The Railway Correspondence & Travel Society had arranged a special train (1L50) to run from Euston to Skipton that, after arriving at Manchester (Victoria), was scheduled for a trip via Rochdale, Castleton East Junction, Bury, Bolton, Blackburn and Hellifield, before arriving at Skipton. It was then booked to run via Colne, Blackburn, Lostock Hall, Ormskirk, Bootle Junction and Rainhill, before returning to Manchester via Earlestown and Kenyon Junction. This train comprised 13 coaches totalling 442 tons and, with engine No 70013 *Oliver Cromwell* and a Lostock Hall crew, I was scheduled to travel as inspector from Lostock Hall, via Rainhill, Manchester Victoria and then onwards to Stockport.

Meanwhile, the Locomotive Club of Great Britain had organised its own railtour (1Z74) from St Pancras to Carnforth which, after arriving at Manchester (Victoria), was scheduled a rather complicated route onwards to Carnforth. From Manchester (Victoria), it travelled via Bolton, Blackburn, Hellifield, Settle Junction and Wennington to Carnforth. It was booked to return by the same route to Blackburn and then by way of Lostock Hall Junction, before rejoining the West Coast Main Line at Farington Junction, to return home via Crewe. Upon arrival at Manchester (Victoria), I was then again rostered to accompany engine No 70013 with a set of Lostock Hall men, double-heading this train via Bolton and Walton Summit to Blackburn.

Another more-locally organised railtour (1T80) from Stockport to Carnforth, was operated by 'GC Enterprises', which, from Manchester (Victoria), followed the same route to Carnforth as 1Z74, but upon arrival back at Blackburn, it then travelled via Darwen and Bolton back to Manchester and Stockport.

The final special train (1T85) was a BR London Midland Region railtour that had the title 'Last Days of Steam', but turned out to be a much less ambitious affair than any of the others, as it only went from Manchester to Southport and back, leaving Manchester Victoria at 14:20 and arriving back at 17:10.

When I arrived at Lostock Hall Shed on Sunday 4 August, at about 09:30, the place was a hive of activity, with numerous engines being prepared to work various stages of the aforementioned specials. Official railway personnel on duty proved to be totally outnumbered both by enthusiasts and other members of the public merely wanting to witness the passing of an era. Some of the enthusiasts had certainly been busy during the night, as they had attempted to make every engine look its best for this, the very last curtain-call for steam.

After watching No 70013 being prepared, I noticed that the engine sported the wooden mock nameplates that seemed to be fitted whenever the engine worked trains organised by the RCTS. According to our engine workings, we were booked off shed at 11:49 and to travel to Manchester light-engine coupled to a 'Black Five', then to work as assistant engine on 1Z74 (the LCGB tour to Carnforth), between Manchester Victoria and Blackburn, departing Manchester Victoria at 13:30 and arriving at Blackburn at 14:22, that is, if everything was running to time. On arrival at Blackburn, after hooking-off, we were timed to run light-engine back to Lostock Hall, in order to be re-manned, before working another enthusiasts' special, 1L50, (RCTS) from Lostock Hall later in the day.

To say that things did not go well would be a gross understatement, as, for a variety of reasons, most of the special trains failed to keep to their booked timings.

We left Lostock Hall shed on time at 11:49, with nothing to delay us en-route. 1Z74 itself, however, eventually ran into Manchester Victoria nearly an hour late and we then experienced further delays at Bolton due to Sunday engineering works. After Bolton, we did enjoy a clear run up the bank to Walton Summit and then down into Blackburn, and, with a load of only nine coaches totalling 314 tons, little effort was required from the two engines as we tried to pull back a bit of the lost time. After hooking-off at Blackburn, we then ran light-engine as scheduled tender-first back to Lostock Hall Shed, via a reversal at Todd Lane Junction Station. This saved turning the engine on the shed for the next stage of our tour of duty. At 16:30, No 70013, now with the fresh set of locomen, was then scheduled to work 1L50 from Lostock Hall Station to Stockport, via Burscough Jct, Ormskirk, Aintree and Rainhill, before returning via St Helens Jct and Earlestown to Manchester Victoria - where we were booked to take water. As was to transpire, by this time the special was running about four hours late and when it did eventually arrive at Lostock Hall, in order to attempt to regain some time, a decision had been taken by the RCTS officials to request Preston Control to permit the special to take a more direct route home. In the event the train took the 'back line' from Lostock Hall Jct to Farington Jct and then ran via Chorley and Bolton to Manchester.

We had a reasonable run from Lostock Hall Jct, but, with a load of all of 13 coaches behind the tender, only a little time could be recovered. To make matters worse, upon our arrival at Manchester Victoria, we discovered that there was no water available from our platform column. A decision now had to be made - should the train be delayed further, by detaching the engine, to source out a supply of water, or should we press on regardless to Stockport? The water-level gauge on the tender tank indicated that we had just below 1000 gallons remaining but, being familiar with the engine, I was aware that this gauge was 'shy', thus intimating that there was always slightly more water in the tender than appeared to be the case. I also climbed onto the tender and shone a 'Bardic' lamp into the tank, before then making the decision to continue to Stockport.

Instead of arriving there at the booked time of 18:56, we were still about 3½ hours late and darkness had already descended on the station. As we were hooking-off to seek that urgently needed refreshment, a mock coffin was being transported down the platform – a token gesture to signify the death of steam traction on British Railways. What moved me most of all, as we pulled away light engine, were the shouts of "Will ye no come back again?" Due to the efforts, particularly of the staff on the Great Central Railway, the wishes of those rail enthusiasts of many years ago have since become reality.

For the passengers on 1L50, they later had the rare privilege of having part of their fare - £1-2s-0d (£1.10) - returned as an offer of 'compensation'. By the time that their train had arrived back at Euston, it was just before 02:00 on the Monday morning - a mere four hours after booked time! Nevertheless, British Railways could not offer the weather as an excuse, as this had been fine and sunny all day long… but, at least the thousands of photographers lining the various routes to record the events enjoyed their day, as conditions had been ideal for them.

To complete the tale, fortunately we did manage to obtain water at Stockport, before proceeding tender-first back to Lostock Hall shed. For myself, I could now make my weary way homewards in the direction of Accrington, for a well-earned rest!

The final dawn for the condemned. A view taken from the top of the Lostock Hall coaling plant, this historically important photograph depicts the last curtain-call of all for steam standing in the yard in all its majesty. All the glory of the occasion obviously centres upon the various 'Farewell to Steam' specials; indeed, there has probably never before been such a concentration of workings of this nature in a single area, since there are no fewer than six steam-hauled trains touring Lancashire today. Rows of immaculate locos reflecting the early morning sunlight, the engine cleaners of the MNA have obviously been busy. Indeed, this is their swansong too – for after today there will be no more! Overnight, no less than an all-time record of 13 engines have been groomed in one session. ALAN CASTLE

"Last sunrise for steam"
- Lostock Hall shed 4 August 1968

Replacement self-adhesive smokebox numerals and shedplates have been applied, bufferbeams repainted, fires banked up, tenders refilled and all that is now needed is for the crews to book on duty. In ones and twos, throughout the morning the last men and machines will gradually depart to their allocated rendezvous points, leaving a shed yard eerily empty and silent. BOB CLARKE

Lostock Hall fitter Tommy Baldwin passes a replica wooden *Oliver Cromwell* nameplate up to fitter Pete Whelan ready to affix to the smoke deflector of No 70013. This particular set of plates, believed to be the property of the RCTS, were always accompanied by a society representative wherever they went, if only to ensure their safe return after use. In view of the large-scale and extremely selfish removal of innumerable smokebox numberplates by persons unknown in the final years of steam, while locomotives still remained in service, this was a very sensible move! MIKE POPE

No 70013 is prepared at Lostock Hall shed, prior to running light to Manchester Victoria. Alongside is No 45110, which had been the rostered loco to take over from 8F No 48476 at Blackburn on 1L50, the RCTS special. However, someone in the BR hierarchy had then decreed that a standby loco should be sent to Manchester for 1T85, and the depot foreman had then selected the equally immaculate and fully lined-out No 45110. The latter, being sent light to Manchester, stood there all day doing nothing, before then returning to the shed – a complete waste of a superb locomotive. MIKE POPE

Lostock Hall fireman Jim Marlor prepares to leave shed with 8F No 48476, coupled to No 73069, running light to Manchester Victoria, where both engines will stand to await the arrival from London of the RCTS special. MIKE POPE

Driver Frank Herdman, a recent transfer from Stockport with the end of steam at 9B, is the booked driver for today's itinerary for No 70013. The loco has a busy day in front of it, for, at different times, it will later be seen at the head of both an LCGB and an RCTS special and, here, Frank is seen awaiting the two 'Black Fives' that will accompany him light-engine to Manchester Victoria. MIKE POPE

For some the time has already come. No 44878, never a popular engine at 10D, ever since it first arrived from Kingmoor, is totally ignored by the cleaners and has already been dumped on No 10 Road to await its inevitable destiny," PETER FITTON

For those who have laboured tirelessly through the night, before the very last steam chase begins, there is now time to cogitate on various successes achieved over the years. "Where will we be going tomorrow? What engines will we be cleaning?" is the previously much-exclaimed question that, even today, is still on most of our lips… for full realisation has yet to hit us. Nevertheless, there is no escaping the inevitable… there is nothing beyond The End. As crews arrive and prepare their allocated steeds, discarded ladders and tins of cleaning oil lie around and, some still with cleaning rags in their hands, our group mills around aimlessly, perhaps looking for *The Answer* in each other. But none is forthcoming. BOB CLARKE

Awaiting the arrival of their respective specials at Manchester Victoria on 4 August 1968, are John Burnett (driver, 73069), Jim Marlor (fireman, 48476), Harold Bolton (driver, 48476) and John Roach (fireman, 73069), all 10D Lostock Hall men. No 73069, last of the Standard 5MTs in service, failed to survive, the type being represented today by much earlier withdrawn examples. BILL ASHCROFT

Manchester Victoria
4 August 1968

Nos 48476 and 73069 stand in the banking engine road at Manchester Victoria, patiently awaiting the arrival of the RCTS special from London – a train that was eventually to end up running four hours late at one stage – but not for reasons attributable to the motive power. Being constructed at Swindon Works in 1945, No48476 was the final GWR-built standard gauge locomotive in BR service. One of the better 8Fs at Lostock Hall, sadly it was denied preservation. BILL ASHCROFT

Nos 70013, 44781 and 45305 arrive at Manchester Victoria, coupled-together light-engine from Lostock Hall. *Oliver Cromwell* and No 44781 will double-head the first steam leg of the LCGB special from London and then No 70013 will head the final stage of the RCTS special, which also originates in London. No 45305 will shortly run up to Cheetham Hill Carriage Sidings to collect the stock of a BR-organised special to the Liverpool and Southport areas. BILL ASHCROFT

My final steam turn

Former Lostock Hall fireman, Paul Tuson, recalls his own involvement in the events of 4 August 1968

The roster-board in the lobby at Lostock Hall shed, for the six specials on the final day, 4 August 1968, in fact originally did not show No 45305 allocated to the duty that it eventually came to work. The actual engine selected by the shed had been No 45407.

On Friday 26 July, a local enthusiast had arranged for No 45305 to be put on 6P16, the 18:15 Ribble Sidings-Carnforth. However, it was removed from that job and No 45212 appropriated instead. When asked for a reason why, it was advised that BR wanted it specially preparing for their special on 4 August and the '15 Guinea Special' the following weekend. No 45305 was, therefore, washed out during the coming week, thoroughly cleaned and put aside, doing nothing further all week.

Meanwhile, No 45110 had been the rostered loco to take over from No 48476 at Blackburn on 1L50, the RCTS special. However, someone in the BR hierarchy had then decreed that a standby loco should be sent to Manchester for 1T85, and whoever it was that was on duty at 10D had then selected the equally immaculate and fully lined-out No 45110. No 45110 being sent light to Manchester, stood there all day doing nothing, before returning to the shed.

In actual fact, No 45305's own booked job had originally been to pilot No 73069 on 1L50, the RCTS special, from Blackburn to Skipton and then back to Farington Junction. As 1T85 was the special organised by BR itself, very clearly, some strings must have been pulled at a high level of management, for some last-minute changes were made and the very unkempt (and uncleaned) standby engine, No 45407, came to be appropriated for 1L50.

On 4 August 1968, I was rostered at 10D Lostock Hall shed as the fireman to work on British Railways' own 'Last Days of Steam' tour (1T85). One of six enthusiasts' special trains running on this, the very last day of steam, my booked locomotive was to be one of the ubiquitous Stanier 'Black Five' 4-6-0s based here, No 45305, and my driver was to be no less than Vinny Commons, a colleague with whom I always found it a real pleasure to work. We booked on together at 10:49 and set to preparing our locomotive for its last moments of glory.

Always one of the externally visually more presentable of the 'Black Fives' on the shed's allocation, No 45305 was also one of the 13 locos that had just previously received a thorough polishing overnight by a group of clandestine engine cleaners.

Light engine to Manchester

All the other locos having departed during the morning to their respective rendezvous points, at around noon we coupled up to No 70013 *Oliver Cromwell* and another 'Black Five', No 44781, and the three of us then set off to proceed light engine towards Manchester. In so doing, the following weekend's event apart, we were probably the last departure from our shed of locomotives still in normal service.

Upon arrival at Victoria station, it was then up to Cheetham Hill carriage sidings, where we turned the engine, before coupling up to our stock waiting for us there. At around 13:45, we dropped the eight-vehicle ECS down the bank to pick up the patiently waiting passengers. The route our special was to take was Manchester (Victoria)-Eccles-Earlestown-Bootle branch-Birkdale-Southport (Chapel Street) avoiding line-Wigan (Wallgate)-Dobbs Brow and back to Manchester (Victoria).

Due to the exceptionally late-running of the RCTS special from London, which was forced to truncate its itinerary, the tour was the only one that day to cover the section of line where the original locomotive trials were held by the Liverpool and

Manchester Railway in 1829 and Parkside, where the Rt Hon William Huskisson MP was killed following the official opening ceremony in 1830.

Two footplate passengers

Upon drawing to a stand in Platform 11 Middle (the long one connecting Victoria with Exchange), we were joined by two footplate passengers, one being a local conductor-driver (my driver didn't know the road between Manchester and Liverpool, it not being a route normally worked by Lostock Hall men) and the other being a rather surly character whose identity we never did discover. Whether he was a footplate inspector, or perhaps some other higher-up official, was unclear, but he did, nevertheless, produce a valid footplate pass.

Right away

Anyway, at around 14:20 we got the 'right-away' and set off along the ex-LNWR line towards Liverpool. No 45305 was steaming well and we soon arrived at Olive Mount Junction, just short of Edge Hill, where our conductor alighted, to be replaced by another man to pilot us onwards towards Southport.

Having turned right at Olive Mount off the direct route down into Lime Street, we then proceeded along the, by now, goods-only line through Stanley and Tue Brook, to gain access near Bootle onto the Liverpool Exchange to Southport third-rail dc electric line.

Not unsurprisingly, there were a few surprised faces hereabouts, for the locals had long become accustomed to seeing EMUs - and not a steam locomotive and 'real' coaches! Indeed, no regular steam passenger workings had passed this way since the through Southport-Euston coaches, normally hauled by 2-6-4 tanks as far as Lime Street, had ceased running some years previously.

At Southport, our second pilot driver alighted, at last permitting the ever-patient Vinny to take over at the controls. We managed a quick dash over the racing stretch of mainly level track of the ex-L&Y route through Burscough Bridge, before coming to a stand at Wigan (Wallgate), in order to take a, supposedly, 10-minute stop for water.

Water supply problems

Having not been used for a while, the bag at the column was leaking badly and this operation was clearly going to take quite some time. Indeed, the tank was filling so slowly, that a decision was soon made to uncouple No 45305 from our stock and to cross over to the opposite platform to fill up there. This move proved to be a sensible one and, eventually, we were able to back up again onto the train.

It was at this point that our 'mystery' passenger assured me that he would 'put a fire on' for the steep climb up to Hindley, however he made no immediate move to do so and, after waiting for a while in anticipation, I eventually had to pick up the shovel to 'gas her up' myself. We had to set off shortly after this and, unfortunately, the fire that I had just put on hadn't had chance to burn through properly.

Nevertheless, off went Vinny, steam pressure and water level both falling steadily, as he hammered No 45305 up the bank with full regulator and probably 40 to 50 per cent cut-off. I decided to give the fire a good root through with the pricker to help it along. This produced plenty of black smoke and would be described in the *Handbook for Steam Locomotive Enginemen* as 'incomplete combustion', but it did produce the required effect and we did eventually top the bank, where the road fortunately eased to permit an uneventful run along the direct line via Crows Nest and Dobbs Brow Junctions back to Victoria and back to Lostock Hall.

For an outlay of a mere £2-0s-0d, passengers had been treated to almost three hours of steam haulage and after all the final photographs had been taken, we took the empty stock back up the bank to Cheetham Hill carriage sidings. As far as Vinny and I were concerned, the day was not quite yet over, for we still had to turn the loco again, before setting off light engine all the way back to Lostock Hall shed. As we booked off duty, so ended our last job with steam and, at the time, we thought the end had also come for No 45305. But that, of course, is quite another story!

The last day specials
4 August 1968

Having endured an extended station stop to take on water, the spotlessly cleaned and fully lined-out Class 5MT No 45305 storms up the bank out of Wigan Wallgate, on the former L&Y main line from Liverpool to Manchester, with the British Railways-organised 'Last Days of Steam' railtour of 4 August 1968. DAVID WHARTON

Lydgate Viaduct, on the Todmorden to Burnley route via Copy Pit. The first of two Stephenson Locomotive Society specials passes over, double-headed by 'Black Five' 4-6-0s No 44871 with driver Cliff Nelson and fireman John Fletcher and No 44894 with driver Ronnie Hall and fireman Tom Jones - an all Lostock Hall crewing! PETER FITTON

On the long slog from Bolton up to Waltons Sidings, No 45156 passes under the ornamental castellated bridge at Turton & Edgworth. This feature was incorporated into the design when the railway was constructed through the grounds of the adjacent Tudor manor house at Turton Tower. MAURICE BURNS

With an unusually matching set of blue and grey stock (perhaps borrowed for the day from Longsight depot and from its more usual workings to Euston) No 45156 passes over the western end of the local beauty spot at Entwistle Reservoir. DEREK HUNTRISS

A view from the opposite side of Entwistle Viaduct, taken much later in the day, No 70013 *Oliver Cromwell* and 'Black Five' No 44781 pass over with the LCGB special, composed of the unfortunately more usual (for the period) rake of mixed-livery stock, which caused so many problems for photography at this time. MAURICE BURNS

With Lostock Hall driver Ronnie Clough and fireman Joseph Booth both surveying the Manchester skyline for their final time behind steam, No 45156 makes a powerful departure for Blackburn and Carnforth past Salford with the 'GC Enterprises' tour. Curiously, the locomotive bears a Stockport Bahamas Locomotive Society headboard, of which the tour organiser was the ex-president. Notice also the, one-time very appropriate, 65B St Rollox shed plate, which had been applied as a finishing touch by the enthusiast who had cleaned this particular engine at Lostock Hall. PAUL RILEY

Working apparently flat-out, the second SLS special storms up the last few yards to Copy Pit summit and, once again, there is an all Lostock Hall crew on board. Motive power is also again 'Black Five' 4-6-0s, this time, No 44874 with driver John Commons and fireman Roy Haythornthwaite and No 45017 with driver Bill Wilson and fireman Billy Bamber. PETER FITTON

...gton and Blackburn, the second SLS special heads ...ownhill stretch of the Blackburn-Bolton line. Passing ...nger traffic) north curve, avoiding Bolton station, ...along ex-L&Y lines via Wigan towards the Liverpool

Heading up the hill in the opposite direction at nearby Turton, the RCTS special is in charge of yet another Lostock Hall crew. 8F 2-8-0 No 48476 with driver Harry Bolton and fireman Jim Marlor, double-heads Standard 5MT 4-6-0 No 73069 with driver John Burnett and fireman John Roach. PAUL RILEY

Literally yards further on Nos 48476 and 73069 are captured yet again, on the climb up to Sough Tunnel. The line climbs at gradients as steep as 1-in-73 for the first six miles out of Bolton and in earlier times many freight trains were banked along this stretch. PETER FITTON

'Black Five' No 44874 still bears its 1Z79 reporting number board from the SLS special that it has worked earlier in the day and one of the loco headlamps also remains in place. Arguably, there seems little point in removing them, for they won't ever be needed again! PETER FITTON

Above: The evening of 4 August 1968 and, for these three engines, it's now all over. With the onset of evening, very few observers remain to witness the bitter end and, by 22:00, there are 16 engines on shed at Lostock Hall that have been in steam today (not all, of course, having been used on line work). With only Nos 70013 and 45156 still awaited back from specials' duty, in the eerie light and shade cast by a few flickering yard lamps, serried ranks of now withdrawn engines stand, many still exuding their final ebbing signs of life. Standard 5MT No 73069 and 'Black Five' No 45017 are both Carnforth engines, but they will never see their home shed again. Likewise for 8F No 48493, which is a Rose Grove engine, its days are ended. The latter has a particular claim to fame in the history books, which, today, has gone almost unrecorded and totally unrecognised. No 48493 has worked the very last steam-operated yard shunt turn, having spent the earlier part of the day marshalling ballast wagons in the sidings at Farington Jct. PETER FITTON

'It's all over'

The last Standard 5MT No 73069 has just been placed on No 2 Road for the last time by Driver John Burnett. Not one of John's favourite classes of engine, this example was, nevertheless, in such good mechanical order that it survived the closure of five previous depots: Neasden, Kentish Town, Leamington, Patricroft and Bolton. Its Bolton maintenance legacy and external smartness brought about its selection from the 'also ran' BR 5MTs at Patricroft for several 'end of steam' specials, which was also probably the main reason why it ended its career at Carnforth – a depot never previously having had any of these on its allocation. Surprisingly, however, it was up to other earlier withdrawn members of the class to represent the type in preservation. PETER FITTON

A study of the front end of Lostock Hall's last working 8F 2-8-0, No 48476, its fire now having been thrown out, it is seen standing on No 2 Road, alongside the ex-LMS coach of the breakdown train in its usual location on No 1 Road. Once again, the loco lamps have not been returned to the stores along with the other footplate tools. PETER FITTON

On the evening of Saturday, 10 August 1968, No 70013 *Oliver Cromwell* is in steam and about to depart light engine for Lostock Hall, where it will spend the night, before continuing to Manchester Victoria the following morning, to await the arrival of 1T57.
MAURICE BURNS

 # Motive power arrangements
11 August 1968
Alan Castle

10 August 1968
Light engine Carnforth-Lostock Hall
Motive power: Class 7MT 4-6-2 No 70013 *Oliver Cromwell* (10A)
Footplate Inspector: Frank Watson

11 August 1968
Light engine: Lostock Hall-Liverpool Lime Street
Motive power: Class 5MT 4-6-0 No 45110 (10D)
Unknown crew
Light engines: Carnforth-Hellifield (reverse)-Carlisle
Motive power: Class 5MT 4-6-0 No 44871 (10A) & Class 5MT 4-6-0 No 44781 (10A) – double-headed. 44871 - Driver: Willie Pape (ex-Carlisle man) / Fireman: John Gorst (both of 10A) / Acting Loco Inspector: Frank Watson. 44781 - Driver: Charlie Wilson / Fireman: Jeff Beattie (both of 10A) / Loco Inspector: Bert Moore (Carnforth)

1T57 the British Railways-organised 'Fifteen Guinea Special'
Liverpool (Lime Street) to Carlisle and return: 10 coaches
Stage 1: *Liverpool Lime Street-Earlestown-Manchester Victoria*
Motive power: Class 5MT 4-6-0 No 45110 (10D)
Driver: Jack Hart (8A) / Fireman: Brian Bradley (8A)
Stage 2: *Manchester Victoria-Bolton-Blackburn Hellifield-Settle-Carlisle*
Motive power: Class 7MT 4-6-2 No 70013 *Oliver Cromwell* (10A)
Driver from Man. Vic to Blackburn: Unknown / Fireman: Tommy Gorman (Preston). Driver from Blackburn to Carlisle: Bob Grogan / Fireman: Raymond Watton. Guard: John Weal / Loco Inspector: Chief Inspector John Hughes

Stage 3: *Carlisle-Settle-Hellifield-Blackburn.*
Motive power: Class 5MT 4-6-0 No 44871 (10A) & Class 5MT 4-6-0. No 44781 (10A) – double-headed.
44871 - Driver: Norman Ashton / Fireman: Tony Helm / Loco Inspector: Chief Inspector John Hughes.
44781 - Driver: Ray Grimshaw / Fireman: David Greenhalgh / Loco Inspector: Bert Moore (Carnforth)
Stage 4: *Blackburn-Bolton-Manchester Victoria, Light Engine direct to Carnforth*
Motive power: Class 5MT 4-6-0 No 44871 (10A) & Class 5MT 4-6-0. No 44781 (10A) – double-headed.
44871 - Driver: Ted Fothergill (10A) / Fireman: Malcolm Thistlethwaite (10A) / Loco Inspector to Manchester: Chief Inspector John Hughes. 44781 - Driver: Jack Simpson (10A) / Fireman: Ian Thistlethwaite (10A) / Loco Inspector: Bert Moore (Carnforth)
Stage 5: *Manchester Victoria-Earlestown-Liverpool Lime Street*
Motive power: Class 5MT 4-6-0 No 45110 (10D)
Driver: Fred Smith (8A) / Fireman: Stephen Roberts (8A) / Loco Inspector: John Hughes.

Light engine: *Liverpool Lime Street-Wigan-Lostock Hall*
Motive power: Class 5MT 4-6-0 No 45110 (10D) Unknown crew
Light engine: *Carlisle-Settle-Hellifield- Blackburn-Lostock Hall*
Motive power: Class 7MT 4-6-2 No 70013 *Oliver Cromwell* (10A)
Driver from Carlisle to Blackburn: Bob Grogan / Fireman: Raymond Whatton / Acting Footplate Inspector: Frank Watson (Carlisle-Lostock Hall-Accrington)
Light engine: Loco went onto Lostock Hall depot for servicing and then straight to Norwich via Doncaster - Healey Mills crew Motive power: Class 7MT 4-6-2 No 70013 *Oliver Cromwell* (32A)

1T57 preparations Frank Watson BA (British Railways 1951-1970)

Upon reporting for duty at Preston Divisional Office on Monday 5 August 1968, I was given my duties as a temporary footplate inspector for the following week, which were mainly associated with the organisation and running of '1T57' the very last steam special to be operated by British Railways, which was to run from Liverpool Lime Street, via Manchester Victoria and Blackburn, to Carlisle and return on Sunday 11 August 1968. On Monday 12 August, I was to return to my normal duties of those as Train Crew Inspector at Accrington Diesel Depot.

This working became better known as the 'Fifteen Guinea Special', as this was the price for anyone who wanted the privilege of riding on the train. Due to the price, it was boycotted by many genuine steam enthusiasts - the cost being about a week's wage after stoppages for the average working man in 1968. This was probably the main reason that the ten-coach train was not a complete sellout, but left with about 50 empty seats for the 314-mile round trip. As both Lostock Hall and Carnforth sheds were shown on special notices to provide steam locomotives for 1T57, I had to check that both depots still had sufficient coal of the right quality in the hoppers for the allocated engines to be coaled-up.

According to the timings published in the Special Traffic Notices N1 and N2, 1T57 was booked to take water at Blackburn station and at Blea Moor in both directions, so I had to check with the outdoor machinery department that these supplies were still operative. To be on the safe side, I also personally visited both sites, but at Blackburn station, due to the design of the swing-type arm on the parachute-type column at the end of the platform, I could not reach the operating wheel without a ladder or a locomotive tender. With neither readily available, I was assured by the station staff that the column had been used the previous Sunday without any problems. As a back-up, I also checked that there was still a water supply in operation at Hellifield and then arranged for the water supply information to be made available to John Hughes, the Chief Footplate Inspector for the London Midland Region of British Railways, who was shown in the Special Traffic Notice to accompany 1T57 throughout its entire journey.

My own personal involvement with the running of 1T57 was more of a supporting role, as my first task was to ride with engine 70013 on Saturday night light engine from Carnforth to Lostock Hall. I left the engine in the care of the British Transport Police alongside D403, a diesel mixed traffic class that had now taken over most of the express passenger work on the West Coast Main Line. I then had to return to Carnforth, where I lodged in private accommodation with the family of a Carnforth fireman, having to be up reasonably early the following morning, to take two light engines to Carlisle via Wennington and Hellifield, as these were diagrammed to work 1T57 from Carlisle to Manchester Victoria.

Before leaving Carnforth at our booked time of 08:09, with engines 44871 and 44781, both engines were topped up with coal from the hopper. After ringing off the shed, there was still one unauthorised person on the footplate, who I had to request to leave before we departed. It was only later that I found out that this was no less than Doctor Beet, a well-respected preservationist of steam locomotives, who was actually in the process of purchasing one of the engines now diagrammed to work 1T57 from Carlisle to Manchester.

After taking water with both engines at Blea Moor, even though 1T57 was not due for another two-and-a-half hours, people were beginning to appear at strategic points at the lineside all the way to Carlisle. Arriving on time at Carlisle with the two light engines, these were then turned and topped-up with water. Prior to the arrival of 1T57, the Carnforth men had been relieved by two sets of Blackburn men, drivers Norman Ashworth and Raymond Grimshaw, with firemen Tony Helm and David Greenhalgh, all rostered to work 1T57 through to Blackburn. My next allotted task was to meet No 70013 on its arrival and then go light engine with it to Lostock Hall shed, via Hellifield and Blackburn, to service the engine before it set out on its final journey to Bressingham later that same evening.

Due to the problems he had encountered obtaining water at Blackburn, John Hughes was not a 'happy bunny' as he stepped down from the footplate upon arrival. Blackburn driver Robert Grogan and fireman Raymond Watton, both former Lower Darwen men, had worked 1T57 from Blackburn to Carlisle and were now rostered to take No 70013 light-engine to Lostock Hall, via Hellifield and Blackburn. I knew them both very well from my days as a Running Shift Foreman at Lower Darwen shed from 1963 to 1966. At Carlisle we were also joined on the footplate by a person from the railway museum at Clapham, London, who had the task of handing over the locomotive to its new owners on arrival at Norwich en-route to Bressingham.

On our departure from Carlisle, we followed 1T57 all the way to Blackburn. As Raymond Watton had already done a reasonable amount of work firing No 70013 from Blackburn to Carlisle over the 'Long Drag', I volunteered to fire the light engine back to Lostock Hall Shed. Unfortunately, by now the coal was way back in the tender and the fire was burning with a distinctly blue-ish tinge, a sure sign of clinker on the fire-bars, caused by a lack of primary air supply through the fire bed, or, to put it in layman's terms, the fire was knackered. (One would never guess that I had been a firing instructor!). Fortunately, No 70013 was equipped with rocker bar grates, so one could remove or lift the smaller one of the two catches holding the grates level and then gently rock them to and fro, which then caused just enough movement to break up the clinker a little and then allowed an increase of primary air through the fire bed, without allowing any of the fire to drop into the ash pan.

Even with our late start from Carlisle, we managed to arrive at Lostock Hall Shed at 19:16, just a few minutes before our booked time of 19:20. During the cleaning of the fire on the ash plant, a small piece of brick arch that had fallen onto the fire bed managed to wedge itself between the open grates as the fire was being cleaned. This meant that the rocking grates were wide open and could not be closed due to the obstruction, which we could not locate looking into the firebox from the footplate. If this problem could not be sorted out, then the engine would be a failure and unable to go to Bressingham later on that night. After about 10 to 15 minutes of feeling along each individual rocking grate with a long 'pricker', the obstruction was eventually located and prised out while the grates were being gently rocked to and fro.

While I was wrestling with my problems, John Hughes had been trying to regain time on the return trip to Liverpool with 1T57, but his attempts to pull back some time resulted in pulling back 5mins by Appleby, but then thwarted for a number of reasons, including coming to a complete stand for a half-minute at Wilpshire, this due to a block failure. After being re-manned at Blackburn, the two 'Black Fives', in an effort to regain time, made such a spirited effort up the bank to Darwen, that they set fire to the railway embankment and Darwen fire brigade had to be called out. So, one could say that steam did go out in a blaze of glory, but more likely a glorious blaze! A fireman, after dealing with the fire, commented unenthusiastically that he was glad to see the back of steam locomotives.

By the time the special train ran into Lime Street station it was only six minutes late, but the press still had a field day with their coverage the next day over British Railways' inability to run the last steam special to time despite the best efforts of the footplate crews and John Hughes, the Chief Footplate Inspector of the London Midland Region, to arrive back at Liverpool on time.

My next, more mundane, task was to depart from Lostock Hall Shed, at our booked departure time of 21:30 with No 70013, to proceed light engine via Blackburn, Accrington, Copy Pit and Hebden Bridge to Norwich, where it eventually arrived at midday on Monday 12 August. It was 18 August before the engine was finally hauled dead to Diss station, in order to be taken by road transport the last three miles to Bressingham. We now had a set of Healey Mills men on the footplate and I was booked to be relieved at Blackburn by a Footplate Inspector from the North Eastern Region. I stayed on the engine to Accrington station, where I alighted from *Oliver Cromwell* for the last time shortly after 22:00, after wishing the person from Clapham Museum a pleasant journey to Norwich.

Upon running into the station, I was astonished to see my wife and a family friend Jack Whalley waiting on the platform. Jack was a rail enthusiast who had been out during the day, watching 1T57 pass through Whalley station in both directions, before calling at our house later that night. He did not believe my wife when she told him that No 70013 and I would be returning through Accrington station at about 22:00 that night, so, leaving his wife babysitting my children, ran my wife Barbara down the station in his car just before 21:45. I still have that vivid memory in my mind of Jack kissing the tender of *Oliver Cromwell*, before she pulled out of the platform.

However, the real bonus for me was that I now had a lift home in his car, particularly as I had to be on duty at 07:00 the next morning at Accrington Diesel Depot, back in my own permanent position as Train Crew Inspector after a reasonably busy and tiring weekend.

1T57 – Aboard the train

11 August 1968

Steve Leyland

I'd never been an ardent railtour supporter (having been a passenger on only four between late 1965 and 1T57) because of cost and a devotion to 'normal service' steam. Though tempted by 1T57, I'd admittedly, baulked at the fare, but it was my mum who, surprisingly, persuaded me to 'lash out' and travel, because she knew what those years of following BR steam, to the 'nth degree', meant to me. I think her gesture was fuelled by relief that it was all over and a hope that her son would now begin to lead the life of a normal 19-year-old!

Lostock Hall shed proved to be the base for Sunday's tour engines. We went to have a look on Saturday morning, but after noting only Nos 45110 and 45305 (both 10D) newly fired, were ejected in no uncertain way! There'd doubtless been lots of enthusiasts, partly at a loose-end, trying to get round Lostock Hall that day and, by noon, the staff were clearly fed up with it all. Part of that very warm afternoon, I watched the summer Saturday go busily by at Preston station, then returned home (loco-hauled) to prepare for the 11th.

No train from Bolton on Sunday would have got me to Liverpool in time. My dad would, doubtless, have obliged with a lift, but it wasn't worth risking even the remotest chance of a delay or breakdown, with so much (let alone the 15 guineas!) at stake. So, I was there by train mid-Saturday evening.

Pictures of Lime Street, showing No 45110, simply adorned with its 1T57 board, the train seemingly hemmed in by countless onlookers filling every available inch of platform and more, yet kept tidily in check by a single visible policeman, are most easily brought to mind by most enthusiasts. My designated seat was at the train's very rear on that first leg to Manchester, so I quickly grabbed a RH drop window in the brake next to the engine.

BR had intended to cater for 470 passengers, but from the surprisingly varied reports that followed, 420 would seem to have been the sum total of tickets sold, but more of the press anon. One minute late, I made it, 5110 with its train of 10 coaches, 364½ tons net, began the very difficult cold start at 09:11, paced briefly, as intended, by the electrically hauled 09:10 to Euston. This pulled ahead quickly, as No 45110, after several slips, plugged away against the 1-in-93 to Edge Hill, attaining 14mph towards the top. It wasn't at all easy, but Jack Hart, the 61-year-old driver now passing close to his old shed would have known what to expect; 59mph followed a check at Edge Hill No 4, but six minutes had been lost to Rainhill, the first commemorative halt.

Cutting down that photographic stop to eight minutes among a sea of freely wandering spectators and passengers was a wonder challenged only by my joining them and returning to find my all-important window still free! On time away, 63mph preceded checks up to, and a halt at, Parkside, to commemorate the unfortunate fatality there in steam's infancy. Though 1T57 made no inroads into the new, but slight arrears, 5110 sounded in fine form chattering across Barton Moss, with such an even exhaust that it could have been a Caprotti. We were up to 63 before Patricroft, then a bad slowing after Eccles put the tour seven late into Victoria.

If we believe the shortlist of locos originally advised by BR, No 45110 had not been under consideration, unless, as I strongly suspect, No 45310 appeared only due to a misprint. Any other misplaced digit would have thrown up a non-existent or long withdrawn loco, thereby eliminating conjecture.

As the morning warmed up outside, I walked back to claim my premier window seat for the next 125¾ miles, immediately behind the engine, on the left and facing too! The generous half-hour allowance at Victoria, again with platforms crammed to the very edges, permitted No 70013 *Oliver Cromwell* to get away only a minute late, but the difficult Platform 14 start wasn't to the Pacific's liking. It slipped time and time again (17 on my recording), but once onto the straight, in true 'Belfast Boat Train' style, leapt ahead,

Liverpool Lime Street station on 11 August 1968. As departure time approaches, Stanier 'Black Five' No 45110, simply adorned with its 1T57 board, is seemingly hemmed-in by countless onlookers occupying every available inch of the platforms and more, yet kept tidily in check by a single visible BT policeman. PETER FITTON

comparatively. 44mph over Agecroft Jct fell to a steady 40 on to Farnworth, marginally improving before we threaded Bolton at close to the prescribed limit, having lost no further time.

I recorded the whole ascent from Bradshawgate Box to Walton's Sidings. The reason that my left arm ached considerably in the closing stages was the 21-minute duration of that climb, the features of which, to any 'first time southerners' would have been handsomely exaggerated. No 70013 started reasonably, but never behaved like a true Class 7 anywhere, in fact, and I can only presume either a persistent, but not serious, shortage of steam on the climb in question, or a degree of brake-drag'.

Maybe the valves were in need of attention, even. But, still, the engine remained entertaining, the 'Brit's' sharp, percussive blast never deserting it. From 23mph at The Oaks, we began to flag from Bromley Cross, really, experiencing a very gradual drop to 14mph at worst, just before Entwistle. Walton's Sidings stopped the train briefly and mysteriously, unless the cautious descent that followed was linked to some verbal message communicated to the crew. 1T57 nevertheless pulled into Blackburn on time, thanks to the unexacting schedule so far.

Due to difficulties watering, No 70013 had to come off the train for that purpose, delaying its departure by half an hour, to the delight of journalists waiting for an irregularity to pounce on.

After some curious playing about with the regulator in the tunnel, our driver wisely decided that a generous opening was best to produce the exciting staccato exhaust we heard so clearly on the climb to Cemetery Hill, surmounted at 36mph.

Since the first call at Walton's, just prior to midday, the stewards had experienced some problems in persuading those standing to sit down for lunch and clearing the tables of equipment for setting. It was good to see that the taking-in of the steam was uppermost in the

No 45110 with its train of 10 coaches weighing 364½ tons net, begins the very difficult cold start at 1-in-93 up to Edge Hill, attaining 14mph towards the top. As planned, the 09:10 to Euston has paced the train on departure, but the electrically hauled express has rapidly pulled ahead by the time that this picture is taken. DICK MANTON

minds of passengers other than me. The 'trimmings' on this tour were of little importance, personally, and I turned down the wine offered.

Sixty-four mph down through Langho helped a fairly swift run on to Hellifield and the 'Brit' had sustained 31mph up Rimington bank, again with a lot of gusto. We'd kept the booking from Blackburn, but water was also deemed necessary at Hellifield, though six minutes only were required for this. A very businesslike start to Long Preston (48mph) preceded an easing until Settle Jct, which could have been taken faster than at 58. At about this stage in the journey we were informed that the souvenir scrolls which were being given out, had not been pre-inscribed with the recipient's name, as intended, and would have to be self-signed.

Thankfully, for the few making tape-recordings from the open stock, unwanted sounds were kept to a minimum. The clinking of plates and the like could hardly be objected to and it even added a degree of authentic class, as the train settled down to 32-35mph on the long climb to Blea Moor, where, if I may juxtapose two parts of commentary from an LP record made of the event

soon after, "Even the lonely moorland that skirts the tracks at Ribblehead was crammed to the doors." Things did get a bit fraught in that locale personally, as I tried to cope with a tape wrap-round, log the run and have my lunch served (two hours after that first call), all at the same time.

It was a friend that later disclosed to me a 'disaster' of his own there. While I'd been struggling to disentangle the twisted tape, he, by the lineside had, in the excitement, forgotten to plug in his microphone!

It was indeed a glorious day for train-watching. Bare legs dangled from walls, even disused platform-edges and other vantage points, as the public turned out in force to wave and cheer us on our way. Morecambe secured the day's sunshine record of 13.2 hours, but it was no less summery elsewhere, even in those fells. Two thousand cars an hour were reported to have been entering Blackpool, but the few byways of Ais Gill were far more inconvenienced by perhaps a tenth of that.

We had been able to omit the booked water stop of five minutes at Blea Moor, but dropped 4mph in two minutes from that signalbox to entering the tunnel at 29mph. A photo-stop lined-up for Ais Gill was cut by five minutes too.

At least the journey continued to be remarkably free of engineering work for a Sunday and No 70013 managed unhindered progress from Ais Gill to Carlisle in 55 minutes. Top speeds of 75 at Ormside and 69 through Little Salkeld were still not fast enough, in view of our lateness and the 51-minute schedule, and we arrived 34 late.

The stop at Carlisle, more than halved to a quarter of an hour, took me unawares and still in my seat at what now was the train's rear. I was to blame and soon paid for my tardiness. Even a futile and largely obstructed walk through ten coaches and back looking for a free window didn't justify a 28-minute gap in my log almost to Culgaith!

The pair of 'Black Fives,' Nos 44781 piloted by 44871, were running very well. Emitting mostly a thin grey exemplary exhaust, they were clearly

Rainhill - 11 August 1968. A scene such as this would, in 2008, cause apoplexy in certain quarters! Given the sea of freely and aimlessly wandering spectators and passengers, it is little short of a miracle that the scheduled photographic stop is reduced to a mere eight minutes. PETER FITTON

In the open countryside on the original Liverpool & Manchester Railway, No 45110 leaves a short tunnel near Kenyon Village. DAVE RODGERS

Manchester Victoria. Fireman Brian Bradley has uncoupled No 45110 from the train and the loco now awaits the road to run up to Miles Platting to turn. Meanwhile, No 70013 *Oliver Cromwell* is backing on to the rear of the train. PETER FITTON

not to be trifled with, gaining five minutes to pass Appleby in just less than 40 at 60mph, after much speeding in the mid-60s. An unfortunate lapse to 36mph by Griseburn, ending the first 1-in-100 stretch, kept the Appleby to Ais Gill average down to a shade under 50mph, but a lively enough 52 over the summit made amends.

Quickly up to 70 over the crest, 1T57 swept round the curves approaching Garsdale at slightly less. Only a slack at Dent really prevented an on-time arrival at the Blea Moor water stop. This was extended to a photo opportunity too, but though descending to the ballast using the steps provided, I stayed at the train's rear, more peacefully obtaining an alternative view and also a shot of the signalbox, recalling, no doubt, the April afternoon spent therein more than two years previously and how so much more than the weather contrasted that day from this. We were away again at 16:21, breaking the thread of any such reverie.

Much less taxed in other departments than on the northbound run, I cheerfully accepted a spare 'high tea' salad, as well as my own, before Blackburn. The day's highest speed of 77mph came briefly approaching Settle, but the 17-minute lateness from Blea Moor was deviated from but a little through to Manchester. Our pair of 5MTs fell from 42mph through Whalley to 37 on the bank by Langho prior to a short signal stop at Wilpshire.

At Blackburn I walked forward again to tape our ascent to Walton's, being loath to let those classic uphill miles, of which I'd become so fond and familiar, slip by unrecorded, but window occupancy, as expected, prevented full absorption of the live event, to say the least. Through the early sunny evening we forged in the mid-30s, an urgent enough exhaust audible from one or both locos intermittently, until their exertions ceased at 31mph over the see-saw summit to which I never expected to return.

Uneventful was the rest of the running, with our double header, as the many familiar features on home ground were passed by, never to be seen again in quite the same way. Thoughts, until now largely distracted by goings on of the day spent steam hauled through town and country, began to turn to the significance of those diminishing miles.

1T57 halved the loco-changing allowance at Victoria to one of only seven minutes. This involved No 45110 coupling to our rear for the final (non-stop) stretch to Liverpool Lime Street. This time I couldn't be caught out by the slick operation!

The 4-6-0 began slowly, very slowly, but more sure-footedly than the Pacific, from Platform 12. It did feel as if the brake drag characteristics, real or imagined, had returned briefly. However, 5110 got away soon after, to hold very similar rates along the flat as it had that morning. A check before Newton we had, then the last highlight in sound with an energetic attack on the short but steep length of railway between St. Helens Jct and Rainhill.

As the lowering sun's rays of that beautiful summer's day played along and through the coach windows of our unnamed farewell train, they were metaphorically setting on so much more, a plain fact that few passengers, as 1T57 rolled its last miles into the city, were not deeply conscious of.

At a few seconds to 20:00, No 45110 came to rest at the Lime Street buffers. After collecting my

A view from 1T57 taken as the special arrives back at Manchester Victoria. Having returned from Lostock Hall after servicing and then turned on the Miles Platting triangle, No 45110 stands alongside Exchange Station, waiting to back onto the rear the special ready to return it to Liverpool Lime Street. The Lostock Hall crew are standing in front of the loco. Driver Ken Mason is on extreme left and fireman Dick 'Roger' Owen is third from left. PETER FITTON

belongings, I stood alone for some time opposite the familiar engine's smokebox, half lost to melancholy thought.

I still went home on the train from Liverpool, probably too late to catch *Flying Scotsman's* non-stop May ECML run on BBC TV (in colour). Maybe I'd shunned it in anticipation of continued inaccurate media representation.

There was plenty of that next morning, as people showed me four newspaper accounts of the 'Fifteen Guinea Special', two of which I'd

dismissed as 'rubbish'. Ill-informed statements such as confusing the day's mileage with the number of passengers were mixed with over emphasis on cost and the leaving behind of careless journalists at stops, which had been shortened to reduce the lateness they also criticised! The *Daily Express's* Alan Bennett at least combined dignity with some useful information in his account. "WHAT A GLORIOUS WAY TO END IT ALL" read the headline. Yes, it had been indeed!

On the 'Long Drag', No 70013 *Oliver Cromwell* is seen near Selside shortly before its scheduled stop at Ais Gill Summit, 1169ft above sea level. DAVE RODGERS

1T57 coasts effortlessly downhill over Smardale Viaduct, the highest viaduct on the S&C railway, towering 131ft over Scandal Beck and built entirely of grey limestone. Although not visible in this view, the trackbed of the closed Kirkby Stephen to Tebay line passes underneath the viaduct. TIM STEPHENS

 # 1T57 – From the lineside
11 August 1968 Alan Castle

The very last two regular BR standard gauge steam-hauled passenger service trains having departed, within minutes of each other, from adjacent platforms of Preston station on the evening of 3 August 1968, there were six special passenger and a solitary ballast working the following day that provided the final duties with steam for many of the crews at my local depot, 10D Lostock Hall.

THAT, as far as most ardent followers of steam in the late 1960s were concerned, really was THE END – a fact that had, indeed, been so poignantly proclaimed on the headboard of our shed's No 45318, which I had photographed, surrounded by massive crowds, standing at the buffer-stops of Liverpool's Exchange station the previous evening. After nearly a century and a half of loyal service of steam to the nation, it was all over – there would be no more! Not REAL steam, anyway.

Following hot on the heels of the announcement of a firm date for the death knell for the last three existing steam sheds, feelings were already running high in some quarters when it was not too long before the news also emerged that, despite nothing at all being planned for the redundant footplate crews themselves, the BRB

had made the incredulous further disclosure that it was to organise a high profile final event after all, this to occur a mere seven days after the disposing of literally hundreds of its loyal steam men, many of whom had devoted their lives to the railways. Some schools of thought considered the insensitive timing to be in extremely bad taste, but whatever the pros and cons of any reasoned argument, certainly such an occasion would somewhat tone-down or divert away from public awareness some of the more embarrassing aspects of how the steam infrastructure and its personnel did actually come to be disposed of.

Many critics of the plans became quite incensed, developing arguably jaundiced views that in all of this the railway societies in particular had perhaps received a raw deal or been cheated in some way. Whether a blatant display of one-upmanship or not, it was also contended that the BRB had taken unfair advantage in making such a move. Potentially, '1T57' came to present a real threat to carefully-made plans to operate the 4 August 'Last Day' specials (which, technically now, wouldn't be operating on the 'last day' after all!). Although, for very valid operational reasons, just about every tour organiser in previous months had been permitted only to use

steam on a severely restricted number of routes (these, essentially, within the environs of Lancashire), the major selling-point for this one was that the final working would traverse that 'Jewel in the Crown' of lines – the Settle & Carlisle Railway – AND in each direction - AND with steam all the way!

In an attempt to place a more-balanced perspective to any argument, others pointed out, perhaps unconvincingly, that surely, ANY steam action must be welcome to a steam enthusiast and, even though we all had a love/hate relationship with BR at some stage during the closing years of steam, it was, after all, trying to run a business and at a profit.

Nevertheless, whatever direction one's views tended to favour, it was an inescapable fact that, in 1968, £15.15s.0d - or 15 guineas - the asking price for a ticket to ride on the train - was more than the weekly wage of many working men. It was this aspect above all else that caused many also to accuse BR of unfair profiteering – despite the undoubtedly high costs involved in setting up such an event. But, conversely, as a public relations exercise, again surely, would not such an expense for the railway be a mere drop in the ocean in the general scheme of things? Why, indeed, DID it have to be so expensive?

Many exclaimed – with more than an element of justification – that the event was clearly a jaunt for the more affluent, or even for 'those with more money than sense'. Certainly, it was a fact that many high-ranking BR managers and BRB members were known to have been aboard and '1T57' did also come to earn a place in the history books not as 'The Final Steam Train', but more so under the unfortunate sobriquet, 'The Fifteen Guinea Special'. In that particular context, as an aside, the fact that there were about 50 seats that did go unsold on the day might have intimated something.

From what we read today, BR all along seemed to have decidedly mixed feelings about its initiative, but then it had spent the previous few years systematically purging the network of steam power and, of course, there were a number of individuals on the Board who were known to be vehemently anti-steam. Notwithstanding all of that, it was also an undeniable fact that some considerable effort had been put into the 'behind-the-scenes' organisation and planning, in order to ensure that the event really turned out to be a success in the end.

The major issue was that five operational steam locomotives had to be retained on the books until week-ending 17 August 1968. This of course, was merely a technicality, for neither before nor after the event, were any of these to be permitted to perform any other duties. But it was all the more fortunate that neither Lostock Hall nor Carnforth motive power depots had completely closed on 5 August and particularly insofar as the coaling and watering facilities were still in-situ and operational, along with enough personnel to perform the tasks to be required of them.

Behind the scenes, special posters headed 'British Rail Runs Out Of Steam', had already been distributed and now special commemorative tickets and brochures were being printed, with restaurant car staff being rostered to work overtime on a Sunday to serve the at-seat service of lunch, high-?tea and other refreshments.

Resulting from the various light-engine movements of the previous Sunday evening, of those five engines still in service, 'Black Five's Nos 45110 and 45305 were sat at Lostock Hall and sister engines Nos 44781 and 44871 along with Britannia No 70013 Oliver Cromwell were at Carnforth.

On Saturday 10 August, No 70013 was lit up again and during the evening, following completion of all the necessary checks, the Pacific started to make its way light-engine to Lostock Hall, where it would again be coaled, watered and made ready to depart once more the following morning. The two 'Black Fives', Nos 44781 and 44871, were also lit-up during the day, in order to play their own later roles in the activities.

Fortuitously, perhaps with the hindsight gained the previous Sunday, two engines had been prepared by the steam-raisers at Lostock Hall. Although the fully lined-out and immaculate No 45305 had all along been the preferred machine of choice, it was soon observed that the fire-grate had fallen in, causing stand-by No 45110 (equally well-presented and in lined-out livery), to be rostered. In the gathering gloom, these two were soon joined by Oliver Cromwell and, surrounded by lines of other now long cold and

Journey's end - the border citadel of Carlisle. No 70013 awaits detaching from the train. Arrival at being some 30min late, the station-time is cut down to about 15 minutes and 'Black Fives' Nos 44781 and 44871 are already backing onto the other end ready for 1T57 to retrace its route back to Liverpool.
PETER FITTON

lifeless hulks, stood awaiting their final hours of glory and the coming opportunity to earn their places in the history books.

And so it was that, at 05:38 the following morning, No 45110 set out light-engine with a Preston crew, heading via Wigan for Edge Hill Depot, where it arrived at 07:20. At 08:36, another Preston crew moved No 70013 off shed heading in the direction of Manchester, arriving at 10:00. Over at Carnforth, at around the same time and coupled together, Nos 44781 and 44871 were slowly backing off-shed to set out towards Hellifield, where they would reverse direction in order to run northwards to Carlisle. The Special Traffic Notices of the period indicate that although the West Coast Main Line over Shap had been closed the previous weekend, it was open on this date. It is, therefore the more curious that the light-engine movements this day did not run over Shap.

The driver of No 44781 was Charlie Wilson, his fireman was Jeff Beattie and they were accompanied by loco inspector Bert Moore (all three being Carnforth-based men). On No 44871, was driver Willie Pape (an ex-Carlisle man) and fireman John Gorst (both of Carnforth)

with acting footplate inspector Frank Watson (from Accrington MPD).

Meanwhile, at 'centre-stage' back in Liverpool, electric No E3083 was soon dropping the 10 coaches of very mixed-livery empty stock down the 1-in-93 into Lime Street station and passengers beginning to present their commemorative tickets at the barrier in order to board. In light of a shortfall in bookings, one vehicle was deleted from the originally proposed 11-coach set. No 45110 had already been waiting at Edge Hill for half an hour and, amid huge crowds lining the platform ends watched over by a solitary BTC policeman, now slowly backed onto the other end.

Having coupled-up and now crewed by Edge Hill driver Jack Hart and fireman Brian Bradley, departure was but a single minute after time at 09:11, and, with some initial rear-end assistance from E3083, No 45110 slowly set out up the incline with its 364½ tons to head for Carlisle. There being a number of high-ranking BR managers and BRB members on board, apart from the fact that the event would, undoubtedly also be closely followed by the media, the loco inspector accompanying the train was no less

Travelling at 50mph, high on the valley side past Mallerstang Common, Carnforth's 'Black Fives' Nos 44871 and 44781 climb with 1T57 on the final stage to Ais Gill Summit. With the roadway far below, this is one of the remoter stretches of track, but close to where the unfortunate tragedy of September 1913 caused the deaths of 14 passengers, when a southbound express passed a signal at danger and collided with the rear of a stationary train.
DEREK HUNTRISS

One thing was for sure, it was by no means certain that the way north would finally become clear until at least the return working had passed and, as about 60 of us had a prior appointment to partake afternoon tea at the Temperance Hotel in Kirkby Stephen, most turned round to make the enormous (but, in the circumstances, faster) detour via Garsdale and Sedbergh. Here, the celebrated Ford Zephyr Mk 1 of Paul Riley (mentioned in an earlier chapter) beats a hasty retreat! ALAN CASTLE

than John Hughes, Chief Inspector for the British Railways London Midland Region and this gentleman was to supervise operations from one or other footplates throughout the day.

1T57 was to cover 314 miles during its 10¾ hour journey and special stops for the benefit of photographers were made during the first stage at Rainhill, where the original 'locomotive trials' were held by the Liverpool and Manchester Railway in 1829, and at nearby Parkside, where the Rt Hon William Huskisson MP, was killed in an accident following the opening ceremony of the Liverpool and Manchester Railway on 15 September 1830.

In order to witness such a uniquely historic event, crowds lined the trackside at both locations. Prominent in the background of most photographs taken at Parkside, was the shining Huskisson memorial. An absolute contrast was evident in early 2008, the monument all but forgotten and with heavily overgrown undergrowth and trees almost obscuring it from view.

Upon arrival at Manchester Victoria, some six minutes behind time, No 45110 left the train and, there now being no operational steam facilities remaining in the Manchester Division, it had to run light back to Lostock Hall shed for servicing. No 70013 was waiting and backed onto the other end of the train to take it forward for the remainder of its journey, a generous 25 minute station allowance permitting an on-time departure. The route now lay via Bolton, Blackburn, Hellifield and Settle, and thence over the 'Long Drag' to Carlisle. The driver working the stage to Blackburn was a Preston man, Harold Bolton, with fireman Tommy Gorman and the guard was John Weal. As 1T57 passed the sidings at Agecroft Power Station, one of the CEGB RSH 0-4-0 saddle-tanks was in steam and whistling its own farewell.

Assurances having been provided during the previous week by Blackburn station staff, that platform-end watering facilities were still in full working order, proved to be ill-founded and, upon arrival, the Britannia now had to be removed from the train in order to access a much faster-running supply nearby. This unexpected additional movement caused a massive delay, however, and Settle Junction was passed some 36 minutes adrift. The Blackburn crew now in control, driver Bob Grogan and fireman Raymond Watton, now found themselves needing to make up some time, and a decision was made to omit the water-stop scheduled to occur in the loop at Blea Moor.

The trip had clearly been well-publicised and, at the lineside, it seemed if the entire population of the North of England (and elsewhere) had turned out to bid their farewells. Blackpool on a Bank Holiday weekend was nothing on this! Cars were parked erratically absolutely everywhere, station platforms and line over-bridges packed with humanity, even the sheep presumably no longer felt safe! We joined in the mêlée. Surveying the number of cars jam-packed right under the arches (and in the shot), the view of Ribblehead Viaduct from the slopes of Whernside might have suggested that a new Battymoss branch of Tescos had just opened and that everything was free for the day!

We moved on, hoping for a little more solitude higher up and further from civilisation. Hopeless! Cars and people were everywhere - the Sunday motorist brigade was out in force and driving at its usual pedestrian pace regardless of the urgency of others! Cresting the hill on the narrow, winding 'Coal Road' above Dent station, we came upon that never-to-be-forgotten vista of absolute gridlock. Bedlam! Very clearly, we were going to make no further progress whatsoever for

Shortly afterwards, and within yards of the summit, the train reaches the head of the beautiful Eden Valley and crosses over the 75ft high Ais Gill Viaduct, one of the most photographed locations on the whole Settle & Carlisle line. MAURICE BURNS

a while in that direction, so, hastily abandoning our vehicle, we made directly across the boggy moorland in the direction of the former water-troughs. Our mad dash being somewhat hastened by the chime-whistle soon heard in the far distance, a somewhat unsatisfactory 'grab-shot' was the best that could be obtained. (Nevertheless, no-one else was in the picture!)

For passengers, there was a planned lineside photographic stop alongside the isolated signalbox at Ais Gill Summit. Word of this had got out, however, and the location being, at 1169ft above sea level, the highest point on any main line in England, it proved to be a magnet for spectators. Those that had arrived early, now causing massive traffic jams on the narrow B6259, literally swarmed across the tracks and prevented any further chance of photography. It really was a case of the best shot being one of the crowds, not despite them – oh, and there might have been a train in there somewhere!

Still running late, a decision was made to cut seven minutes from this brief sojourn and, as soon as the tracks had been safely cleared, No 70013 proceeded upon its way. Long after its departure, however, the highway alongside remained totally blocked with stationary traffic and the AA and RAC were going to be busy for hours rescuing numerous vehicles that had become bogged-down in the soft verges, or had totally expired through overheating in the queues. One thing was for sure, it was by no means certain that the way north would finally become clear until at least the return working had passed and, as about 60 of us had a prior appointment to partake in afternoon tea at the Temperance Hotel in Kirkby Stephen, most turned round to make the enormous (but faster) detour via Garsdale and Sedbergh. In retrospect, looking at the photos I did get, maybe that was where I should have headed in the first place! After all, I did already possess far happier memories of the 'Long Drag' along with the photographs to support these.

Perhaps the most vivid memory that many of us might retain of that sultry afternoon may well have been the impromptu football match between the North Yorkshire Moors Railway and the Severn Valley Railway that occurred on a far from level stretch of moorland immediately above the southern portal of Birkett Tunnel!

Arrival at Carlisle was some 33min late at 15:29, but by cutting the station time down to about 15 minutes, some of the lateness came to be reduced and, now with Nos 44781 and 44871 at the head, 1T57 set out again to retrace its route back to Liverpool. The driver of No 44871 was Norman Ashton and the fireman Tony Helm with Chief Inspector John Hughes accompanying them. Aboard No 44781 were driver Ray Grimshaw and fireman David Greenhalgh, with footplate inspector Bert Moore.

These Preston crews had travelled up to Carlisle 'on the cushions' on the morning Manchester-Glasgow (1S45). With two engines in perfect mechanical condition, along with the sultry conditions that afternoon, very little exhaust was evident as the train bowled along at something approaching 50mph all the way to Ais Gill Summit.

Cromwell returned light-engine some 15min behind the train, heading to Lostock Hall for servicing. Still crewed by driver Grogan and Fireman Watton with acting Footplate Inspector Frank Watson, these men worked the engine through to Blackburn. After 1T57 had passed on

In a scene is dominated by the imposing masses of Simon Fell and Whernside, a scheduled water-stop at Blea Moor, one of the few remaining operational water-columns on the Settle & Carlisle, is extended to a photo stop, this ably superintended by a mere two BT police officers and a single lookout man. Blea Moor is home to one of the loneliest of Britain's signalboxes lying some ¾ mile from the nearest road adjacent to open moorland, where it bears the brunt of inclement winter weather. PETER FITTON

Having traversed the picturesque Ribble Valley line from Hellifield, a crowd of young admirers gather to witness Nos 44871 and 44781 joining the East Lancashire line at Daisyfield Junction, on the approach to Blackburn. Most of what can be seen here, both on the skyline and at the lineside, having been swept away during the course of the intervening years, one of the most significant changes today is the intrusive and intensely unsightly high-security fencing that now deters youthful trespassers such as these. Nevertheless, it has to be emphasised that no children were harmed during the taking of this photograph. PETER FITTON

its way, those few who lingered for a while on the hillsides in the vicinity of Mallerstang Common - perhaps reflecting upon the fact that they really had just witnessed the end of an era - could not help but to notice just how insignificant the Britannia appeared, as it almost silently passed through the glorious valley in the hazy afternoon sunlight. Dramatic scenery certainly, but without a steam engine working hard against the gradient, not even the noisiest of diesels could ever come even close to exuding the atmosphere. Most of us thought this was our last time here, we wouldn't return. Many didn't.

No 70013 took on coal and water at Lostock Hall as planned, after which it departed at 21:30, running to Doncaster shed via Blackburn, Copy Pit, Todmorden and Wakefield, now with a Healey Mills crew and a Leeds locomotive inspector. Although this movement was supposed to be a secret, we all knew that the locomotive was en route to Bressingham Gardens for preservation.

For the Blackburn-Bolton-Manchester Victoria leg and, afterwards, to return the light engines back to Carnforth, on No 44871 driver Ted Fothergill (of 'Belfast Boat Express' fame) took over.

He was accompanied by fireman Malcolm Thistlethwaite, one of Carnforth's celebrated Thistlethwaite brothers. The other brother, Ian was also present, firing No 44781 for Carnforth driver Jack Simpson and accompanied by loco inspector Bert Moore.

For the final stage, onwards from Manchester

Victoria, via Earlestown, to Liverpool (Lime Street), No 45110 had leisurely returned from coaling and watering at Lostock Hall and now with Lostock Hall's driver Ken Mason and fireman Dick 'Roger" Owen in charge, set off running only about five minutes behind booked time. In no time at all, the final 30 miles or so were rattled off and, as the 'Fifteen Guinea Special' arrived at its destination at 19:59 some 9 minutes behind schedule, the sun was setting literally on the train and figuratively on the very end of an era. People everywhere were not quite so merry.

After the ECS had been removed at Lime Street, No 45110 lingered at the buffer stops of No 5 platform for some time, as though reluctant to depart the scene, finally moving very slowly out before a strangely silent throng of observers. As it drew away, fireman Roger Owen shouted, "No more dirty hands!" The engine returned light directly to Lostock Hall, withdrawal from service and, as believed at the time would inevitably occur, the last journey in convoy to the scrapyard.

Ironically, although 1T57 may very well have been the last train to be worked by a British Railways-owned steam locomotive, it wasn't the last steam locomotive to leave Lime Street – indeed only a few weeks were to pass before No 4472 *Flying Scotsman* also came to depart, on 26 October and, more importantly perhaps, also heading for Carlisle! It was to be many more years before something like that would happen again – but happen again it would!

Rose Grove, August 1968. With connecting rods neatly tied to their running-plates, rows of withdrawn 8Fs await their final journeys from which there will be no return. MIKE TAYLOR

"Perchance it is not dead... but sleepeth"

Alan Castle

After 4 August 1968, officially no further steam movements over BR metals occurred (apart from, that is, those in connection with the following weekend's 'Fifteen-Guinea Special'). Off the record, however, that was not quite the case. It has, nevertheless, taken 40 years to finally dispel some of the myths of 'ghost' steam happenings that emanated from all three of the final depots, the tales of some of which are still being told today and, of which, many grow ever taller as the years go by.

Doubtless, there were a number of clandestine happenings that, essentially, had to be just that, for fear of being halted should the upper echelons of management have got wind of them. That being the case, some, in fact, went totally unrecorded anywhere. Notwithstanding that, those detailed below definitely did happen.

One such seldom-reported steaming occurred on Thursday 8 August and some four days after the end of steam. At Rose Grove shed (which, at the time, was still open for diesels), Stanier 8F No 48773 was lit-up again by driver Winston Hartley and moved around the yard for watering and coaling, in preparation for a light-engine journey to Bescot and thence onwards to Bridgnorth, Severn Valley Railway. Unfortunately, however, management, in the shape of Preston Control, got wind of the plans and the engine never got beyond the shed limits. Control reminded Rose Grove that there was now a ban in place preventing any further steam

locomotives operating over BR tracks. No 48773 was, therefore, placed safely back inside the shed, with the instruction that its connecting rods were to be removed to prevent any further recurrence. Some time later, on 13 September, the 8F did move again, and did reach the SVR by rail, but this time it was towed by a diesel to Tyseley and then on to Bewdley.

Regardless of the official edict, some shed-masters and managers became quite adept at bending the rules … if only to make life easier for everyone. Well outside the jurisdiction of Preston Control, on 24 August, the now privately-owned 'Black Five', No 45428, journeyed light under its own steam from Leeds Holbeck shed to its new home at Tyseley. It had spent almost a year since withdrawal awaiting such a move and, still bearing its tangerine-painted 55A shed plate, it was seen that day taking water in Derby station.

On 20 September 1968, the probably deliberately sparse information available today suggests that another hush-hush move occurred in moving Standard 5MT No 73050 in steam from Manchester to Peterborough. The Rev Richard Paten had purchased the, then sole preserved member of the class for £3,000, its scrap value. His intention being to display it on a plinth outside the local Technical College, ultimately the locomotive was found to be in such good condition that there was resistance to this idea and it eventually found a home on the Nene Valley Railway. On 15 November 1968, Jubilee No (4)5596 *Bahamas* worked in steam from storage at Bury electric car sheds to its

new home at the Dinting Preservation Centre.

There were other movements of main-line locos by rail that year, these including several 'Black Fives'. No 45025 went from Carnforth to the Hunslet Engine Co in Leeds and then to its first home on the Keighley & Worth Valley line, No 45110 went from Lostock Hall to Ashford and No 45212 from Lostock Hall to Keighley. During the week between the 4th and the 11th of August, No 44888 was also sent to Derby for a BR open day there. It was still there three months later, but eventually quietly disappeared for scrap. All of these movements were 'out-of-steam' and behind diesels. However, much later, in travelling back from Ashford to Bridgnorth, on 17 August 1970 at Bescot Depot, the coupling-rods were replaced back onto No 45110 and the engine worked forward from Bescot in 'light steam'- in fact pushing the accompanying Class 40. Once on the Severn Valley line, it might be added that, with pressure rapidly falling on the final stretch downhill to Bridgnorth, the tender contained nothing but spare fire-bars and fresh air, all the coal having been used up!

The following year, another example of an in steam movement was that of the, now preserved, J27 0-6-0 No 65894 from the NCB works at Philadelphia to Thornaby MPD in 1969. The Divisional Maintenance Engineer, the late John Bellwood, not only drove it down the coast line through Hartlepool but, in order to turn the engine, he then took No 65894 over the Tyne bridges into Newcastle Central station in full daylight, to the amazement of waiting passengers!

In October 1969, following its first restoration, NELPG members also steamed Q6 No 63395 at Thornaby depot and ran the loco up and down the yard, within shed limits, but on BR tracks, and even turning it on the depot's roofless roundhouse turntable several times for photographs. Indeed, the engine then moved to Grosmont on 25 June 1970 towed by a diesel but, once again, in steam. There were one or two more instances of movements by 'industrials' over BR metals, particularly NCB locos. The Lambton 0-6-2 tanks Nos 5 and 29 from Philadelphia for example, made various journeys towed in light steam, before eventually arriving on the North Yorkshire Moors Railway.

Of course, there were numerous other workings over closed lines, where a preservation society was still negotiating for purchase, for example from Bewdley to Hampton Loade on the Severn Valley line. IOW O2 0-4-4T No W24 Calbourne ran under its own steam on the island during a stock move, over then still BR tracks, in about 1970. One thing is for certain, the publishing of this article will, doubtless, reveal many other previously unreported happenings that, in some cases, blatantly occurred very much behind the backs of authority!

Although the demise of BR steam had long been forecast, when the end actually came in August 1968, many of those involved with railways felt a distinct sense of unreality - it being extremely difficult to comprehend that steam really had ended – one week it was there, the next week it had gone. There was, of course, still industrial steam at work in a number of locations, and a few more engines soldiered on hauling engineering trains for London Transport, but, at most of these locations this, too, was in rapid decline. Remarkably, however, some survivors remained at work into the early 1980s – even on NCB lines. In addition, it should not be forgotten that, although BR had finished with standard-gauge steam working, for some years to come it would retain the 1ft 11½in gauge Vale of Rheidol tourist railway in West Wales, running from Aberystwyth to Devil's Bridge.

After 1T57 had departed from Carlisle on 11 August 1968, many of those who turned out to be involved in that sad occasion clearly felt that it really now was all over. Nevertheless, as came to transpire, it was only just over a month later that, on 26 October, steam in the form of *Flying Scotsman* materialised in the border city. Alan Pegler, owner of the preserved Gresley Pacific

The scene at Lostock Hall on 10 August 1968. There are at least 25 withdrawn locomotives in this view.
PETER FITTON

since 1963, had adeptly negotiated an agreement with British Railways that assured that No 4472 would be kept employed on main line excursions well into the early 1970s and a special that had also originated in Liverpool, worked to Carlisle, this time over Shap Fell. Not only that, but on 1 June 1969, *Scotsman* headed yet a further special over Shap to Carlisle, this time starting out from its birthplace at Doncaster.

Outside the North West, there were other specials planned for No 4472, of course, but these occasional forays constitute the early beginnings of the main-line preservation era and do not really play a part in this account.

The last loco to leave Rose Grove in March 1969 was No 44899, a former 12A Carlisle Kingmoor loco transferred there in December 1967. It was collected in a convoy, including Lostock Hall's Nos 45444 and 45318, that had called en-route to Draper's scrapyard in Hull. The shed continued to be used as a stabling point for diesel locomotives for several months, until this facility was transferred to a part of the remaining sidings area near the station. The depot building soon became derelict and was finally demolished in 1973, the site today being unrecognisable, as part of the M65 motorway now crosses it.

The situation over at Carnforth probably needs little further explanation. As at Rose Grove, diesels continued to use the premises here, until 31 March 1969, the remaining steam engines stored in the sidings gradually being towed away over the coming months. Several others had been purchased with a view to them being used on the hopefully soon-to-be preserved Plumpton Junction to Windermere (Lakeside) branch, being stored meanwhile at the depot. From Christmas 1968, two shed roads were leased for this

purpose and as many as possible were then moved under cover. Following closure, the entire site was handed over - by now in sadly run-down condition - to a company that eventually became 'Steamtown Carnforth'. Although for many years an excellent collection of motive power was maintained here, at times faithfully exuding the air of an LMS loco shed, the Lakeside Railway eventually went its own way and some of the locomotives went with it. Others went elsewhere, but Steamtown, however, had been born, and was to come to be an important asset to the railway preservation movement, before it too finally closed in 1997. Following this, the site was taken over by the West Coast Railway Company, which still uses it as a maintenance depot, albeit with visitors no longer being accommodated other than on rare occasions.

At Lostock Hall, during this period, the rows of withdrawn and abandoned steam locomotives outside the shed, awaiting their final call for the cutter's torch, made visitors feel like they were intruding upon a mass grave. It was, in fact, to be another nine months or so after the closure to steam, before the final few went their way, with Nos 44894, 45017 and 45388 believed to have been the very last to leave – from any depot – on 28 April 1969.

However, as one of the photographs shown here so graphically depicts, for one withdrawn 'Black Five', a final job awaited. The plans for this, unfortunately, included a bizarre conclusion. The 'Fifteen-Guinea Special' celebrity, No 44781 ended its existence in the limelight in September 1969, as a major film-prop - ostensibly in the Malayan jungle during the state of emergency there in the early 1950s - but in actuality somewhat nearer to home, at Bartlow on the, then recently-closed, branch-line to Audley End in deepest Essex.

Having been sold to Columbia Pictures, No 44781 was disguised as a tank engine (most curiously, without a chimney!) for a scene in the black comedy, *The Virgin Soldiers*. The plans calling for the train, it was ostensibly hauling, to be deliberately derailed and 'wrecked' and, after the cameras had done their job, even though at least one expression of interest in preservation was made, recovery then proved to be prohibitively expensive and the loco was broken-up on site. Sadly, apart from its historical associations with the final steam passenger train of all, No 44781 would have been the only long-wheelbase Walschaerts valve-gear 'Black Five' to have survived.

Back at Lostock Hall, even after these last few rusting relics of a past age had departed and the weeds started to grow between the abandoned

531.03 (alias No 44781) derailed in the Malayan Jungle near Bartlow, Essex. September 1969. TIM STEPHENS

In the final three years of existence, no less than nine locomotives ending their days on 10D's allocation, found their way into preservation. 'Black Five' No 45110 saw purchase from an unlikely source, by members of the Flairavia Flying Club, based at the former RAF Biggin Hill airfield in Kent. The engine soon moved to Ashford for storage before ending up on the Severn Valley Railway. DAVID HARDMAN

The shedmaster's office, Lostock Hall, a typical feature of ex-L&Y depots - and former domain of Mr Mr Harold Sedgbeer. In 1988, this part of the structure, covering the offices, workshops and stores, still retained the typical L&Y 'sawtooth' roof, the remainder having been totally rebuilt in 1954. TONY GILLETT

The roof having been destroyed in a fire some time earlier, and the rails also having been removed, demolition has commenced on the remainder of the structure in this view looking down No 7 road in January 1990. For some however, the ghosts of long-vanished Aspinall, Barton-Wright and Hughes machines still haunt the eerie emptiness. BOB GREGSON

The scene shortly after demolition. An overall view taken from Watkin Lane, surveying the scene by the site of 'Bowden's Gap'. Access problems preventing development, there is currently no other practical use for the site (although it will later be taken over as a gypsy encampment and even, at one stage, by a travelling circus), the mere outline of the concrete walkways between the filled-in inspection pits today still bears silent witness to the age of steam, albeit now through a rapidly-advancing forest of ever-encroaching vegetation. BOB GREGSON

sidings, the ghosts still lingered. Shortly before all the steam-age infrastructure was swept away, Bob Gregson was one of the few who cared enough to eventually came back to say his own farewell to 24C/10D.

Lostock Hall Revisited – a closing tribute by Bob Gregson

Diesel locomotives continued to use Lostock Hall depot until 1973, when all motive power was transferred to the north of Preston Station, and it was then used as a Carriage & Wagon repair depot, following the closure of the old C&W Works at nearby Todd Lane South. The Preston breakdown train and maintenance vehicles were also still based here, until a fire destroyed a section of the roof covering six of the eight roads. The two remaining roads were partitioned-off from the roofless section and, there, the business of vehicle maintenance continued up until January 1988, when all operations ceased and the building was closed down altogether.

In April 1988, I decided to revisit old haunts. Having passed by countless times over the years, I now felt obliged to pay my respects after so long an absence. It was a beautiful, fresh spring morning, similar to the one I experienced during my first visit of some 26 years previously, but with a silence more profound than that of 5 August 1968. For the first time in my life, I had the entire place to myself.

I passed through the opening by the old oil stores and entered this ruined temple of nostalgia. Memories of better times came flooding back, as I stood amongst the decaying wreckage. Nature was slowly taking over; young trees, plants and grasses growing in profusion, spreading a green shroud over the rusting steel and rotting timbers.

The partition doors to the old L&Y section were open and, here, apart from the atrocious work of vandals, I noticed very little had changed over the years. I walked across the yard to the shed-master's office, with its characteristic bay window façade and here, too, the vandals had been hard at work – papers, books and furniture being strewn across the floor and, everywhere, a sea of broken glass – indeed, not a window-pane intact! I passed through to the signing-on lobby and stood there awhile, in the gloomy silence, deep in thought; wondering how many generations of railwaymen had passed this way.

Visions of familiar faces from long ago flitted before my eyes. A sudden chill in the atmosphere awoke me from my grip of melancholy and I walked out into the warmth and sunlight – back into the world of the living.

I wandered along by the inspection pits, trying to visualise how it all had been in happier times. Everything of interest in the yard had long since disappeared; save for two decapitated cast iron lamp standards that once illuminated the water columns. These were originally gas lamps and had probably been there since the shed was built. And there they remained, still standing side-by-side,

like sentinels, faithfully guarding the entrance to the very last steam shed, their withered arms pointing defiantly towards the encroaching mass of trees and vegetation.

The building was eventually demolished in January 1990. Today, merely the outline of the concrete walkways between the filled-in inspection pits bears silent witness to the age of steam. It is difficult to imagine that it once contained a busy eight-road engine shed, coaling plant and turntable etc, once having an allocation of 50 plus locomotives.

1968 marked the 50th anniversary of the end of the First World War, and I remember seeing footage of the old veterans revisiting the Flanders fields, and hearing comments such as, "It's changed a bit since then" and "Who will remember it when we've gone?" A similar theme was passing through my mind as I stood near the filled-in 'trenches' (inspection pits) at 10D.

For the railway enthusiast of the late 1960s, the passing of steam had left a great void, one that, we knew, the few preserved railways then in existence could never fill with quite the same authentic 'feel'.

The story of main line steam had been concluded … or so we all then thought ... that is, until 15 September 1971, when a 'secret' trial run from Hereford to Newport proved to be the portent of much greater things to come. What arose as a consequence of that brave pioneering exercise is, however, as they say, quite another story!